A SHEARWATER BOOK

Faith in a Seed

Henry D. Thoreau

Faith in a Seed

The Dispersion of Seeds
and Other Late Natural History Writings

Edited by Bradley P. Dean

Foreword by Gary Paul Nabhan
Introduction by Robert D. Richardson, Jr.
Illustrations by Abigail Rorer

ISLAND PRESS / Shearwater Books

Washington, D.C. • Covelo, California

A SHEARWATER BOOK

PUBLISHED BY ISLAND PRESS

The original manuscript pages for *The Dispersion of Seeds*
reside in the Henry W. and Albert A. Berg Collection
of English and American Literature,
The New York Public Library.
Text design by David Bullen

LIBRARY OF CONGRESS CATALOGING-IN-PUBLICATION DATA
Thoreau, Henry David, 1817–1862.
Faith in a seed : the dispersion of seeds & other late natural
history writings / Henry D. Thoreau ; edited by Bradley P. Dean ;
foreword by Gary Paul Nabhan ; introduction by Robert D.
Richardson, Jr. ; illustrations by Abigail Rorer.
p. cm.
Includes index.
ISBN 1-55963-181-3 (cloth : acid-free paper).
1. Seeds—Dispersal. 2. Natural history—New England.
3. n-usn. I. Dean, Bradley P. II. Title.
QK929.T48 1993
582'.0467—dc20 92-35896
CIP

Printed on recycled, acid-free paper
Manufactured in the United States of America
10 9 8 7 6 5 4 3 2 1

Though I do not believe
that a plant will spring up
where no seed has been,
I have great faith in a seed.
Convince me that you have a seed there,
and I am prepared to expect wonders.

HENRY D. THOREAU

Contents

Learning the Language
of Fields and Forests

IN EACH of our lives, there is a time, and often a person, that sets us on
our trajectory. At a time in my youth when I wanted to be both a poet
and a biologist, those who were close to me—academic advisors, friends,
parents—told me that I must choose between these two incompatible pursuits. Faced with this career choice between the arts and the sciences, my
response was pure flight behavior: to withdraw from others, to walk for
hours on end, and to read Thoreau. About that time, a friend offered me a
retreat—a chicken coop that had been converted to a cabin. There I secluded myself, wrote, pored over biology texts, and read each morning
from the journals of Thoreau.

That morning reading ritual was among the most precious I have ever
performed. Each dawn, I would contemplate the passages that Thoreau
had written on the very same calendrical day more than one hundred years
before. As I worked at tasks through the morning, afternoon, and evening,
Thoreau's words would burrow deeper and deeper into the soil of my soul,
in much the same way as certain awned grass seeds twist and drill their way
into the earth before germinating. Somehow, in some way, Thoreau al-
tered my life then, for my course as field biologist *and* writer finally
emerged out of those months of doubt and difficulty. Although it took sev-

eral more years of schooling in ecology, literature, and ethnobotany to clarify my course, I eventually settled down to study and write about seeds and their conservation in soils, gene banks, and cultures.

In retrospect, I see that I became anchored by the steadiness of Thoreau's voice and by his persistent faith in the natural order of the world. In reading his journals, I gained a sense of how one might integrate a scientist's skill for detailed observation with a poet's command of language. In Thoreau, I first encountered someone who saw no polarity between poetry and nature's economy, but instead envisioned a vast ecology that spans both and enriches our senses, our hearts, and our minds.

It is not surprising that I feel a special connection with this remarkable treatise, *The Dispersion of Seeds*—the book within the covers of *Faith in a Seed*. Yet this book, which has taken more than a century to reach publication, is remarkable not only because it strikes a personal chord but also because it conveys several important messages, not least of which is that Henry D. Thoreau did *not* choose between the arts and the sciences. Robert D. Richardson, Jr., who contributed the introduction to this book and who wrote *Henry Thoreau: A Life of the Mind*, has commented that Thoreau, Emerson, and their colleagues "recognized no 'two culture' split between literature and science; they believed that to study nature and to know oneself came at last to the same thing, which it was the purpose of literature to express." Accordingly, it can be argued that Thoreau began to rough out a literary ecology of North America, a work in progress that is still being shaped by dozens of landscape writers and literate biogeographers who are active today.

Fortunately, other talented individuals have followed in Thoreau's path to build ever-stronger bridges between ecology and literature—from Vladimir Nabokov, John Steinbeck, Loren Eiseley, and Archie Carr to David Ehrenfeld, Barbara Kingsolver, David Quammen, Jean Craighead George, and Robert Michael Pyle. They have written creatively about the cryptic creatures, hidden habitats, and natural curiosities that they have encountered in their work as biologists and have enriched us all by exposing us to these seldom-seen universes.

It is ironic that Thoreau's involvement in purely scientific inquiry has been ignored for so long by so many and pooh-poohed by the few scholars of American literature who were familiar with this hitherto unpublished work. In the years between the publication of *Walden* and his death, Thoreau's four thousand or so journal pages and his unfinished "Kalendar," or "Book of Concord," were devoted primarily to detailed observations of local natural history. Literary critics have never been captivated by these digressions into "technical writing." For example, Odell Shepard, editor of *The Heart of Thoreau's Journals*, considered Henry's seedy inquiries to be a chapter of his lifework best left unpublished. According to Shepard, Thoreau's journals after 1857 wallowed in parochial and pedantic preoccupations: "From this point in the Journals, to the end, we watch the gradual conquest of the thinker and poet in Thoreau by the observer. The 'views as wide as heaven' are being 'narrowed down to the microscope' as he had feared. . . ."

Although always committed to broadening his biological knowledge, Thoreau occasionally worried about whether this immersion in science would take a toll on his art. In 1851 he asked, "What sort of science is that which enriches the understanding but robs the imagination?" Still, he proceeded over the next decade to hone his skills as a scientific observer, to inject more precision and authority into his work. In 1852, when he received an edition of Asa Gray's *Manual of Botany*, Thoreau finally had in his hands the tool that would help him probe the composition of the local forests. And early in 1860, when he acquired a copy of Darwin's *On the Origin of Species*, he at last had an overview of evolution and natural selection that provided an authoritative context for his observations.

In much the same way that literary critics have dismissed the quality of

Thoreau's later scientific writing, botanical and zoological taxonomists have maligned his early attempts at plant and animal study. Modern scientists have largely ignored the fact that he did not have reliable keys to the flora and fauna of North America until the last decade of his life—hence, most of his early misidentifications of biota are excusable. Even so, taxonomy was never his forte, a "failing" that has inspired certain botanical historians such as Ray Angelo—in his *Botanical Index to the Journal of Henry David Thoreau*—to chide Thoreau for not being able to distinguish poison ivy from poison sumac and for not knowing that only one species of spruce grew in Concord. Other scientists familiar with Thoreau's writings have also noted that his field identifications of common plants and animals generally left something to be desired.

But they miss the point, for they judge Thoreau as a biologist solely on the basis of his lackluster skills in taxonomy while underestimating his remarkably acute ecological insights into plant-animal interactions. Indeed, we learn from his treatise *The Dispersion of Seeds* that Thoreau was the first Anglo-American field ecologist to be influenced by Darwin's theory of natural selection and adaptation. Thoreau's writings between 1856 and 1861, which were shaped not only by Darwin's works but also by those of pre-Darwinian theorists, clearly anticipate issues in plant population biology and coevolution that did not become fully articulated in evolutionary ecology until the early 1970s. He launched inquiries into numerous topics—the demographic consequences of seed dispersal by adhesion to animal fur, deposition by birds, ingestion and defecation by mammals, and transport by wind and water—that remain vital areas of interest to evolutionary ecologists. His observations on dispersal distances of fleshy fruits carried by animals remain important a century and a half later for their precision and anticipation of plant-animal mutualism arguments.

Although the theory of natural selection had dawned on both Charles Darwin and Alfred Russel Wallace during their travels in tropical archipelagoes quite distant from the temperate forests, Thoreau realized that

xiv

their principles should be as evident in his local community as they were in exotic lands. In studying the evolutionary adaptations characteristic of various seed dispersal syndromes evident right around his home, Thoreau was far ahead of his time. For several more decades, biologists who investigated seed movement simply accumulated anecdotes about extreme cases of long-distance dispersal by trade winds, migratory waterfowl, or floating rafts of vegetation. Such anecdotes considered only the heroic anomaly—the one seed in a billion that lands on a distant island to colonize a newly formed lava flow. In contrast, Thoreau's approach included testing hypotheses, carrying out field experiments, quantifying data, and confirming empirically that bird B did indeed disperse fruit C to place A. His inquiries more reasonably explained the fate of 99 percent of the seeds that are dispersed no more than a couple hundred yards from their mother plants.

The result of this painstaking work was that Thoreau gradually elucidated most of the dominant patterns of seed dispersal and tree seedling recruitment within an afternoon's walk of his home. He deduced these patterns by way of ingenious inferences; by measuring the distances between trees of the same species; by counting, weighing, or floating certain seeds; by noticing which accumulate in windrows, ruts, and animal burrows; and by observing how far nesting birds and mammalian residents could carry the fruits around his neighborhood. His particularist approach to community ecology—a thoroughly modern one by today's standards—offered him more than enough to study in his own backyard: "I shall never find in the wilds of Labrador any greater wildness than in some recess of Concord."

In 1856, while in the midst of researching his essays on seed dispersal and forest succession, Thoreau met Walt Whitman. Whitman spoke to him as a representative of the American soil, as a voice of what is native and unique to his home ground. Within a year's time, such metaphors had infused Thoreau's botanical pursuits:

If a man is rich and strong anywhere, it must be on his native soil. Here I have been these forty years of learning the language of these fields that I may better express myself. If I should travel to the prairies, I should much less understand them, and my past life would serve me but ill to describe them. Many a weed here stands for more of life to me than the big trees of California would if I should go there.

Thoreau became obsessed with "learning the language of these fields" in the years just prior to his death. For him, the forest was a book waiting to be read: one simply had to devote sufficient time to grasp its grammar, to learn the rhythms of its syntax. His faith in natural order made him believe that there was a deep structure to all vegetational patterns that could be ascertained by any diligent student.

It is amazing how far Thoreau went beyond taking mere snapshots of the forest that stood before his eyes to explore the processes that led to its regeneration. More than any other botanist of his time, Thoreau moved past the mere naming of trees—the nouns of the forest—to track its verbs: the birds, rodents, and insects that pollinate flowers or disperse seeds, and all the other agents that shape the forest's structure.

It is a difficult language to learn. As ecologist Henry Howe conceded in 1986,

plants have an ancient and uneasy relationship with vertebrate animals which eat their fruits, and either digest or disperse their seeds. . . . In contemporary forests, as many as 45 to 90 percent of the tree species bear fleshy fruits apparently evolved for consumption by birds and mammals. [And yet], given the prevalence of seed dispersal by animals, it is puzzling that neither the advantages of seed dissemination to the plant nor the means to bring it about are well understood.

Thoreau's dedication to the task of learning the language of the forest is humbling. He knew Concord's forests like the back of his hand. Daily walks, years of land surveying, and communication with other local naturalists enabled him to know the distances between every new patch of tree seedlings and the nearest sexually mature tree of the same species. Yet despite his detailed knowledge of the local landscape, Thoreau was ultimately attracted to this field of inquiry because it was so full of the unexpected: "Though I do not believe that a plant will spring up where no seed has been, I have great faith in a seed. Convince me that you have a seed there, and I am prepared to expect wonders."

"The very earth itself is a granary," Thoreau concluded. What Thoreau the ecologist may have lacked in training and technology he made up for in his capacity for protracted attention to the land's dynamics and in his considerable talent for metaphorical thinking. The loveliest passages in his treatise on seeds are those in which his deep reservoir of literary knowledge wells up into his science. In them we experience the precision and grace with which he encounters the earth:

Touch-me-not seed vessels, as all know, go off like pistols on the slightest touch, and so suddenly and energetically that they always startle you, though you are expecting it. They shoot their seed like shot. They even explode in my hat as I am bringing them home.

Look under a nut tree a month after the nuts have fallen. . . . The ground looks like a platform before a grocery, where the gossips of the village sit and crack nuts and less savory jokes. You have come, you would say, after the feast was over, and are presented with the shells only.

The scales of all our birch cones are three lobed, like a typical spearhead . . . but those of this species are peculiarly interesting, having the exact form of stately birds with outspread wings, especially of hawks sailing steadily over the fields, and they never fail to remind me of them when I see them under my feet.

It was on the wings of seeds that Thoreau sailed home, where he found peace before he died. Although often itching to travel to the far reaches of the world, and always cosmopolitan in his readings, Thoreau gradually became convinced that what he could learn closest to home was what was ultimately of the greatest value. If literary historians sense that he had ceased to emulate Wordsworth and Goethe in his poetry and lofty philosophical essays, they misread his intentions. Instead of turning his back on these literary traditions, Thoreau tried to incorporate them into his search for a language more difficult but more enduring: the language of the forest itself.

Gary Paul Nabhan

Faith in a Seed

Thoreau's Broken Task

M<small>OST</small> of Henry Thoreau's work after *Walden* has never been published. When he left the pond, he said he had several more lives to live. One of these was a life in science, about which we know very little. Thoreau's 354-page manuscript on *The Dispersion of Seeds*, his 631-page manuscript on *Wild Fruits*, his more than 700 pages of notes and charts of natural phenomena in Concord in the 1850s, and his 3,000 pages in twelve notebooks on aboriginal North America remain unknown to the general public—and, with a handful of exceptions, even to specialists in American literature. The existence of these manuscripts is not a secret. They are for the most part raw material and rough drafts. Scholars have assumed that they deal with dry and unprofitable matters, that they present insurmountable editorial problems, and that they add little to what we know about Thoreau. The present volume is dramatic evidence to the contrary.

In *Faith in a Seed*, Bradley P. Dean has meticulously assembled some of Thoreau's late natural history writings and placed as the centerpiece the complete manuscript of *The Dispersion of Seeds*—the first new book of Thoreau's to appear in one hundred twenty-five years. It adds a whole new chapter to our understanding of Thoreau's life. The writer of *The Dispersion of Seeds* has traveled a long road from *Walden*, although he has not yet

3

gotten farther than Concord. *Walden* is a great—perhaps our greatest—celebration of the sweet freedom of a life in nature that is single, unattached, and uncommitted. *The Dispersion of Seeds*, in contrast, celebrates fertility, fecundity, and interconnectedness. *Walden* is about the growth and cultivation of the self; *The Dispersion of Seeds* is about the growth of communities and the rise of new generations. *Walden* is the acknowledged masterpiece of Thoreau the poet-naturalist; *The Dispersion of Seeds*, even in its rough-draft form, is the culminating work of Thoreau the writer-scientist.

After *Walden* was published in 1854, Thoreau lived for eight more years. During that time he published little, even though he did a great deal of reading and writing. In 1855 part of *Cape Cod* appeared in *Putnam's Magazine*. In 1856 Thoreau surveyed in New Jersey, met Walt Whitman, and lectured on "Walking." In 1857 he made his last trip to Cape Cod and his last trip to the Maine woods. In 1859 he became caught up, for a time, in the John Brown affair. In 1860 he wrote and published an essay on "The Succession of Forest Trees." Despite being ill during most of 1861, he journeyed to Minnesota for his health. On this trip he made botanical notes, and he heard the great leader of the Santee Sioux, Little Crow, just one year before the beginning of Little Crow's War, an early step on the road to Wounded Knee. Back home, even as he lay dying in the early months of 1862, he was hard at work on his manuscripts, selecting and readying small portions for publication.

Shortly after his death in early May of 1862, a number of Thoreau's short pieces appeared in a volume called *Excursions* (1863). The first half of *Excursions* reprints early essays; the second half is made up of a group of late essays. These pieces, "The Succession of Forest Trees," "Walking," "Autumnal Tints," "Wild Apples," and "Moonlight," are related, although they do not form any sort of coherent whole. They are tiny, disconnected fragments of a vast enterprise, or series of overlapping enterprises, on which Thoreau lavished his formidable attention for most of the last decade of his life. Ralph Waldo Emerson was acutely aware of the problem of Thoreau's late work. Shortly after Thoreau's death, his friend wrote:

The scale on which his studies proceeded was so large as to require longevity, and we were the less prepared for his sudden disappearance. The country knows not yet, or in the least part, how great a son it has lost. It seems an injury that he should leave in the midst his broken task which none else can finish, a kind of indignity to so noble a soul that he should depart out of nature before yet he has really been shown to his peers for what he is.

Thoreau himself wrote, just six weeks before his death, "I have not been engaged in any particular work on Botany, or the like, though, if I were to live, I should have much to report on Natural History generally."

During the years from 1852 to 1862, Thoreau accumulated primary material in three main sets of notebooks. First and most important was his huge journal, which in the 1906 edition comes to roughly six thousand printed pages. Thoreau also hived up information and notes on aboriginal North America in another set of twelve notebooks, which comprise some three thousand manuscript pages. His third major repository was a pair of large notebooks containing extracts from his reading in natural history, along with his comments on his readings.

Sometime in the late 1850s Thoreau began a massive rereading of all this material, with the specific purpose of listing all the natural phenomena in Concord and the order in which they appeared each year. He made a list of which fruits ripened on what day during one month of one specific year; then he made a similar list for the same month of the next year, and so on. He made a list of the first appearances of birds for each of the years 1852 to 1861. Another set of lists recorded the sequence in which trees and shrubs leafed out in the spring. Still other lists—hundreds of pages of them—recorded sightings of quadrupeds, of reptiles, of fishes, of insects, and of flowers. When he was finished, Thoreau had a huge pile of lists, each one detailing the occurrences of one class of natural phenomena for one month of one year. He had leafing for April 1853, leafing for April 1854, leafing for April 1855, and so on through all the categories for each month of each of the ten years for which he had adequate data.

Next, from all these lists he laboriously assembled large charts that enabled him to track his observations over time. (An illustration of one of these charts appears on page 222.) One chart might record the first appearance of April flowers over ten years. Above the ruled columns at the top of the chart, Thoreau wrote the years. Down the side he put the days of the month. In the boxes he inserted whatever flowered on each day in April in each of ten years.

After Thoreau had committed a huge portion of his energies to this large-scale tabular, statistical survey of natural phenomena in Concord, he became particularly interested in how different kinds of forest trees succeed each other in nature, and in how seeds disperse. Roughly half the manuscript here printed—the first half—seems to derive from Thoreau's list-and-chart work. Exactly what that project was aiming toward—and what part, if any, *The Dispersion of Seeds* material was to have in the larger project—we do not know. The publication of *The Dispersion of Seeds* does not clarify the overall intention of Thoreau's late works. Indeed, it raises more questions than it settles; but at least the general drift is, with this volume, out in the open, and Thoreau's importance to science as well as to literature is immediately a little clearer, as Gary Nabhan convincingly shows in his Foreword.

Thoreau's interest in science makes no sense apart from his Transcendentalist background. Because American Transcendentalism insisted on strengthening the relation between human beings and nature, Emerson and Thoreau considered science both important in itself and inextricable from other kinds of knowledge. One of the most valuable legacies of

Transcendentalism is the realization that science has a necessarily subjective side. Science, for Emerson and Thoreau, cannot be considered separately from the people doing the science. As Emerson might have put it, there is ultimately no science, only scientists.

The precursors of Transcendentalism thought similarly. Montaigne observed of natural science that "in words are its questions asked, in words are they answered." Goethe did work in optics, botany, and anatomy. In "The American Scholar," Emerson could insist on the fundamental relation between the self-knowledge dear to the Stoics and the scientist's knowledge of nature. The student, he says, "shall see that nature is the opposite of the soul, answering to it part for part. One is seal and one is print. Its beauty is the beauty of his own mind. Its laws are the laws of his own mind . . . So much of nature as he is ignorant of, so much of his own mind does he not yet possess. And, in fine, the ancient precept 'Know thyself,' and the modern precept 'Study nature,' become at last one maxim." Emerson, too, thought at one time that he would become a naturalist. Insofar as Transcendentalism was a premonition of the interconnectedness of all of nature, the work of Darwin and Wallace did not destroy, but rather confirmed, the basic insights of Emerson and Thoreau.

Thoreau was interested in science from early in his life. An extended passage on scientific method in the "Friday" section of *A Week on the Concord and Merrimack Rivers* (1849) shows his enthusiasm for rigor and precise observation, as well as his interest in the observer. "The most distinct and beautiful statement of any truth must take at last the mathematical form," he says, and goes on to say immediately afterward, that "the fact which interests us most is the life of the naturalist. The purest science is still biographical." Thoreau's early comments on how science proceeds are still pertinent today. "The process of discovery is very simple," he says with his usual maddening aplomb. "An unwearied and systematic application of known laws to nature causes the unknown to reveal themselves. Almost any *mode* of observation will be successful at last, for what is most wanted

7

is method. Only let something be determined and fixed around which observation may rally."

It is true that Thoreau later voiced reservations about certain aspects of science, but it was a lover's quarrel, and his reservations were those of a person with a lifelong commitment to the scientific enterprise. When Thoreau says "The man of science, who is not seeking for expression but for a fact to be expressed merely, studies nature as a dead language," he is not attacking science, but blinkered fact-collecting in the name of science. Thoreau had many links to the scientific community of his time; nevertheless, it must be remembered that his active decades, the eighteen forties and fifties, were the exact period when American science was becoming professionalized, and a part of Thoreau resisted this professionalization. The word "scientist" was not yet in common use, and even Darwin preferred to call himself "a person interested in natural history."

Thoreau was a member, after December 1850, of Boston's new and energetic Society of Natural History. In 1859 Harvard appointed him to the Visiting Committee in Natural History, which was charged with annual evaluation of the college curriculum. From 1847 on, he was a member of Louis Agassiz's far-flung network of local specimen collectors. As the years passed, Thoreau came to doubt Agassiz's well-known belief in the permanence of species. Agassiz was a famous European scientist, a magnetically compelling teacher and lecturer, a scientific empire builder, the darling of Harvard and the rising federally funded science establishment. Agassiz was the most powerful scientist of his day, whereas Thoreau was a minor—if reputable—local naturalist. Yet on the big issue Agassiz was wrong and Thoreau was right.

Agassiz believed that the "facts demonstrated that species were immutable," and that "species do not pass insensibly one into another, but that they appear and disappear unexpectedly without direct relations with their precursors." In 1850, in a volume called *Lake Superior*, Agassiz wrote, "The more intimately we trace geographical distribution, the more we are impressed with the conviction that it must be primitive . . . that animals must have originated where they live, and have remained almost precisely within the same limits since they were created." The basis of Agassiz's work was not scientific, despite his claims; it was theological, and has persisted as the theory of special creation. Agassiz believed that the geographical distribution of species was "regulated by the limits marked out on the first day of creation."

By March of 1857 Thoreau had become critical of the way Agassiz's mind worked. After a dinner with Agassiz at Emerson's home, Thoreau recorded their conversation. "When I began to tell him of my experiment on a frozen fish, he said that Pallas had shown that fishes were frozen and thawed again, but I affirmed the contrary, and then Agassiz agreed with me." By June 1858 Thoreau had become skeptical of Agassiz's main point. Climbing Mount Monadnock and observing some toad-spawn in a shallow pool near the summit, Thoreau speculated on how it got there. In the middle of a long discussion of possibilities he remarked, with curt dismissal, "Agassiz might say that they originated on top."

During the late 1850s, when Thoreau was beginning the vast job of overhauling his journals and drawing up his exhaustive list of natural phenomena, he was acutely aware of current studies in botany and zoology. He seems to have been working toward a grand calendar of Concord, the fullest possible account of a natural year in his hometown. No hint of Thoreau's exact plan has survived, but the materials and their preliminary organization suggest that the calendar was to include scientific attention to detail as well as some sort of seasonal structure.

The idea of such a volume was scarcely new. Emerson, as early as 1835 had considered writing a "natural history of the woods around my shifting camp for every month in the year." In the seventeenth century John Evelyn had published a *Kalendarium Hortense*, a book about gardening with a calendar structure. Gilbert White originally undertook *The Natural History of Selborne* as a "natural history of the twelve months of the year." Daines Barrington extracted a "Naturalist's Calendar" from White's papers and also published a sixty-five-page blank book for readers to assemble their own natural calendar. William Howitt's *Book of the Seasons: or A Calendar of Nature* (1831) was a mild, pastoral calendar.

Thoreau was familiar with all of these, except perhaps Barrington's. Where his own work seems to have differed is in breadth and in detail. Thoreau aimed to pin down exactly when each tree and shrub leafed out, exactly when every single fruit in Concord became ripe. By reducing the scope to Concord, he could aim at comprehensiveness. He seems to have wanted to produce a microcosmic version of Alexander von Humboldt's *Cosmos*, a multivolume work of the 1840s that aimed to give a complete account of the natural world, including the history of previous attempts at the same subject. Thoreau's attention to detail is far greater than that in, say, George B. Emerson's *Report on the Trees and Shrubs of Massachusetts* or F. A. Michaux's *North American Sylva*, both standard works of the time. The level of detail in *The Dispersion of Seeds*—a level easily matched elsewhere in Thoreau's unpublished work—is comparable to that found in the work of Alphonse De Candolle and of Charles Darwin himself. It is not always recalled that Darwin wrote whole books on *The Fertilization of Orchids* (1862), *Variation of Plants and Animals under Domestication* (1868), *Insectivorous Plants* (1875), *Climbing Plants* (1875), and *The Power of Movement in Plants* (1880).

After Thoreau's death his friend H. G. O. Blake edited four volumes culled from the journals, called *Early Spring in Massachusetts* (1881), *Summer* (1884), *Winter* (1888), and *Autumn* (1892). Blake's work has been neglected, but it is possible that he knew of Thoreau's grand seasonal ambition and was doing what he could to honor Thoreau's intentions.

It is hard to say where Thoreau's examination of the seasons might have led him. He knew, for example, that the Roman agricultural writer Varro had divided the year into the conventional four seasons, then had suggested a six-season year as well: Preparing Time, Planting Time, Cultivating Time, Harvest Time, Housing (Storing) Time, and Consuming Time. Thoreau also knew that the American Indians regard each month as a season. The Oglala Sioux begin the year with the Moon of Frost in the Teepee, and call the summer months the Moon of Making Fat, the Moon of Red Cherries, and the Moon of Black Cherries. It is possible that Thoreau also knew that the Chinese traditionally divide the year into twenty-four seasons. Beginning of Spring starts on February 4, Rain Water on February 19, Waking of Insects on March 6, Spring Equinox on March 21, Pure Brightness on April 5, Corn Rain on April 20, and so on. From Stoever's life of Linnaeus, Thoreau copied a passage which showed that Linnaeus " 'demonstrated how accurately flowers perform the service of a time-piece, in which the hour of the day can be precisely ascertained; he composed a calendar . . . and pointed out from this calendar in what manner the time best calculated for certain labors of rural economy may be chosen, &c.' " It is possible, then, that Thoreau spent the best energies of his later years on the first stages of a book in which he would have revealed the world around us in so concentrated and passionate a way as to convince us that every single day is a whole new season.

By late 1859 the calendar project was still in a very early stage. Its form was not clear, and there were serious problems. Thoreau had far too much material, there was no central focus, and it would be almost impossible to cast the book as an "excursion," which was now his preferred literary form. Smaller, more manageable topics kept suggesting themselves. At this time Thoreau became involved in the fate of John Brown and wrote a series of pieces defending him. And in early 1860 he became interested in Charles Darwin.

On New Year's Day of 1860 Charles Brace, a New York social worker, came to Concord carrying a copy of Darwin's just-published *On the Origin of Species*, which he had obtained from his brother-in-law Asa Gray, a

Harvard botanist and correspondent of Darwin's. Brace, Bronson Alcott, and Frank Sanborn (one of John Brown's New England backers and later the author of books on both Thoreau and Emerson) had dinner with Thoreau and discussed the new book. Darwin's ideas fell on fertile ground. Thoreau had long been interested in the geographical distribution of plants and animals around Concord. Well read in the general subject, he was already skeptical of Agassiz's confident assertions about special creation and immutable species. Three days after the dinner, Thoreau acknowledged the effect of Darwin on his own slowly ripening projects in one of the shrewdest comments ever made on the actual working mechanism of influence:

A man receives only what he is ready to receive, whether physically or intellectually or morally ... We hear and apprehend only what we already half know ... Every man thus *tracks himself* through life, in all his hearing and reading and observation and travelling. His observations make a chain. The phenomenon or fact that cannot in any wise be linked with the rest which he has observed, he does not observe.

Thoreau had read *The Voyage of the Beagle* years before. Now he copied extracts from *On the Origin of Species* into his natural history notebook, and he made comments that show he followed Darwin's argument closely. He copied, for example, the passage in which Darwin asserts that "nearly all the plants and animals of the Galapagos archipelago, of Juan Fernandez, and the other American Islands [are] related in the most striking manner to the plants and animals of the neighboring American mainland." To this passage Thoreau appended his own anti-Agassiz conclusion, "hence not created there."

Much of Darwin's argument that species are merely strongly marked varieties depends on the elaborate demonstration in the early chapters of *On the Origin of Species* of the innumerable and largely unobserved means by which animals and plants disperse themselves over the surface of the earth. The opening chapters of Darwin's famous book are in fact largely concerned with dispersion. Darwin's work accelerated and concentrated Thoreau's own attraction to the subject. Darwin showed Thoreau that his already strong interest in how seeds get planted was important because it was related to larger, currently pressing issues.

The Dispersion of Seeds is, then, a very early draft of Thoreau's book-length study, in minute detail, of "how, according to my observations, our forest trees and other vegetables are planted by Nature." The manuscript incorporates most of Thoreau's late essay "The Succession of Forest Trees," and it is obviously related to the still unpublished "Wild Fruits" project, of which, in turn, the posthumous essays "Wild Apples," "Autumnal Tints," and "Huckleberries" are small parts. The draft is so rough that its final form is not entirely clear; but what we have here, in Bradley P. Dean's meticulous and principled edition, is sufficient to elucidate the general direction of Thoreau's thought.

The Dispersion of Seeds is an argument against the then-prevalent concept that some plants spring up "spontaneously"—that is, not from a root, cutting, or seed. The idea is a mistaken commonplace of the time and can be found, for example, in successive editions (from 1846 to 1875) of George B. Emerson's *Report on the Trees and Shrubs of Massachusetts*. Thoreau, on the other hand, reports that in all his years of observation, he has never found a true case of spontaneous generation, but has determined that if one excludes plants that grow from cuttings or from roots, plants always grow from seeds that have been dispersed in a variety of ways, many of them previously unnoticed.

Thoreau began as a minor associate of Louis Agassiz. In this manuscript he emerges as a major ally of Charles Darwin. *The Dispersion of Seeds* argues against the concept of special creation, instead making a positive case for Darwin's developmental concept of continuous creation. "We find ourselves," says Thoreau, "in a world that is already planted, but is also still being planted as at first."

Here we see Thoreau's interests shifting from the human world to the world of nature, from the cultivated fields to the wild woods. In *Walden*, with its famous bean-field, agriculture is a metaphor for human self-cultivation. In *The Dispersion of Seeds*, wind, water, and animals are the agents for nature's self-cultivation. Thoreau is interested in how plants are seeded in the wild, and in the natural succession of plants. He pulls the reader's attention to the details themselves. "As I was passing through a pitch-pine wood, where as usual, the ground was strewn with twigs, I observed one eleven inches long and about half an inch thick, cut off close below two closed cones, the stem of one cone also being partly cut." We soon learn that it is the squirrels who trim the cone-bearing twigs for convenience of transport. At first glance, such unremitting detail would seem to make for slow and unexciting reading. But, as "Autumnal Tints" shows, Thoreau retained his power as a writer to the end of his life, and we are dealing here with the earliest stages of a book.

There are many passages in *The Dispersion of Seeds* that show the heights the whole might eventually have reached. Take, for instance, the wonderful description of milkweed seeds. "When I release some seeds, the fine silky threads fly apart at once, opening with a spring, and then ray their relics out into a hemispherical form, each thread freeing itself from its neighbor, and all reflecting prismatic tints." He watches one particular seed sailing like a balloon higher and higher until he loses sight of it. The passage goes on, itself rising like the milkweed seeds and giving us a glimpse of a larger subject in the distance. "I am interested," says Thoreau, "in the fate or success of every such venture which the autumn sends forth. And for this end these silken streamers have been perfecting themselves all summer, snugly packed in this light chest, as perfect adaptations to this end—a prophecy not only of the fall, but of future springs." Thoreau's prose at the end rises like a winter's daydream. "Who could believe in prophecies of Daniel or of Miller that the world would end this summer, while one milkweed with faith matured its seeds?"

With uncanny insight, Joel Porte has called Thoreau's lifework "a fable of dissemination." But this was far from evident in *Walden*, where the long first chapter, "Economy," ended with a fable of freedom. "I read in the Gulistan, or Flower Garden, of Sheik Sadi of Shiraz, that 'they asked a wise man, saying: Of the many celebrated trees which the Most High God has created lofty and umbrageous, they call none azad, or free, excepting the cypress, which bears no fruit; what mystery is there in this?'" The general answer Thoreau gave is that only those are truly free who are detached from the endless biological round of production and reproduction. Exactly how much Thoreau has changed by the early 1860s can be judged from the very opening of *The Dispersion of Seeds*:

Pliny, whose work embodies the natural science of his time, tells us that some trees bear no seed. "The only ones," says he, "among the trees that bear nothing whatever, not so much as any seed even, are the tamarisk, . . . the poplar, the Atinian elm, . . . and the alaternus" and he adds that "these trees are regarded as sinister [or unhappy, *infelices*] and are considered inauspicious."

There can be little doubt, I think, that *The Dispersion of Seeds* was to be not only a contribution to science, but a fable of dissemination as well. The reader feels that there is, behind the details and animating them, an insistent interest in fecundity. Starting, as Darwin started, from Malthus's astonished observation that "the germs of existence contained in this earth, if they could freely develop themselves, would fill millions of worlds in the course of a few thousand years," Thoreau quotes Darwin's patient but no less amazing experiments. "I took in February, three table-spoonsful of mud," Darwin says, "from three different points, beneath water, on the edge of a little pond; this mud when dried, weighed only 6¾ ounces. I kept it covered up in my study for six months, pulling up and counting each

15

plant as it grew; the plants were of many kinds and were altogether 537 in number; and yet the viscid mud was all contained in a breakfast cup!"

Thoreau further noted that another writer had calculated that the fifth year's crop from the single seed of a common thistle would be "more than sufficient to stock not only the surface of the whole earth, but of all the planets in the solar system, so that no other vegetable could possibly grow, allowing but the space of one square foot for each plant."

Thoreau's project is in the end not about speciation—as was Darwin's—nor about population control—as was Malthus's. From behind the pressing issue of fecundity in Thoreau's manuscript there emerges, tentatively and incompletely, but unmistakably, a powerful metaphor of death and rebirth. The seed was the favorite metaphor of the Quakers, especially of the Quaker leader George Fox. Thoreau knew about Fox, having inherited his copy of William Sewall's account of Fox and the founding of the Quakers from his Quaker grandmother on his mother's side. It was Emerson who picked out the image. "George Fox's chosen expression for the God manifest in the mind is the Seed. He means the seed of which the Beauty of the world is the flower and Goodness the fruit." In the light of this metaphor *The Dispersion of Seeds* expands to reach its full meaning. The seed means not only birth but rebirth. Every plant can be born again in every seed. Every day is a day of creation and at the same time a day of rebirth. "The very earth itself is a granary and a seminary," says Thoreau in one of the great passages of this new book, "so that to some minds, its surface is regarded as the cuticle of one living creature."

In the early 1850s most of New England's grand white pines, with their pagoda-like tiers of branches and their feathery needles, had been cut down for lumber. Here and there a solitary white pine still stood on a hilltop, visible for miles around, a giant with no companions left. The white pine bears seed sparingly, in cones that mature and open high on the tree. Although it scatters less seed than most other pines, it does manage to propagate itself. The white pine, Thoreau once said, "is the emblem of my life."

Henry Thoreau died in 1862 of tuberculosis and complications brought on by a cold he caught on December 3, 1860. There is something almost eerie in the fact that this exact date figures prominently in this book. Thoreau taught that we are linked to all things living and dead, and our link to him is a little tighter for knowing that this present work was what occupied his mind as he tramped the Concord woods on December 3, 1860, counted tree rings on stumps, and caught the cold that finally killed him. He died on May 6, 1862, at home and surrounded by friends and family. He had memorable last words for everyone. For an aunt who asked if he had made his peace with God, he said he didn't know that they had quarreled. To a question about the afterlife he replied—perfectly—"One world at a time." No one has loved the green world more. To his friend Ellery Channing, Thoreau said one day in the woods, "When I die you will find swamp oak written on my heart." On my next visit to Walden Pond, I think I will put an acorn instead of a stone on the growing cairn that marks the place where he lived.

Robert D. Richardson, Jr.

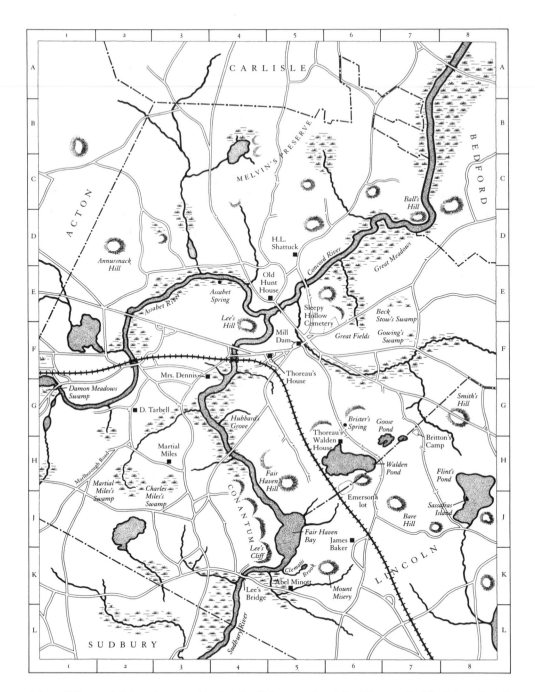

Map of Concord, Massachusetts, showing localities mentioned by Thoreau in *The Dispersion of Seeds*. (From a map compiled by Herbert W. Gleason in 1906.)

As I went by a pitch-pine wood the
other day, I saw a few little ones
springing up in a pasture from seeds which
had been blown from the wood. . . .
In a few years, if not disturbed, these
seedlings will alter the face of Nature here.

The Dispersion of Seeds

The Dispersion of Seeds

Pliny, whose work embodies the natural science of his time, tells us that some trees bear no seed. "The only ones," says he, "among the trees that bear nothing whatever, not so much as any seed even, are the tamarisk, which is used only for making brooms, the poplar, the Atinian elm [*Ulmus campestris* rarely does in England], and the alaternus"; and he adds that "these trees are regarded as sinister [or unhappy, *infelices*] and are considered inauspicious."

As there is even yet a lingering doubt in many minds with regard to some trees, whether they bear flowers and seed or not, it is the more important to show not only that they do, but for what purpose.

We are so accustomed to see another forest spring up immediately, as a matter of course, when one is cut down (whether from the stump or from the seed), never troubling ourselves about the succession, that we hardly associate seeds with trees, and do not anticipate the time when this regular succession will cease and we shall be obliged to plant, as they do in all old countries. The planters of Europe must therefore have a different and much more correct notion of the value of seeds than we. To speak generally, they know that forest trees spring from seeds; but we know only that they come out of the earth when we cut them down, as regularly as the fur grows on the hides of animals after the summer has thinned it. As time elapses and the resources from which our forests have been supplied fail, we too shall of necessity be more and more convinced of the significance of the seed.

My purpose in this chapter is to show how, according to my observation, our forest trees and other vegetables are planted by Nature.

When, hereabouts, a forest springs up naturally where none of its kind grew before, I do not hesitate to say that it came from seeds. Of the various ways by which trees are known to be propagated—by transplanting, cuttings, and the like—this is the only supposable one under these circumstances. No such forest has ever been known to spring from anything else. If anyone asserts that it sprang from something else, or from nothing, the burden of proof lies with him.

It remains, then, only to show how the seed is transported from where it grows to where it is planted. This is done chiefly by the agency of the wind, water, and animals. The lighter seeds, as those of pines and maples, are transported chiefly by wind and water; the heavier, as acorns and nuts, by animals.

To begin with the pitch pine. All my readers probably are acquainted with its rigid conical fruit, scarcely to be plucked without a knife—so hard and short that it is a pretty good substitute for a stone. Indeed, this is the use to which the Romans once put their kind. They called it the pine nut, and sometimes the apple of the pine, whence pine-apple. It is related that "when Vatinius gave a show of gladiators to conciliate the people, by whom he was much hated, they pelted him with stones. The ediles made an order forbidding the people to throw anything but apples within the arena; and on this the people pelted Vatinius with the apples of the pine tree. The question was, then, whether this was to be considered as a defiance of the law; and the celebrated lawyer Cascellius being consulted, replied, 'The pine nut, if you throw it at Vatinius, is an apple.' "

If not plucked, these cones hold on all winter and often many years. You see old gray cones, sometimes a circle of them (which the Romans appear to have called *azaniae*) within two feet of the ground on the trunks of large trees, having been formed there when the tree was young twenty or thirty years before—so persistent are they.

Within this strong, prickly, and pitchy chest are contained about a hundred dark brown seeds in pairs, each pair occupying a separate apartment behind its prickly shield. A very thin membrane or wing about three-fourths of an inch long extends from one end of each seed, which it clasps in its divided extremity like a caged bird holding the seed in its bill and waiting till it shall be released that it may fly away with and plant it.

For already some rumor of the wind has penetrated to this cell, and preparation has been made to meet and use it. According to Darwin, Alphonse De Candolle has remarked that winged seeds are never found in fruits which do not open. They were designed for flight. This wing is so independent of the seed that you can take the latter out and spring it in again, as you do a watch crystal.

The sun and wind, which have the key to these apartments, begin to unlock them with a crackling sound in the second or third fall and continue to do so here and there all winter long, and there they lie exposed with their thin, curved handles upward and outward to the wind, which ever and anon extracts them and conveys them away. If they chance to be released in calm weather, they fall directly to the earth, rapidly whirling all the way; but if there is any wind, they are borne more or less to one side. They remind me most, after all, of some deep-bellied fish—an alewife or shad—with their flanks and a tail curving to this side or that, the whole of whose flexible body is a sort of wing or fin fitted not for the varied and prolonged flight of birds, but to steer and assist its course in the stronger or grosser current in which it floats—schools of brown fishes which perform this short migration annually.

Nature always adopts the simplest modes which will accomplish her end. If she wishes one seed to fall only a little to one side from a perpendicular line, and so disseminate its kind, perhaps she merely flattens it into

25

a thin-edged disk—with some inequality—so that it will "scale" a little as it descends. In course of time, when it contemplates a more distant and wider flight from the pine-tree tops to the earth, moveable edges, called fins or wings, may be added to this simple form.

The pitch pine is a very seedy tree and is peculiarly bent on extending its domains. It begins to bear when very small—sometimes when less than two feet high.

I have noticed that where, on account of the poverty or rockiness of the soil, these trees find it hard to live at all, they bear the more fruit. I have counted on a solitary pitch pine, which was only three feet high and as broad as high, spreading flat over a rock on a hilltop, more than one hundred cones of different ages. Having scaled this rocky citadel, its first care, though in a crippled state, was to call a hundred followers about it and so get undisputed possession.

Michaux observes that "wherever these trees grow in masses, the cones are dispersed singly over the branches, and . . . they release the seeds the first autumn after their maturity; but on solitary stocks, the cones are collected in groups of four, five, or even a larger number, and remain closed for several years."

Not only is it the outside trees that bear the most seed, where it is most required, but only a considerable wind, which can transport the seed to a distance, is able commonly to set it free, so that it does not fall at once to the ground, where it would be wasted. All have noticed the dense groves of pitch pine of uniform height, which were perhaps planted in a single gale, and you can often tell what tree the seed came from. In my mind's eye, and sometimes partially with my bodily eye, I see the seeds from which they sprang falling in a dense shower which reaches twenty or thirty rods on one side, like grain scattered by the hand of the sower.

Sometimes a man cuts off a lot of young pitch pines, leaving only the old parent tree to seed the ground again. They are not commonly noticed till half a dozen years old.

As I went by a pitch-pine wood the other day, I saw a few little ones springing up in the pasture from these seeds which had been blown from the wood. There was a puny one which came from the seed this year, just noticeable in the sod, and I came near mistaking it for a single sprig of moss. It was, as it were, a little green star with many rays, half an inch in diameter, lifted an inch and a half above the ground on a slender stem. What a feeble beginning for so long-lived a tree! By the next year it will be a star of greater magnitude, and in a few years, if not disturbed, these seedlings will alter the face of Nature here. How ominous the presence of these moss-like stars to the grass, heralding its doom! Thus, from pasture this portion of the earth's surface becomes forest—because the seeds of the pine, and not of moss and grass alone, fell on it. These which are now mistaken for mosses in the grass will perhaps become lofty trees and endure two hundred years.

Pitch-pine seeds

Unlike the white pine, the pitch pine is opening its cones and dispersing its seed gradually *all winter*, and it is not only blown far through the air, but slides yet further over the snow and ice. It has often occurred to me that it was one value of a level surface of snow, especially a crusted snow, that by its smoothness it favored the distribution of such seeds as fell on it. I have many times measured the direct distance on a snowy field from the outmost pine seed to the nearest pine to windward, and found it equal to the breadth of the widest pasture. I have seen that the seed thus crossed one of our ponds, which is half a mile wide, and I see no reason why it should not be blown many miles in some cases. In the fall it would be detained by the grass, weeds, and bushes, but the snow having first come to cover up all and make a level surface, the restless pine seeds go dashing over it like an Esquimaux sledge with an invisible team until, losing their wings or meeting with some insuperable obstacle, they lie down once for all, perchance to rise up pines. Nature has her annual sledding to do, as well as we. In a region of snow and ice like ours, this tree can be gradually spread thus from one side of the continent to the other.

By the middle of July, I notice on the shore of the above-mentioned pond, just below the high-water line, many little pitch pines which have just sprung up amid the stones and sand and muck, whose seed has been blown or drifted across. There are some places for a row of pines along the water's edge, which at length, after fifteen or twenty years, are tipped over and destroyed by the heaving of the frozen shore.

I noticed lately a little pitch pine which had come up on the sandy railroad embankment in our meadows, just sixty rods by pacing from the nearest pine tree; nor is this uncommon. I have seen a single pitch pine spring up spontaneously in my yard in this village, about half a mile from the nearest of its kind, with a river and its deep valley, and several roads and fences between, and it grows there yet. This tree would soon sow itself in all our yards if they were neglected.

Every year the seed of the pines is blowing thus from our pine woods and falling on all sorts of ground, favorable and unfavorable. When the circumstances are propitious, a forest of pines springs up, especially if the land to leeward is open or has been lately cleared, or plowed, or burned over.

One man accordingly tells me, and there are countless cases like it, that he had a lot of pines, which being cut, shrub oaks came up. He cut and burned and sowed rye, and, it being surrounded by pine woods on three sides, the next year a dense growth of pines filied the ground.

Squirrels also help to disperse the pitch-pine seed. I notice every fall, especially about the middle of October, a great many pitch-pine twigs or plumes, which have evidently just been gnawed off and left under the trees. They are from one-half to three-fourths of an inch in thickness, and often have three or four branches. I counted this year twenty under one tree, and they were to be seen in all pitch-pine woods. It is plainly the work of squirrels. As I had not chanced to detect their object, I resolved last fall to look into the matter.

Accordingly, thinking it over one night, I said to myself, "Anything so universal and regular, observed wherever the larger squirrels and pitch pines are found, cannot be the result of an accident or freak, but must be connected with the necessities of the animal." I have found that the necessaries of my life are food, clothing, shelter, and fuel; but the squirrels use only food and shelter. I never see these twigs used in constructing their nests; hence, I presume that their motive was to obtain food, and as its seeds are all of the pitch pine that I know them to eat, my swift conclusion was that they cut off these twigs in order to come at the cones, and also to make them more portable. I had no sooner thought this out than I as good as knew it.

A few days after, as I was passing through a pitch-pine wood, where as usual, the ground was strewn with twigs, I observed one eleven inches long and about half an inch thick, cut off close below two closed cones, the stem of one cone also being partly cut. Also in open land three or four rods from this grove, I saw three twigs which had been dropped near together. One was just two feet long and cut off more than a foot below three cones which were still left on it, two on one branch and one on another. One of the others was longer still.

Thus, my theory was confirmed by observation. The squirrels were carrying off these pine boughs with their fruit to a more convenient place either to eat at once or store up. You would be surprised to see what great limbs they carry, and to what distances sometimes. They are stronger than we suppose. A neighbor tells me that he had a gray squirrel which would take a whole and large ear of corn, run out of a broken window of his corn barn and up the side and over the roof, or perhaps high into an elm with it.

Most of the twigs which you see in the woods, however, are smaller, mere single plumes, which have been sheared off above the cones, whether to lighten the load or to come at the cone. They were so generally cut off last fall, when comparatively few pitch pines bore any cones, that I commonly detected the fertile trees when going through a grove by seeing these green twigs strewn on the brown ground beneath them.

It is surprising how rudely the squirrels strip and spoil the trees on which they depend. I often thought what a hue and cry I should have made about it, if they had been orchard trees and belonged to me. Even the pitch pines thus get *trimmed* after a fashion, and perhaps for their benefit.

In most cases, evidently, they carry off the cone alone; but perhaps a strong squirrel prefers to carry three cones, twig and all, at one trip than come three times after single cones. I frequently see where they have dropped the bare cones, having been interrupted, and I once counted twenty-four such cones quite fresh and unopened brought together under a solitary pine in a field, evidently ready to be transported to another place.

It chanced that I did not see last October where any of these cones had been eaten or stripped, as I often do. I conclude therefore that most of them must have been collected into holes in trees or in the earth, where the squirrels live, and possibly some are buried singly as nuts are.

Think how busy the squirrels are in October, in every pitch-pine grove all over the state, cutting off the twigs and collecting the cones. While the farmer is digging his potatoes and gathering his corn, he little thinks of this harvest of pine cones which the squirrel is gathering in the neighboring woods still more sedulously than himself.

In this way even the squirrels may spread the pine seed far over the field. I frequently see a pitch-pine cone far out in an open field, where it was dropped by a squirrel when on its way toward some tree or wall or stump—or oftener by the side of a fence on which the squirrel travelled at a considerable distance from the woods; and there it will sometimes lie covered by the snow all winter, and not expand and shed its seeds till the snow goes off and it feels the heat of the sun.

The pitch-pine cones have very stout and tough stems, the woody part alone being often a quarter of an inch in diameter; and they are scarcely so long as wide, which makes them hard to come at. But rigid and unmanageable as they are, almost every fresh cone of this kind which you see on the ground was cut off by a squirrel, and you can plainly see the marks of its teeth on the stem. He cuts it as he bends it, and a very few cuts suffice to separate it from the branch.

When he has thus plucked it, sitting on a fence-post or other perch, he begins at the base of the cone and gnaws off the scales one after another, devouring the seeds as he goes, leaving only half a dozen empty scales at the extremity. The close-shaven cone presents thus a pretty flower-like figure, which it would take a long time to produce with a knife.

This plucking and stripping a pine cone is a business which he and his family understand perfectly. It is their forte. I doubt if you could suggest any improvement. After ages of experiment perhaps, their instinct has settled on the same method that our reason would, finally, if we had to open a pine cone with our teeth; and they were thus accomplished long before our race had discovered that the pine cone contained an almond.

Observe more particularly how this one proceeds. He does not prick his fingers, nor pitch his whiskers, nor gnaw into the solid cone, any more than is necessary. Having sheared off the twigs and needles that may be in his way (sometimes even the cheeks of the twig, for like the skillful woodchopper he first deliberately secures room and verge enough), he neatly cuts off the stout stem of the cone with a few strokes of his chisels, and it is his. To be sure, he may let it fall to the ground and look down at it for a moment curiously, as if it were *not* his, but probably he is taking note where it lies and adding it to the heap of a hundred like it in his mind, and it is only so much the more his for his seeming carelessness. When he comes to open it, he holds it in his hands, a solid embossed cone so hard it almost rings at the touch of his teeth, pausing for a moment, perhaps, not because he does not know how to begin, but only to hear what is in the wind. He knows better than to try to cut off the tip and work his way downward against a *chevaux-de-frise* of advanced scales and prickles. If there ever was any age of the world when the squirrels opened their cones wrong end foremost, it was not the golden age, surely. He knows better than to gnaw into the side for three-fourths of an inch in the face of many armed shields. But he does not have to think what he knows. Having heard the last Aeolian rumor, he whirls the cone bottom upward in a twinkling, and beginning where the scales are smallest, and the prickles slight or none, and the short stem is cut so close as not to be in his way—for the same strokes which severed it from the twig have exposed its weak side—he proceeds to cut through the thin and tender bases of the scales, and each stroke tells, laying bare at once a couple of seeds. Thus, he strips it as easily as if the scales were chaff, and so rapidly, twirling it as he advances, that you cannot tell how he does it till you drive him off and inspect his unfinished work. Dropping this, he resorts to the pines for another, till quite a pile of scales and of these interesting cores is left on the snow there.

In April of last year I found under one small pitch pine in a little grove of these trees on the top of Lee's Cliff, a very large heap of cones which had been thus cut off and stripped evidently by the red squirrel the previous winter and fall, they having sat upon some dead stubs a foot or two above the while. Probably there was a hole in the ground there where they lodged. I counted 239 cores of cones under this tree alone, and most of them lay within an area of two feet square upon a mass of the scales one to two inches deep and three or four feet in diameter—showing that these had been stripped by but few squirrels, possibly only one. They had brought them all to this stub to be eaten, in order that they might be near their hole in case of danger. There were also many similar cores of cones under the surrounding pines. They appeared to have devoured all the fruit of that pitch-pine grove; and who had a better right to it?

The red squirrel thus harvests the fruit of the pitch pine annually. His body is about the color of its cone, and he who can open them so dexterously is welcome to what he can find in them. The cones to him who can open them. As for the seed of new plantations, Nature will be contented with the crumbs which fall from his table.

Such are the principal ways in which the pitch-pine wood is planted. I know the history of many of them.

It is pleasant to observe any growth in a wood. There is the tract northeast of Beck Stow's Swamp, where some years since I used to go a-blackberrying and observed that the pitch pines were beginning to come in; and I have frequently noticed since how fairly they grew, clothing the plain as evenly as if dispersed by art. At first the young pines lined each side of the path like a palisade, they grew so densely, crowding each other to death in this wide world. Eleven years ago I was first aware that I walked in a pitch-pine wood there, and not a blackberry field—which erelong, perchance, I shall survey and lot off for a wood auction, and see the choppers at their work. These trees, I said to myself, are destined for the locomotive's maw; but fortunately it has changed its diet of late, and their branches, which it has taken so many years to mature, are regarded even by the woodman as trash.

There is also the pitch-pine plain behind James Baker's, which I remember as a bare pasture. Ten years ago it was already an open pitch-pine wood, where I used to cut off long and broad capes in my walk, gliding easily between the trees without disturbing the fretful watchdog, and unseen from the house, whose tinkling industry I heard. Nay, I sometimes went near enough to catch glimpses of a row of shining milk pans between the trees. These are among our pleasantest woods, so open and level—half field, half wood. On the outskirts, the trees are far apart and have room enough, making here and there only a carpet of pine needles, with wiry grass and goldenrod, St. John's-wort, and blackberry vines, and younger pines between; further in, wild pinks and lady's slippers in their season; and further still, you come to moss-covered patches, dry, deep, white moss, or almost bare mold, half covered with pine needles. Thus begins the future forest floor.

Nor would I forget the dense pitch-pine wood east of the Deep Cut, which I remember as an open grassy field with a pigeon place in it, where also I used to gather blackberries. It contains now one of our pleasantest wood paths, which we call Thrush Alley, because the wood thrush sings there in the shade of the pines in the heat of the day. I have heard this bird sing in several of these groves where I remembered a bare pasture. It is an era when the wood thrush first sings in a new pine wood.

As for the white pine, you have all observed its clusters of sickle-shaped green cones at the top chiefly of the tallest trees, well nigh inaccessible to man. About the middle of September these turn brown and open in the sun and wind, and, as in the case of the pitch pine, away go the seeds of future forests flying far and wide.

How little observed are the fruits which we do not use! How few attend to the ripening and dispersion of the white-pine seed! In the latter part of September in a fruitful year, the tops of high trees for six or ten feet are quite browned with the cones, hanging with their points downward and just opened. They make a great show even sixty rods off, and it is worth the while to look down from some favorable height over such a forest—to observe such evidence of fertility in this which commonly we do not regard as a fruit-bearing tree. I occasionally go to the white-pine woods merely to look at their crop of cones, just as a farmer visits his orchards in October.

White-pine seed

These seeds all fall in September, except a few which are left glued to the cones by the pitch. They have one advantage at least over the pitch pine, that growing commonly in the tops of lofty trees they will be wafted to a greater distance by the wind in proportion as they fall further.

The white pine bears much more sparingly than the pitch, and one would say that the latter, though more difficult to transplant, was more likely, both on account of the abundance of its seeds and their falling all

34

winter, to disperse itself and maintain its ground here. Yet it is to be remembered that the white pine has a wider range, since it not only grows well in open ground, but springs up in the midst of the woods far more readily than the pitch pine.

However, in the fall of 1859 the white pines bore a peculiarly abundant crop, as I observed not only in this town but in all this part of the country and as far off as Worcester. I could see its burden of brown cones half a mile distant.

You may often see amid or beside a pine grove, though it may be thirty or forty years old, a few yet larger and older trees from which their seed came, rising above them like patriarchs surrounded by their children, while a third generation shows itself yet further off.

Short, and on some accounts unfavorable, as the season is during which the white-pine seed is falling, it appears to be blown to no less distance than that of the pitch pine. I frequently pass by some wet and bushy meadow in the midst of open land, which is being rapidly filled with little white pines whose seeds must have been blown fifty or sixty rods at least. They are now rapidly spreading over the northeast part of Fair Haven hillside, though the nearest seed-bearing pines are across the river from thirty to sixty rods off. Also, I notice for a quarter of a mile along the corner road beyond Abiel Wheeler's, where it runs through a broad, open tract, quite a number of white pines springing up against the south wall, which must have come from seed blown from Hubbard's Grove, some fifty rods east; and I observe the same thing in other parts of the town. They run forward and entrench themselves like the French soldiers in Sevastopol, and ere long we begin to see the plumes waving there.

The last is a single line of trees of various sizes and much interrupted, from seeds which have gradually been caught and protected by the wall; for I find that, however few they may be, they drift according to the same law with snow. Indeed, I am quite satisfied that there is no part of this town so remote from a seed-bearing pine but its seed may be blown thither, and so a pine spring up there. These which we see springing up thus in distant and neglected meadows and by fences show what would happen over all the intervening space if it were not for our cultivation—that there is nothing to prevent their springing up all over the village in a few years but our plows and spades and scythes. They grow slowly at first, but after they get to be four or five feet high they will frequently increase seven feet in the next three years.

For many years the daily traveller along these roads—nay, the proprietor himself—does not notice that there are any pines coming up there, and still less does he consider whence they came; but at last his heir knows himself to be the possessor of a handsome white-pine lot, long after the wood from which the seed came has disappeared.

We need not be surprised at these results when we consider how persevering Nature is and how much time she has to work in. It does not imply any remarkable rapidity or success in her operations. A great pine wood may drop many millions of seeds in one year, but if only half a dozen of them are conveyed a quarter of a mile and lodge against some fence, and only one of these comes up and grows there, in the course of fifteen or twenty years there will be fifteen or twenty young trees there, and they will begin to make a show and betray their origin.

In this haphazard manner Nature surely creates you a forest at last, though as if it were the last thing she were thinking of. By seemingly feeble and stealthy steps—by a geologic pace—she gets over the greatest distances and accomplishes her greatest results. It is a vulgar prejudice that such forests are "spontaneously generated," but science knows that there has not been a sudden new creation in their case but a steady progress according to existing laws, that they came from seeds—that is, are the result of causes still in operation, though we may not be aware that they are operating.

It is a boy's statement, and does not imply much wisdom, to discover that "little strokes fall great oaks," for the sound of the axe invites our attention to such a catastrophe. We can easily count each stroke as it is given, and all the neighborhood is informed by a loud crash when the deed is consummated; but they are few who consider what little strokes, of a different kind and often repeated, *raise* great oaks or pines. Scarcely a traveller hears these or turns aside to communicate with that Nature which is steadily dealing them.

Nature works no faster than need be. If she has to produce a bed of cress or radishes, she seems to us swift; but if it is a pine or oak wood, she may seem to us slow or wholly idle, so leisurely and secure is she. She knows that seeds have many other uses than to reproduce their kind. If every acorn of this year's crop is destroyed, or the pines bear no seed, never fear. She has more years to come. It is not necessary that a pine or an oak should bear fruit every year, as it is that a pea vine should.

However, Nature is not always slow in raising pine woods even to our senses. You have all seen how rapidly, sometimes almost unaccountably, the young white pines spring up in a pasture or clearing. Small forests thus planted soon alter the face of the landscape. Last year perhaps you observed a few little trees there, but next year you find a forest.

In an account of Duxbury in the *Massachusetts Historical Collections* written in 1793, it is said: "Capt. Samuel Alden, who died twelve years since, recollected the first white pine in the town. Now the eighth part, perhaps, of the woodland is covered with this growth." Pigeons, nuthatches, and other birds devour the seed of the white pine in great quantities, and if the wind alone is not enough, it is easy to see how pigeons may fill their crops with pine seed and then move off much faster than a locomotive to be killed by hundreds in another part of the county, and so plant the white pine where it did not grow before.

If you set out for the first time in your life to collect white-pine seed hereabouts, you will probably be indebted for every one you will get to the labor of the red squirrel. As I have said, this seed ripens in September, when the cones open, and the seed is quickly blown out; but the cones hang on all winter, only falling from time to time in high winds. If you wait till a cone may chance to fall thus, you will surely find it empty. I think that I may venture to say that every white-pine cone that by good rights falls to the earth naturally in this town before opening and losing its seeds (and almost every pitch-pine one that falls at all) is cut off by a squirrel; and they begin to pluck them long before they are ripe, and when the crop is a small one, as it commonly is, they cut off thus almost every one before it fairly ripens. I think, moreover, that their design, if I may so speak, in cutting them off green is partly to prevent their opening and losing their seeds, for these are the ones for which they dig through the snow in the winter and the only white-pine cones which contain anything then. Most of these cones appear to be soon carried off by them—fresh to holes in the earth.

Though the seed of pines cannot otherwise be relied on commonly when it is more than a year or two old, it is stated in Loudon that "the seeds of most species, when allowed to remain in the cone, preserve their vegetative power for several years." So few sound seeds as there appear to be in these cones, the squirrel may occasionally plant a pine tree, as well as lay up food for itself, and this might explain a pine's springing up where no seed had fallen for several years—for I often see white-pine cones which have been transported a considerable distance. If you walk through a white-pine wood in the latter part of September, you will find the ground strewn with green cones that have been thus dropped, while those left on the trees are all open. In some woods, every one will be on the ground.

In August and early in September, they are exceedingly busy cutting off cones in all white-pine woods, for they know well the nature of the tree. Perhaps they also store up the seeds separately, for by the middle of September a great part of those left on the ground will have been already stripped by them, they beginning at the base, as with the pitch-pine cone. Many of these, however, cut off late, open of themselves on the ground and shed their seeds there.

The first season that I set out to gather white-pine seed, I was as green at the business as the cones before they have opened and put it off too late. The next year, every one that I got had been gathered for me by the squirrels, but many of these were immature. The third year, I tried to compete with the squirrels and climbed the trees in good season myself. Hear my experience:

September 9th, 1857

To the woods for white-pine cones. Very few trees bear any, and they are on their tops. I can easily manage small trees, fifteen or twenty feet high, climbing till I can reach the dangling green pickle-like fruit with my right hand, while I hold to the main stem with my left; but I am in a pickle when I get one. The cones are now all flowing with pitch, and my hands are soon so covered with it that I cannot easily cast down my booty when I would, it sticks to my fingers so; and when I get down at last and have picked them up, I cannot touch my basket with such hands but carry it on my arm, nor can I pick up my coat which I have taken off unless with my teeth—or else I kick it up and catch it on my arm. Thus I go from tree to tree, rubbing my hands from time to time in brooks and mudholes in the hope of finding something that will remove pitch, as grease does, but in vain. It is the stickiest work I ever did; yet I stick to it. I do not see how the squirrels that gnaw them off and then open them, scale by scale, keep their paws and whiskers clean. They must possess some remedy for pitch that we know nothing of, for they can touch it and not be defiled. What would I not give for the recipe! How fast I could collect cones if I could only contract with a family of squirrels to cut them off for me!—or what if I had a pair of shears eighty feet long and a derrick to wield them with!

At length, after two or three afternoons, I get a bushel of them home, but I have not got at the seeds yet. They are more effectually protected than a chestnut in its burr. I must wait till they please to open and then get pitched once more.

These green cones collected in my chamber have a strong spirituous scent, almost rummy, or like a molasses hogshead, which would probably be agreeable to some.

In short, I found the business far from profitable, for commonly the trees do not bear more than enough for the squirrels.

———

The seeds of the hemlock and larch are falling all winter and are dispersed in a similar manner to those of the pitch pine. Much hemlock seed is also floated upon the surface of the streams which they overhang. I can thus easily tell when it begins to fall.

So far as I have observed, if coniferous trees bear much seed one year, they bear little or none the next year. In 1859 the white pine, hemlock, and larch bore abundantly, so that the northern birds which feed on their seeds (redpolls and goldfinches and others) were very numerous, and the following spring I saw the crossbills here for the first time in my life. Indeed, I think that I can tell by the numbers of the above birds in our woods whether there is a good crop of these and of birch seeds. But in 1860 I did not chance to see a single fresh hemlock or larch cone, and I am not sure that I saw a ripe white-pine cone of that year—neither did I see any of the above-named birds the following winter.

In the previous winter of 1859–60 I saw large flocks of lesser redpolls feeding on the seeds of the hemlocks—their conical tops, in which the seed was most abundant, being quite alive with them. The snow and ice under the hemlocks on the Assabet were strewn with cones, scales, and seeds, which the wind and the birds had loosened—literally blackened with them for many a rod—and tracked up by redpolls, chickadees, and squirrels, which had been attracted by the seed. A bountiful supply of winter food was here furnished for them. No sooner had a fresh snow fallen and covered up the old layer, than down came a new supply, all the more distinct on the spotless surface. This happened many times during the winter.

As I stood there one day, there came a little flock of chickadees, attracted by me as usual, boldly perching close by; then, descending to the snow and ice, they picked up the hemlock seed which lay all around them, occasionally taking one to a twig and hammering away at it under their claws in order to separate it from the wing or even from the shell. I have seen the same birds dart down to seedless wings of pitch-pine seeds on the snow and then up again as if disappointed, and I have no doubt that they eat those seeds as well as that of the hemlock.

One old hunter tells me of the pigeons alighting in great numbers on the tops of hemlocks in March, and he thinks that they eat the seed.

The following April I saw the crossbills busily feeding upon and under those same hemlocks—the first crossbills that I ever saw alive.

The same winter I saw flocks of redpolls picking the seeds out of the larch cones. They perch on the slender twigs, which are beaded with cones, and swing and teeter there, while they perseveringly peck at the cones, trying now this one, now that, sometimes picking out and swallowing the seeds quite fast. And thus they helped to disperse them.

I see the young hemlocks and larches springing up on suitable soil, to which the wind has wafted their seed, in the same manner as pines—though they are seldom forced upon my notice since those trees are comparatively rare hereabouts. I saw, for instance, the other day many little larches in the meadow, which had evidently sprung from seed blown from a clump of large ones a dozen rods distant and across a road.

The spruce cones do not open till spring. I see, however, in November where the squirrels have stripped them as they do the pine cones.

The birds said by Wilson and others to feed on *pine seed* are the two crossbills, which have bills expressly formed to open the cones, the red-bellied nuthatch, purple finch (Giraud), brown creeper, chickadee, pine finch, pine warbler—and I may add the lesser redpoll and pigeon.

Birches, of the four kinds common in this state, bear an abundance of winged seed. On some yellow birches, by the middle of October, the short, thick, brown cones are nearly as numerous as the leaves were, causing the trees to appear still a dark mass against the sky.

Birch seed begins to fall in October and continues to fall all winter. It is similar in all our species. The fruit of our commonest kind, the small white birch, consists of numerous pendulous cylindrical aments, composed of imbricated scales, with three winged seeds under each. It is remarkable that it so much resembles the fruit of a very different family of trees, the coniferae, that it is often called by the same name, namely, a strobile or cone (*strobos* from στρέφω); and I find that as the scales of the pitch-pine cone are arranged always in just thirteen spiral lines around it, so are the scales of the white-birch cone, making about one turn—as you may easily prove by counting the fine lines made by the projecting points of the middle lobes of the scales. It might be worth the while to inquire why Nature loves the number thirteen in these cases.

White-birch scale

The scales of all our birch cones are three lobed, like a typical spearhead (or *fléur de luce*); but those of this species are peculiarly interesting, having the exact form of stately birds with outspread wings, especially of hawks sailing steadily over the fields, and they never fail to remind me of them when I see them under my feet.

Volatile as these appear and are, the seeds which they cover, and for which they are often mistaken, are practically far more bird-like and are wafted much further by the wind. Indeed, they can easily be separated from the scales by winnowing. They are much smaller and of a livelier brown, with a very broad transparent wing on each side and two little dark brown persistent styles in front, just like an insect with its antennae. They may pass for tiny brown butterflies.*

When the cones are perfectly ripe and dry, these scales and seeds, being blown or shaken, begin to flake off together like so much chaff or bran, commencing commonly at the base of the cone, and falling gradually throughout the winter, leaving a bare, thread-like core. Thus, unlike the pines, the whole cone loses its cohesion and is disintegrated.

Each catkin, one inch long by a quarter of an inch wide, contains about one thousand seeds, which would suffice to plant an acre of land with birches seven feet apart each way. No doubt many single trees contain seed

*Thoreau included sketches in his journals to illustrate his observations, like the one to the left. These drawings are reproduced throughout the text.

enough to plant all the old fields in Concord several times over. At this rate you could carry the seed for a thousand acres in a box of three inches cubed.

The seed is so small, and so exceedingly light and chaffy, that it does not fall to the earth in a perfect calm without many gyrations; and when there is considerable wind, it floats on it almost like a mote—disappearing at once from your sight like those little insects which the Indians call "no-see-'ems."

Some fall at the slightest jar, and some is left tossing about incessantly on the light spray till the latest gales of spring. In sudden gusts of wind such seeds as these, and even much heavier ones, must be carried over our highest hills, not to say mountains, and it is evidently one of the uses of such winds, which occur especially in the fall and spring, to disseminate plants. Alphonse De Candolle quotes Humboldt as saying that M. Bousringault had seen seeds (*graines*) elevated 5,400 feet (*pieds*) and fall back in the neighborhood (apparently among the Alps). I think that I could arrange a trap by which I could catch some of the birch seed which might be floating in the air, in very windy weather in the winter or spring in any part of this county.

White-birch seed

This is eminently one of those northern "grains" which Nature sows broadcast on the snow and with it—as man does with some seeds occasionally. No sooner has the first snow fallen than I begin to see where these pretty brown bird-like scales and winged seeds have been blown into the numerous hollows of the thin-crusted surface. Indeed, all this part of New England is dusted over with them, throughout almost all woods and many fields, as if they had been regularly sifted on it; and each successive snow is newly covered with them—furnishing ever fresh and accessible repasts to the birds. It would not be easy to find a considerable area in the woodland of this county which is completely clear of them. For how many hundreds of miles this grain is scattered over the earth—under the feet of all walkers, in Boxborough and in Cambridge and the like, and rarely an eye distinguishes it.

Whoever faithfully analyzes a New England snowbank will probably report a certain percentage of birch seed. Where a birch has been bent down and jarred, or run over by a sleigh in a woodland path, you will often see the snow perfectly browned with its fruit so as to be conspicuous a long way off.

It is also blown far over the snow like the pine seed. Walking up our river on the 2d of March 1856—by Mr. Prichard's land, where the shores and neighboring fields were comparatively bare of trees—I was surprised to see on the snow over the river a great many birch scales and seeds, though the snow had but recently fallen and there had been but little wind. There was one seed or scale to a square foot; yet the nearest birches were a row of fifteen along a wall thirty rods off. When, leaving the river, I advanced toward these, the seeds became thicker and thicker, till at half a dozen rods from the trees, they quite discolored the snow; while on the other side, or eastward of the birches, there was not one. These trees appeared not to have lost a quarter part of their seeds yet. As I returned up the river, I saw some of their seeds forty rods off, and perhaps in a more favorable direction I might have found them much further; for, as usual, it was chiefly the scales which attracted my attention, and the fine winged seed which it is not easy to distinguish had probably been winnowed from them. It suggested how unwearied Nature is in spreading her seeds. Even the spring does not find her unprovided with birch—aye, and alder and pine—seed. A great proportion of the seed that was carried to a distance lodged in the hollow above the river and, when the river broke up, was carried far away to distant shores and meadows. For, as I find by experiment, though the scales soon sink in water, the seeds float for many days.

I notice accordingly that near meadows where there is a very gentle inclination over which water has flowed and receded, birches often grow in more or less parallel lines, the seed apparently having been left there by a freshet or else lodged in the parallel waving hollows of the snow.

I observed last summer that the seeds of a few black birches, which grow near one side of one of our ponds (which contains sixty acres), had been drifted to other shores and had just sprung up at high-water mark there.

It is evident that the seeds which are dropped on the surface of a pond or lake, by the wind or any other agent, will be drifted to the shore unless they sink, and thus collected into a comparatively small area—whence their progeny, if fitted for it, may at length spread inland. I have no doubt that if such a pond were to be now dug in the midst of our woods, the willow, birch, alder, maple, and so on would from these and similar causes soon be found skirting its shores, even though none of these trees grew near it before.

Alphonse De Candolle says that M. Dureau "cites a fact according to which seeds of mustard and of birch preserve their vitality after twenty years' immersion in fresh water."

You will often see white birches growing densely in perfectly straight rows in the ruts of old woodpaths now grown up, the seed having been blown into the long hollows in the snow above the ruts.

Birch seed being thus scattered over the country like a fine grain or a shower of dust, which most do not distinguish for seed, suggests how still more impalpable seeds, like those of fungi, are diffused through the atmosphere—and enables us to realize that truth.

No wonder, then, that the white birch is so prevalent and characteristic a tree with us and that the seedling birches spring up every year on so many neglected spots, but especially where the surface has been cleared or burned.

I noticed the other day a little white birch a foot high which had sprung up in the gutter on the main street in front of my house, and it looked about as strange there as it would in State Street in Boston. It had perhaps been wafted thither in some gale or blown out of a woodman's cart. It suggested how surely and soon the forest would prevail here again if the village were deserted.

Birch seedling

Yet it is stated in Loudon's *Arboretum* that the small white birch is "rarely found in groups; and single trees are met with only at considerable intervals." This is not true of this part of the country. As a consequence of its seeds being almost universally dispersed, and the soil being adapted to it, it not only forms peculiarly dense and exclusive thickets in open land but is pretty generally distributed throughout pine and oak woods. So that it is very common hereabouts to cut out all the birches when they begin to decay, and leave the longer-lived trees, which are only one-fourth or half grown and are still as dense as they ought to be. If the seeds fall on water, they are drifted to the shore and spring up there, though they are very often killed by the water standing long around them.

It is generally observed that the canoe birch is one of the first and commonest trees to spring up when an evergreen forest is burned, in Maine and elsewhere in the north, forming dense and extensive woods as if by magic where, as is stated, this tree was "not before known." But it is forgotten, or not known, how abundant and volatile the seeds of the birch are, and that these trees are almost universally distributed throughout those woods. Within the last fifteen years I have had occasion to make a fire out of doors in the wilds of Maine about a hundred times, in places wide apart, and I do not remember that I ever failed to find birch bark at hand for kindling. It is the common kindling stuff.

Blodget, in his *Climatology*, says, "The birch abounds in such forests as exist at the Arctic Circle, and for all the distance southward to the 41st parallel it is common in the woodlands, both of the general surface and of the highest mountains." It appears that the same is true of the north of Europe and of Asia.

Loudon, speaking of the European variety of the common white birch, says, "According to Pallas, the birch is more common than any other tree throughout the whole of the Russian Empire; being found in every wood and grove from the Baltic Sea to the Eastern Ocean." Loudon also learns from a French author that "in Prussia, the birch is planted everywhere; and it is considered to afford security against a dearth of fuel, and to insure the prosperity of the woods by the dissemination of its seeds, which fill up every blank that occurs."

Seedling white birches can easily be obtained for transplanting. They are one of the earliest shrubs to leaf out, and so are easily detected. In a walk in the spring of 1859, coming across a bed of them, seedlings of the previous year, in the grass by the side of an old grain field, and knowing that a neighbor wanted to get a quantity of birches, I pulled up just a hundred of them, to see what I could do, and bound them in moss at the next swamp I came to. The next time I met my neighbor, I took this package out of my pocket and presented him with one hundred birch trees for his plantation. I could have collected a thousand thus in an hour or two; but I would recommend to let them grow two or three years before transplanting, when they will bear the drought better. In August 1861 I found sixty of these birches alive and from one to five feet high.

As it comes up commonly in open land and in exhausted soil, this is in some places called old-field birch.

I frequently see a young birch forest springing up very densely over a large tract which has been neglected only a year or two, tinging it pink with their twigs, and I have been surprised when the owner, as if he had never noticed this godsend, has concluded that he will skim that pasture once more, get one more crop of rye from it, before he lets it lie fallow—and so destroyed some such two-year-old birch wood, in which I could not help taking an interest, though he knew nothing about it. Having in the meanwhile cut down the seed trees, he will now wait twenty years perhaps in the expectation of seeing a forest spring up; whereas if he had let them alone, he would have had a handsome birch wood, ready to be cut, in two-thirds that time. In 1845 or 1846 I pulled up a white birch some two and a half feet high in the woods, brought it home in my hand, and set it out in my yard.

After ten years it was much larger than most birches when they are set. It is now [Blank space in manuscript.] inches in circumference at one foot from the ground.

If the winds are not amply sufficient, we may be indebted to the various birds which feed on the birch seed and shake down ten times as much as they consume. When this seed is most abundant, great flocks of lesser redpolls come down from the north to feed on it and are our prevailing winter bird. They alight on the birches and shake and rend the cones, then swarm on the snow beneath, busily picking up the seed in the copses. Though there may be but few birches, white or black, in the midst of a wood, these birds distinguish their tops from afar. When I hear their notes, I look round for a birch and generally descry them on its top. Mudie says, "It is very pretty to watch one picking the catkins on the long pendulous twigs of a weeping birch over a mountain stream. These twigs are often twenty feet long, and little thicker than packthread. On the points of these the little birds may sometimes be seen, swinging backwards and forwards like the bobs of pendulums, busy feeding, and never losing their perch."

I also see the goldfinch, which the last so much resemble, eating the birch seed in the same manner.

But, to say nothing of these cones on the trees, we have seen what a bountiful table is already spread for the birds, and is kept spread for them all winter, on the snow beneath, all over the country.

Seed of saw-leaved alder

The seeds of the alder, which is closely allied to the birch, are distributed in a somewhat similar manner, though they are not winged. They too are falling all winter and dusting the snow beneath and around the bushes, and being flat and thin edged—though both larger and heavier than the birch—they may be blown to a considerable distance. There is, of course, less need that they be winged, since they grow along streams or in wet places, whither their seeds may be floated in freshets; but the birches, though they have a wide range, grow chiefly in dry soil, often on the tops of dry hills. This may account for the fact that one of our alders, the mountain alder, which grows on mountains in the northern part of New England, has winged seeds, apparently in order that the seeds may be spread from one ravine to another and also attain to higher levels.

The seed of the hoary alder floats at first, but afterward sinks to the bottom. I see it falling still and floating off in the spring, as soon as the ice melts, and also washed up in windrows on the shore in such places as the trees commonly occupy. The farmers, accordingly, often see it springing up in their meadows in pretty straight lines, corresponding to some high-water mark. It is also drifted into shallow bays when the water is high, and there form at last an alder grove, what the French call an *aulnage*, a convenient word for which we have no equivalent in English.

The same birds feed on the alder as on the birch seeds. Frequently, as I am walking up our frozen and snowy river, I see a flock of lesser redpolls eating the seeds of the alder by the riverside, picking them out of the cones as they do the larch and hemlock seeds, often hanging head downward about it; and I see where they have run underneath and picked up the fallen seeds, which they perhaps have shaken down, making pretty meandering chain-like tracks in two parallel lines.

I even see where squirrels have fed on alder seeds, stripping the cones just as they do the pine cones, and this suggests that they may also feed on the birch seeds, which it requires no such trouble to come at.

The maple seed is another kind which is distributed both by wind and water, as well as by animals. All New Englanders are familiar with the very handsome scarlet fruit of the red maple, and they who paddle on our river may observe the much larger keys of the white maple floating on its surface about the 1st of June. They are nearly two inches long by one-half inch wide, with veined inner edges to the wings like green moths, ready to bear off their seeds. I notice that their fall takes place about the time that the great emperor moth (*Attaeus cecropia*) comes out of its chrysalis, and I sometimes find them in the morning wrecked on the surface of the river amid the maple seeds. The seed of the sugar maple does not ripen until the first severe frosts of the fall, generally in October, and many hold on till winter.

Gerarde's old account of a European species will suffice for all. Having described the flowers, he adds, "After them cometh up long fruit fastened together by couples, one right against another, with kernels bumping out near to the place in which they are combined; in all the other parts flat and thin like unto parchment, or resembling the innermost wings of grasshoppers." Being conspicuously nerved, these have more resemblance to wings than the seed of the pines.

In all our maples a thin membrane, in appearance much like an insect's wing, grows over and around the seed while the latter is being developed within its base. Indeed, this is often perfectly developed, though the seed is abortive—Nature being, you would say, more sure to provide the means of transporting the seed than to provide the seed to be transported. In other words, a beautiful thin sack is woven around the seed, with a handle to it such as the wind can take hold of, and it is then committed to the wind, expressly that it may transport the seed and extend the range of the species; and this it does as effectually as when seeds are sent by mail in a different kind of sack from the Patent Office. There is a Patent Office at the seat of government of the universe, whose managers are as much interested in the dispersion of seeds as any body at Washington can be, and their operations are infinitely more extensive and regular.

It is remarkable how commonly the white maple is found on the banks of rivers and in the swamps which border them. It is accordingly called by some the river maple. It is very local in this town, being confined, so far as I have observed, to the *immediate* bank of the Assabet, and of the Concord or the main stream below its mouth, where it is a characteristic tree; but it is not found on the Concord above the mouth of the Assabet for some ten miles, though it reappears higher up in Sudbury. It is undoubtedly far more common in the section of country watered by the Assabet, and its seeds have probably come down from that way. Most other trees, even including the red maple, if they stand by the water's edge, show some timidity or reserve at least, holding up their boughs as if they were afraid they would be wetted; but the white maple was evidently made to stand on the bank with the black willow and trail its branches in the stream as one of its peculiar ornaments. Probably its great seeds are more indebted to the water than the wind for their transportation.

The red maple forms dense woods by itself in low ground almost anywhere, called maple swamps, and it is also found scattered throughout other woods, both on low and high ground, though it does not attain to perfection on high ground.

About the middle of May, the red maples along the edges of swamps, their fruit being nearly ripe, are among the most beautiful objects in the landscape, especially if seen in a favorable light with respect to the sun. The keys are high colored, a sort of pink scarlet commonly, dangling at the end of peduncles three inches or more in length and only a little darker shade than themselves. The lit masses of these double samarae, with their peduncles gracefully arching upward and outward a little before they curve downward in order to spread the fruit and give it room, are unequally disposed along the branches, where they tremble in the wind and are often tangled by it. Like the flower of the shadbush, this handsome fruit is seen for the most part against bare twigs, it is so much in advance of its own and of other leaves.

Early in June the causeways are strewn with the seed blown far and wide, and, a month later perhaps, I am surprised to see along our river dense groves of the young maples an inch or more high, which have sprung from seed of the same year, in pure sand, whither it has been drifted and the requisite moisture supplied, at the water's edge—especially on the shores, whether sandy or muddy, of bays where there is an eddy.

If you look carefully through a dense red-maple swamp anywhere at midsummer, you will commonly find many of these little maples—but only in the most favorable spots, as in the little beds of sphagnum, which appear to have concealed the seed at the same time that they afforded the necessary moisture. There is the little tree already deeply rooted, while the now useless seed, with its fragile wing half wasted away, lies empty nearby, no longer attached to the plant and as if wholly unrelated to it—so speedily has it performed its office.

Red-maple seedling

I noticed last September where a great many little red maples had sprung up in a potato field, apparently since the last plowing or cultivating of that year. They extended more or less thickly as much as eleven rods in a northwesterly direction from a small tree, the only red maple in that neighborhood, occupying an oval or conical space as the seed was blown, and it was evidently owing to the land having been cultivated that year that the seed vegetated there. The previous year, and for many years, it had been a pasture, and no one suspected that any maple seed fell on it. It is evident that land may be kept as a pasture and covered with grass any number of years, and though there are maples adjacent to it, none of the seed catches in it; but at last it is plowed, and that year the seed which falls on it may germinate; and if it chances not to be plowed again, and cattle are kept out, you may have a maple wood there. So of other light-seeded trees.

The sugar maple, though it is called the most common species in the United States, I have found indigenous in only one place in this town. It grows chiefly on high land (hills and mountains). Since it retains some of its seeds so late, I suspect that their distribution may be somewhat aided by the snow.

Animals also may have something to do with the transportation of maple seed. Loudon recommends to plant it in the spring rather than in the fall, to avoid the moles which devour it.

The 13th of May 1858, as I sat in my boat in a calm and sunny bay on the Concord, just above the mouth of the Assabet, I saw a red squirrel steal slyly up a red maple as if he were in search of a bird's nest, though it was early for most kinds, and I thought I would see what he was at. He crept far out on the slender twigs, which bent beneath him, and, reaching with his neck, nibbled off the clusters of the fruit, sometimes bending them within reach with his paw, and then drawing back a little and squatting on the branch, he voraciously devoured the half-grown keys as if they were a sweet and luscious fruit to him, using his paws to direct or stuff them into his mouth. Bunch after bunch he plucked and ate, letting many fall, and he made an ample if not sumptuous feast, the whole tree hanging red with fruit around him. It seemed like a fairy fruit, as I sat looking toward the sun, with the red keys made all glowing and transparent by its rays between me and the body of the squirrel perched high on that slender twig. It was certainly a cheering sight; and I thought what an abundance and variety of food was now ready for him. At length, when the wind suddenly began to blow hard and shake the twig on which he sat, he quickly ran down a dozen feet.

This will partly account for the rapid disappearance of maple seeds after their fall. You will be surprised on looking, at midsummer, through a large maple swamp which six weeks before was red with seed falling in showers around, at the very small number of maple seeds to be found there, and probably some of these will be empty. You do not generally find any correspondingly dense groves of little trees springing up, but comparatively few, where the seeds have fallen into crevices in the moss and leaves and so escaped being devoured.

By the 10th of May at least, the winged seeds or samarae of the elms give them a leafy appearance, or as if covered with little hops, before the leaf buds are unfolded. A day or two later, especially after rain in the night, you will see the seed generally fallen or falling. It strews not only the streets and puddles but the surface of the river, floating off in green patches down the stream and over the meadows to plant other shores, and thus these trees are found bordering the stream. This must be the earliest of trees and shrubs to go to seed with us.

All gardeners know that it is somewhat troublesome to keep their borders clean of the young trees. The seeds lodge against fences, and in a neglected garden more than enough elms spring up thus to set before the house. Even this seed is sought after by birds, and so also distributed. Kalm, in the account of his travels in this country more than a hundred years ago, says that when he was near Lake Champlain one of his companions shot a great number of pigeons "and gave us some, in which we found a great quantity of the seeds of the elm, which evidently demonstrated the care of Providence in supplying them with food; for in May the seeds of the red maple, which abounds here, are ripe and drop from the trees and are eaten by the pigeons during that time; afterwards the seeds of the elm ripen, which then become their food till other seeds ripen for them." However, according to my observation, the elm seed ripens before that of the red maple. I have observed that the rose-breasted grosbeak feeds on the seed of the elm.

So also the white ash, whose knife-shaped seeds are said to remain on often all winter, is dispersed in a similar manner to the elm and maple, springing up in corners and along fences where the seed had been caught and defended—and also floating off on the streams in whose neighborhood it grows.

The black ash, which is such a lover of the water, is still more indebted to it for the transportation of its seed.

I often see a small clump of maples, elms, or ash trees, and various shrubs in the midst of our river meadows, growing about a rock which is concealed by their leaves; or sometimes, on a firmer shore, two or three elms stand close around a bare rock, which lifts its head above the water in the spring as if protecting it—preventing its being wasted away—and my first thought is how it might have floated in between them. But in truth they owe their origin and preservation to it. It first detained the floating seed, protected the young trees, and now preserves the very soil in which they grow.

Thus, the boulder dropped anciently in a meadow makes at length a clump of trees there and is concealed by its beneficiaries.

As for willows and poplars, their downy seeds fill the air in May and June and also form a thick scum on the surface of water. The barren and fertile flowers are almost always on separate plants. It chances that most of the foreign white willows set out on our causeways are sterile. You can easily distinguish the fertile ones at a distance, when the pods are ripe and bursting, by their hoariness. It is said that no sterile weeping willows have been introduced into this country, that we have but one-half the tree, and accordingly no perfect seeds are formed here. Also, I have detected but one sex of two of the indigenous willows common on the brink of our river, and most of our balm of Gileads are fertile ones.

The fertile catkins of the willow are those green caterpillar-like ones, commonly an inch or more in length, which develop themselves rapidly after the sterile yellow ones are fallen or effete. A single catkin consists of from twenty-five to one hundred little pods, more or less ovate and beaked, each of which is closely packed with cotton, in which are numerous seeds so small that they can scarcely be discerned by ordinary eyes. At maturity the pod opens its beaks, each half curving backwards, and releases its downy contents like the milkweed. Except for size, it is much as if you had a hundred milkweed pods arranged cylindrically around a pole.

Prairie-willow pod

The seed is still smaller and lighter than that of the birch—a mere atom, as I measure, almost one-sixteenth of an inch in length by one quarter as much in width—and is surrounded at the base by a tuft of cotton-like hairs about a quarter of an inch long rising irregularly around and above it. These render it the most buoyant of the seeds of any of our trees. It is borne the furthest horizontally with the least wind. It falls very slowly, even in the still air of a chamber, and rapidly ascends in the heated air over a stove. It floats the most like gossamer of any, in a meandering manner and, being enveloped in this cobwebby tuft somewhat like a spider, the seed is hard to detect. It would take a delicate gin indeed to separate these seeds from their cotton.

By the 13th of May the very earliest of our willows (*Salix discolor*), about the warm edges of meadows, show great green wands, a foot or two long, consisting of curved worm-like catkins three inches long. Like the fruit of the elm, they form conspicuous masses of green before the leaves are noticeable. But some have now begun to burst and show their down, and thus it is the next of our trees and shrubs to shed its seeds after the elm.

Three or four days later, in dry hollows in the woods and by woodsides, the *Salix humilis*, and in high and very dry woodpaths, the smallest of our willows, *Salix tristis*, begin to show their down. The twigs of the latter are soon thickly covered with cotton, like hoary wands, containing little green seeds like excrements of caterpillars.

At the same time also, the down of the early aspen (*Populus tremuloides*) begins to appear. The *Populus grandidentata* is considerably later. The pods of these are subject to a singular monstrosity, growing very large and turning bright yellow, so that they look like a handsome ripe fruit.

In the first half of June, willow down and seeds of various species are blowing over the causeways and meadows.

On June 9th, 1860, we had half a dozen distinct summer showers, from black clouds suddenly wafted up from the west and northeast, and also some thunder and large hail. Standing on the Mill Dam in the afternoon, just after one of these showers, I noticed the air as high as the roofs full of some kind of down, which at first I mistook for feathers or lint from some chamber. It rose and fell just like a flight of ephemerae, or like huge white dancing motes, from time to time coming to the earth. Next, I supposed it to be some gauzy, light-winged insect. It was driven by a slight current of air between and over the buildings and went flying in a stream all along the street, and it was very distinct in the moist air, seen against the dark clouds still lingering in the west. The shopkeepers stood in their doorways wondering what it could be. This was white-willow down which the rain had loosened, and the succeeding slight breeze set a-going, bearing its minute blackish seed in its midst. The earth having just been moistened, this was the best time to sow it. I traced it to its source in a large willow twenty rods distant and a dozen rods from the street, behind the blacksmith's shop.

Such is the way in which this tree sows its seed, and possibly some of these downy atoms, which strike your cheek without your being conscious of it, may come to be pollards five feet in diameter.

Again a week later, on the 15th of June, being on the Concord River, I noticed something whitening the leeward shore, where there was a sort of bay, a gap in the black willows and buttonbushes. It was conspicuously white for two or three rods and reminded me of white rags which I once saw washed up from a wreck on the seashore, also of feathers. Turning aside to it, I found it to be the down of the white willow, as usual full of little seeds, collected by the wind, like a dense white foam a foot or two wide along the water's edge, covering the surface like a fleece or batting, and also heaped or ridged like foam on the outer edge. I had not thought of willow down before, because the white willow does not border the river, and it was not time for the black willows in that neighborhood. The wind was southwest, and it had come from some white willows on a causeway twenty rods off in that direction, having first been blown fifteen rods over land.

Black-willow pod

This downiness is one of the peculiarities by which willows and poplars are generally known. It is a common objection to the balm of Gilead that its down litters the yard—and one species, the *Populus laevigatus*, which does not grow in Concord, is called *cotton*wood.

Pliny thought that the willow lost its seed before it attained to maturity, going off into a cobweb—*"in araneam abit."* Homer, in the *Odyssey*, refers to the willow as ὠλεσιχάρπου, which Pliny and some commentators interpret to mean "fruit-losing," though others suppose it to mean "that produces barrenness." Circe, directing Ulysses to the Infernal Regions, says (according to Pope's translation):

> Soon shalt thou reach old Ocean's utmost ends,
> Where to the main the shelving shore descends;
> The barren trees of Proserpine's black woods,
> Poplars and willows trembling o'er the floods.

From this I infer that the shores of the Styx must present an appearance almost exactly like those of the Saskatchewan and Assineboin and many of our northwestern prairie rivers. The poets get their idea of the Infernal Regions from the most remote and barren part of the Supernal Regions. The explorers of our immense northwest plains, from Mackenzie to Hind, report that the prevailing trees, and these are confined to the immediate river valleys, are small aspens and willows; and some think that if the prairies were not annually burned by the Indians, these at last might make a soil for nobler forests.

I have often noticed in the wilds of Maine, and even hereabouts, how rapidly the poplar springs up on burnt lands. It is remarkable that just those trees whose seeds are the finest and lightest should be the most widely dispersed—the pioneers among trees, as it were, especially in more northern and barren regions. Their tiny seed is buoyed up and wafted far through the atmosphere, and speedily clothes the burnt tracts of all British America and our own northern wilds, affording both food and shelter for the beaver and the hare; and the water also assists in transporting them, while the heavy-seeded trees for which they may prepare the way are comparatively slow to spread themselves.

No soil is so dry and sandy, none so wet, scarcely any so alpine or arctic, but it is the peculiar habitat of some species of willow. When I was at the White Mountains in July 1858, considerable tracts of its alpine region were hoary with the down of the little bearberry willow (*Salix uva-ursi*), a densely tufted trailing shrub on which you trod as on moss. Its seeds were just bursting away with irrepressible elasticity and buoyancy, and spreading its kind from peak to peak along the White Mountain range. Another also found there, *Salix herbacea*, the smallest of all willows if not of all shrubs, is said, together with the *Salix arctica*, to extend the furthest northward of all woody plants.

Though we do not commonly observe these seeds floating through the air, yet suitable tests will almost everywhere reveal them. If you lay bare any spot in our woods, however sandy, by a railroad cutting for instance, or if the frost prevents other trees from springing up there, no shrub or tree is surer to plant itself there sooner or later than a willow (*Salix humilis* or *Salix tristis*) or poplar.

The seeds of the poplar seem, like those of the milkweed, to settle mostly in hollows, where there is a lull of the wind. Or they may happen to grow there chiefly because these places, being frosty, are slow to be clothed by less hardy plants. In this neighborhood there are many such poplar hollows.

Build a causeway through almost any open meadow and, if man does not interfere, it will soon be fringed on each side with a hedge of willows (not to mention alders and so on), though none may have grown near there before and no plants or seeds have been introduced by man. Hence, man has learned to protect his causeways against floods by setting willows of the largest species there.

About 1844, when our railroad was built, there was a large, open tract, for the most part meadow, south of the west end of the village and between it and the woods, in which no bushes of any consequence were allowed to grow. Through this the railroad causeway, a sandbank fifteen or more feet in height, was built, running north and south about at right angles with the

59

river; and some ten years afterward I was struck by the fact that a continuous natural willow hedge had been formed, especially on the east side of the embankment along its base, where there was a fence beginning about half a mile from the river and stretching an equal distance to the woods. This hedge was, of course, as straight as the railroad or its bounding fence.

Here was, in fact, quite a natural *Salictum*, very convenient for me to study, consisting of eight species of willows, or about one-half of all the kinds that I find in Concord: namely, *Salix rostrata, humilis, discolor, alba, torreyana, sericea, pedicellaris*, and *lucida*—all but one indigenous. You might have thought that the seeds or twigs were brought with the sand when the causeway was built, from the neighboring deep cut in the woods; but only the first three of these willows *at most* grew there. The last four were not to be found elsewhere nearer than the river meadows, half a mile northward, the other side of the village—and indeed, they are in this town, generally speaking, confined to the river's brink and the adjacent meadows. Especially I should be surprised to find the last two in places remote from the river meadows, so local are they here. The *Salix alba* is the only one which I know to have grown near the causeway before.

Hence, I saw that the seeds of at least one-half of these kinds, and probably most of the others, had been blown hither from a distance and were caught by the bank, lodging against its foot, somewhat as a snowdrift accumulates there; for I saw several ash trees among them, which had come from an ash ten rods east in the meadow, though none had sprung up elsewhere. There were also a few alders, elms, birch, poplars, and some elder. Thus, if the other conditions are favorable, you may surely expect the willows to spring up, for there will always be found seed enough of these trees floating in the air.

For years a willow might not have chanced to take root in the open meadow, but run a barrier like this through it, and in a short time it will be lined with them; for it both collects the seeds and defends the plants against man himself, as well as other foes. They plant themselves along its base only, as exclusively as along the shores of a river. The sandbank is a shore to them, and the meadow a lake; for here they enjoy the warmth and shelter of the sand while their roots are revelling in the moisture of the meadow. The very trees and weeds, if we consider their origin, have often drifted thus like snow against the fences and hillsides, where their growth is encouraged and protected.

How impatient, how rampant, how precocious these osiers. *Some* derive their Latin name *Salix* from *salire*, "to leap," they spring up so rapidly—they are so salient. They have hardly made two shoots from the sand in as many springs, when silvery catkins burst out along them, and anon golden blossoms and downy seeds, spreading their race with incredible rapidity. Thus, they multiply and clan together, taking advantage even of the railroad, which elsewhere invades and disturbs the domains of the trees.

But though the seeds of the willow thus annually fill the air with their lint, being wafted to every cranny in the woods and meadows, apparently only one in a million gets to be a shrub or tree. Nevertheless, that suffices; and Nature's purpose is completely answered. Many of the *Salix alba* have been set along our causeways, but very few have sprung up naturally and maintained their ground elsewhere, and I suspect that more of these have come from twigs accidentally dropped than from seeds. Even the few which have planted themselves with the black willow on the brink of the stream may have sprung from twigs which have been drifted from the causeways. The oldest and largest of these trees standing about houses, if we may believe tradition, have but one history, the same story being told of nearly all. The portly grandfather who sits within remembers that when he was a little boy playing horse in the yard, he at length stuck his willow switch in the ground and forgot it, and now it has grown to yonder tree, which all travellers admire. Of course, it will not do to let many of these willow seeds, comparatively, succeed, for if every white-willow seed were to become a tree like this, in a few years the entire mass of the planet would be converted into willow woods, which is not Nature's design.

White-willow catkin

Another foreign species, the *Salix purpurea*, came into this town by accident a few years ago, as a withe tied round a bundle of other trees. A curious gardener stuck it in the ground, and now it has descendants.

About the middle of June, the black willow, which borders our river, goes to seed, and its down begins to fall on the water and continues to fall for more than a month. It is most conspicuous on the trees in the last week of this month, giving them a particolored or spotted white-and-green look, quite interesting, like a fruit. It is then also most abundant on the water.

Some of these seeds, which I put in a tumbler in my window on the 7th of June, germinated in two days, showing little roundish green leaves. This surprised and interested me because botanists generally complain of the great difficulty of making willow seed germinate.

I think that I see how this tree is propagated. Its minute brown seeds, just perceptible in the midst of the cotton, are wafted with this to the water—most abundantly about the 25th of June—and there they drift and form a thick white scum, together with other matter, especially against some alder or other fallen or drooping shrub by the side of the stream, where there is less current than usual. This scum commonly takes the form of narrow crescents, ten or fifteen feet long, at right angles with the bank and curving downstream, and is so thick and white as to remind me of hoar-frost crystals. There within two or three days a great many germinate and show their two little roundish green leaflets above the white, more or less tinging with green the surface of the scum, somewhat like grass seed in a tumbler of cotton and water. Many of these are drifted in amid the buttonbushes, willows, and other shrubs and the sedge along the riverside; and perhaps the water falling just at this time when they have put forth little fibers, they are gently deposited on the mud just left bare in the shade, and thus probably many of them have a chance to become perfect plants. But if they do not drop into sufficiently shallow water and are not left on the mud at the right time, they probably perish. I have seen the mud in many such places green with them, and perhaps the seed was often blown directly through the air to such localities.

But if they do not succeed in this way, they have other resources. For instance, like some other species along our river, this, by a singular provision, is so brittle at the base of the twigs that they break on the least touch, as if cut square off—though they are as tough above as they are brittle below and could no doubt be twisted into a strong cable by which to moor your vessel, a use to which willow twigs are put in some countries. But these twigs are only thus shed like seeds which float away and plant themselves in the first bank on which they lodge.

One June I noticed, in a mass of damp shavings, leaves, and sand left bare on the sandy shore of the Assabet, a little prostrate black willow just coming into flower; and pulling it up I found it to be a twig sixteen inches long, two-thirds buried in the damp mass. This was probably broken off by the ice, brought down, washed up, and buried there like a layer; and now for two-thirds its length it had put out rootlets an inch or two long abundantly, and leaves and catkins from the part above ground; and thus you had a tree which might at length wave high over the shore—so vivacious is this willow, availing itself of every accident to spread along the river's bank. The ice that strips it and breaks it down only disperses it the more widely.

I commonly litter my boat with a shower of these twigs whenever I run into the black willows, for they are low and spreading, even resting on the water; and heretofore I had ignorantly pitied the hard fate of the tree that was made so brittle and not yielding like a reed. But now I admired its invulnerability. I would gladly hang my harp on such a willow, if so I might derive inspiration from it. Sitting down by the shore of the Concord, I could almost have wept for joy at the discovery of it.

Ah willow, willow, would that I always possessed thy good spirits;

would that I were as tenacious of life, as *withy*, as quick to get over my hurts.

I do not know what they mean who call the willow the emblem of despairing love!—who tell of

"the willow worn by forlorn paramour!"

It is rather the emblem of triumphant love and sympathy with all Nature. It may droop, it is so lithe, but it never weeps. The willow of Babylon blooms not the less hopefully here, though its other half is not in the New World at all and never has been. It droops not to commemorate David's tears, but rather to remind us how on the Euphrates once it snatched the crown from Alexander's head.

Weeping-willow catkin

No wonder that willow wood was anciently in demand for bucklers; for, like the whole tree, it is not only soft and pliant but tough and *resilient*, not splitting at the first blow but closing its wounds at once and refusing to transmit its hurts. It is a tree whose ordinary fate it is to be cut down every two or three years, and yet it neither dies nor weeps but puts forth shoots which are all the more vigorous and brighter for it, and it lives as long as most. It is observed in Fuller's *Worthies* that "this tree delighteth in moist places and is triumphant in the Isle of Ely, where the roots strengthen their banks, and lop affords fuel for their fire. It groweth incredibly fast, it being a by-word in this country that the profit by willows will buy the owner a horse before that by other trees will pay for his saddle."

Herodotus says that the Scythians divined by the help of willow rods, and where could they have found any better twigs for such a purpose? I begin to be a diviner myself at the first sight of one.

When I pass by a twig of willow, though of the slenderest kind, rising above the sedge in some dry hollow early in December, or above the snow in midwinter, my spirits rise as if it were an oasis in the desert. The very name "sallow" (*salix*, from the Celtic *sal*, "near," and *lis*, "water") suggests that there is some natural sap or blood flowing there. It is a divining wand that has not failed but stands with its root in the fountain.

Aye, the willow is no tree for suicides. It never despairs. Is there no moisture longer in Nature which it can transmute into sap? It is the emblem of youth, joy, and everlasting life. Where is the winter of its discontent? Scarcely is its growth restrained by any season, but its silvery down begins to peep forth in the warmest days in January.

Nor were poplars ever the weeping sisters of Phaeton, as some pretend, for nothing rejoices them more than the sight of the sun's chariot, and little wreck they who drives it.

It would perhaps be shorter to tell how such a tree as the willow does not propagate itself than how it does. I do not know of any animals which disseminate it, unless those birds which use the down in their nests may do so. Jardine, in a note to Wilson, says that the nests of the lesser redpoll, which he has often found in a young fir plantation in the north of Britain, being constructed late in the season, "were invariably lined with the wool of willow catkins." This may sometimes be the case with our goldfinches' nests. Mudie says that the English goldfinch sometimes lines its nest with willow down. Wilson says that the purple finch feeds on the seeds of the poplar.

The buttonwood, according to Michaux the largest deciduous tree in this latitude, has seeds which, though much larger than those of the birch and willow, are smaller than those of most garden vegetables. Each of its balls, which are about seven-eighths of an inch in diameter, consists of three or four hundred club-shaped seeds about a quarter of an inch long, standing on their points like pins closely packed in a globular pin-cushion, surrounded at the base by a bristly down of a tawny color, which answers the purpose of a parachute. These balls, dangling at the end of long but tough and fibrous stems, on lofty trees—and when there is a small crop, on the tops of the trees, as I have noticed—are shaken and tossed about by the storms of winter and spring and so gradually loosened and the seeds set free, perhaps in a driving snowstorm. Under these circumstances the seed, though it is not remarkably buoyant, stands a chance of being carried a long way. I have noticed that it sows itself readily anywhere within ten or twenty rods of the parent tree. And I read that "poplars and cottonwood [or sycamore (*Platanus*)] make up a large share of the tree growths of the interior woodlands on alluvial or prairie soils." Wilson says that the orchard oriole usually lines its nest with the buttonwood down or wool and that the purple finch feeds on its seeds in the winter. Giraud also says that the last seems to be very fond of those seeds.

From such small beginnings—a mere grain of dust, as it were—do mighty trees take their rise. As Pliny says of the cypress, "It is a marvellous fact, and one which ought not to be overlooked, that a tree should be produced from sources so minute, while the grains of wheat and of barley are so very much larger, not to mention the bean." He adds that the ants are remarkably fond of its tiny seed, and his wonder is excited by the fact that "an insect so minute is able to destroy the first germ of a tree of such gigantic dimensions."

Or as Evelyn writes, who appears to have been inspired by Pliny:

And what mortal is there so perfect an anatomist, who will undertake to detect the thousandth part or point of so exile a grain, as that insensible rudiment, or rather halituous spirit which brings forth the lofty fir tree and the spreading oak? [Or who is prepared to believe] that trees of so enormous an height and magnitude, as we find some elms, planes, and cypresses, some hard as iron and solid as marble (for such the Indies furnish many), should be swaddled and involved within so small a dimension (if a point may be said to have any) without the least luxation, confusion, or disorder of parts, and in so weak and feeble a substance; being at first but a kind of tender mucilage, or rather rottenness, which so easily dissolves and corrupts substances so much harder when they are buried in the moist womb of the earth, whilst this, tender and flexible as it is, shall be able in time to displace and rend asunder whole rocks of stones, and sometimes to cleave them beyond the force of iron wedges, so as even to remove mountains? For thus no weights are able to suppress the victorious palm; and thus our tree (like man whose inverted symbol he is), being sown in corruption, rises in glory by little and little ascending into a hard, erect stem of comely dimensions—into a solid tower, as it were; and that which but lately a single ant would easily have borne to his little cavern is now capable of resisting the fury and braving the rage of the most impetuous storms.

What would Pliny and Evelyn have said of that eighth wonder of the world, the giant sequoia of California, which springing from so small a seed (the cones are said to be shaped like those of a white pine, but to be only two and a half inches long) has outlasted so many of the kingdoms of the world?

If we suppose the earth to have sprung from a seed as small in proportion as the seed of a willow is compared with a large willow tree, then the seed of the earth, as I calculate, would have been equal to a globe less than two and a half miles in diameter, which might lie on about one-tenth of the surface of this town.

Of course, there is no necessity for supposing that the various trees of which I have spoken, which bear such an abundance of seeds, provided with wings or down expressly for their transportation, should have sprung up from nothing; and I am aware that I am not at all peculiar in asserting that they come from seeds, though the mode of their propagation by *Nature* has been but little attended to. Most of them, or the corresponding species, are extensively raised from the seed in Europe, and they are beginning to be here. So much, then, for the light and winged seeds of trees.

As for the heavy seeds and nuts which are not furnished with wings, the notion is still a very common one that when the trees which bear these spring up where none of their kind were noticed before, they have come from seeds or other principles spontaneously generated there in an unusual manner, or which have lain dormant in the soil for centuries, or perhaps been called into activity by the heat of a burning. I do not believe these assertions, and I will state some of the ways in which, according to my observation, such forests are planted and raised.

Every one of these seeds, too, will be found to be winged or legged in another fashion. Surely it is not wonderful that cherry trees of all kinds are widely dispersed, since their fruit is well known to be the favorite food of various birds. Many kinds are called bird-cherries, and they appropriate many more kinds which are not so called. Eating cherries is a bird-like employment, and unless we disperse the seeds occasionally, as they do, I shall think that the birds have the best right to them.

See how artfully the seed of a cherry is placed in order that a bird may be compelled to transport it—in the very midst of a tempting pericarp, so that the creature that would devour this must commonly take the stone also into its mouth or bill. If you ever ate a cherry and did not make two bites of it, you must have perceived it—right in the center of the luscious morsel, a large earthy residuum left on the tongue. We thus take into our mouths cherry stones as big as peas, a dozen at once, for Nature can persuade us to do almost anything when she would compass her ends. Some wild men and children instinctively swallow these, like the birds, when in a hurry, as the shortest way to get rid of them. It is only princes who can afford to have their cherry puddings stoned, and so make their lives more completely luxurious and useless; and perhaps they expect to atone for this by their planting a tree with a flourish of trumpets now and then.

Thus, though these seeds are not provided with vegetable wings, Nature has impelled the thrush tribe to take them into their bills and fly away with them; and they are winged in another sense, and more effectually than the seeds of pines, for these are carried even against the wind. The consequence is that cherry trees grow not only here but there. The same is true of a great many other seeds.

If this seed had been placed in a leaf, or at the root of the tree, it would not have got transported thus.

I very often see the stones of the cultivated cherry left in the nests of birds in the woods, at a great distance from a cherry tree (in gardens they are often full of them); also while stooping to drink at springs, I see them on the bottom, where birds that came to drink like me must have dropped them, half a mile from the nearest cherry tree—and thus the tree gets planted. In short, it is notorious how busy the birds are in distributing cherry stones, since it is difficult for you to save any cherries for the table. Yet it is to be noticed that they do not always take the stone with them.

A neighbor tells me that the birds do not touch his inferior mazzard cherries until they have finished all the grafted kinds—and even the small wild black cherries that may be near—but after that they strip his mazzard trees also.

Accordingly, the cultivated cherry will spring up far and wide, in sproutlands or wherever the earth is bared of trees, like the wild ones; but as both the forest and cultivation destroy them, they attain to a size which attracts our attention only in sproutlands or along fences. This species appears to prefer a hilltop—whether the birds are more inclined to carry the seeds there, or they find there the light and exposure and the soil which they prefer.

There are a dozen or fifteen handsome young English cherry trees on a hilltop in the woods by Walden Pond, which was cut off a dozen years ago, and I remember much larger ones on Fair Haven Hill enclosed in the woods. I dug up three of the former last fall and set them in my garden, and they were handsome trees and growing faster than any I could find in the last nursery which I visited—showing a clear and vigorous growth—but with large and bad roots for transplanting.

The black, or rum, cherry is far more widely dispersed by the same means and is a common shrub in sproutlands. The birds convey its seeds in great quantities into the midst of the densest woods, and when the woods are cut these are among the first and commonest shrubs to spring up there. But this, too, soon dies out there, and I rarely if ever see a large tree in the woods. You have only to let one stand by your house, or the edge of your field, to have flocks of birds—cherry-birds, kingbirds, and rob-ins—coming and going directly from and to a great distance every day when the fruit is ripe.

Dr. Manasseh Cutler, in 1785 speaking of the northern wild red cherry at the White Mountains—a tree comparatively rare in this town—said, "In land where there is no kind of cherry trees, after the old growth, which consists chiefly of spruce, pine, beech, and birch (exceedingly tall and large), has been felled and burnt on the ground, there springs up the next summer an immense number of these cherry trees."

Michaux also refers to the same fact, saying that "this species of cherry tree offers the same remarkable peculiarity with the canoe birch of repro-ducing itself spontaneously" under these circumstances.

I have noticed in Maine what dense thickets of this tree spring up on the sites of loggers' camps, and at carries, where small areas have been cleared, or even where a solitary traveller has camped for a night—so forward is this fruit, as well as raspberries and strawberries, to come, as it were, at the first beckoning of man, for they love the same light and air that he does. Mr. George B. Emerson, in his *Report on Trees*, says that in climbing the wild hills of Maine and New Hampshire he has "repeatedly observed in the beds of the streams, often the most practicable paths, surprising numbers of the nuts of this cherry, though there were no trees of the kind within a great distance." They were probably washed down by torrents, as well as left there by birds and quadrupeds. However, even the dense thickets of this tree which spring up under these circumstances are easily accounted for, when you consider how regularly and widely its seeds are dispersed by birds.

Probably the fruit of no tree is more regularly sought after by them than that of cherry trees, both wild and cultivated, though some of the former are far from agreeable to our taste; and a great proportion of these birds are such as are likely to carry the seed into the depth of the woods. As I learn from the ornithologies and my own observation, the most common cherry-eating birds are the robin, cherry-bird, catbird, brown thrasher, kingbird, jay, pigeon woodpecker, red-headed woodpecker, bluebird, and cardinal grosbeak.

The ancients, having observed how commonly some seeds were planted by birds, inferred that birds were indispensable agents in their planting. Evelyn, speaking of the seeds of the holly, of which bird-lime is made, says, "There goes a tradition that they will not sprout till they be passed through the maw of a thrush; whence the saying *Turdus exitium suum cacat*."

If you would study the habits of birds, go where their food is; for example, if it is about the first of September, to the wild black-cherry trees, elder bushes, pokeweed, and mountain-ash trees. Excepting the whortle-berries, which are drying up, the wild cherries and elderberries are then the two prevailing wild fruits in this town.

As I was walking at this date in 1859 in a sproutland far in the woods in Lincoln, I came to a small black cherry full of fruit, of which I plucked some, and there for the first time for a long while I saw and heard cherry-birds—their shrill and fine *seringo*—and robins, which of late had been scarce. Indeed, I had remarked to my companion on the general scarcity and silence of the birds. We sat on a rock near this tree and listened to these now unusual sounds. From time to time one or two birds came dashing from out the sky toward this tree till, seeing us, they wheeled, disappointed, and perhaps alighted on some neighboring twigs to wait till we were gone.

The cherry-birds and robins seem to know the locality of any wild cherry tree in the town, and you are as sure to find them on these trees now as to find bees and butterflies on the thistles. If we stay long, they go off with a fling to some other such tree which they know of but we do not. The neighborhood of a wild-cherry tree full of fruit is now, for the notes of birds, a little spring come back again.

At length we continued our walk through silent and deserted fields and woods, and when, a mile or two from this, I was plucking a basketful of elderberries by a fence, I was surprised to find that I had come upon a flock of young golden robins and bluebirds, apparently feeding on them, flitting before me from bush to bush. Thus, whenever we came to the localities of these fruits, we found the berry-eating birds assembled.

To what an extent, then, must cherry stones, especially the smaller or wild kinds which the birds can readily swallow, be sown annually in fields and woods!

There is no mystery about new trees coming up where there has been a fire, because either the young and feeble plants, whose roots escape the fire but which would die if the wood was left, can now grow there, or else, the ground being thus cleared, the seeds can catch there.

It is remarkable how generally wild fruits, berries, and seeds are the food of birds, mice, and so forth. Judging what I do not know from what I do, I am inclined to say that all are—however hard or dry, sour, bitter, tasteless, or minute—for their tastes are not like ours. How many kinds of birds, for instance, feed on the berries of the red cedar in the fall and winter? According to ornithologists, the most common are the robin, cherry-bird, myrtle-bird, bluebird, purple finch, mockingbird, pine grosbeak, and, as I have noticed, the crow; and probably the same ones eat the berries of the creeping juniper also. Wilson says that the cherry-bird is "immoderately fond" of the fruit of the red cedar and that "thirty or forty may sometimes be seen fluttering among the branches of one small cedar tree, plucking off the berries"; and Audubon observes that "the appetite of the cedar-bird [for it is called both cherry- and cedar-bird] is of so extraordinary a nature as to prompt it to devour every fruit or berry that comes in its way. In this manner they gorge themselves to such excess as sometimes to be unable to fly, and suffer themselves to be taken by the hand."

We have very little red cedar in Concord, especially in the south part of the town, and I used to wonder accordingly where a little one which I observed twenty years ago, springing up on one of our hills, had come from. But one hard winter, when I chanced to be watching the crows which regularly visited each hole which the fishermen had made in the ice of Walden Pond as soon as the latter had withdrawn, for the sake of the bait which was left there, I found that they dropped on the ice the seeds of the cedar and barberry in abundance. The nearest cedars which then bore fruit were a grove by the side of Flint's Pond in Lincoln, a mile eastward, where the barberry, which also does not grow at Walden, is plentifully mingled with them. I saw that the crows, after eating cedar berries and barberries there, and having picked up the bait which the fishermen had left on Flint's Pond, had come over to Walden to see what they could glean here. Therefore I have not been surprised to see since that date many more little cedars springing up on that hill.

Barberry seeds, sour as the fruit is, are extensively planted by crows—like apple seeds, in little thickets—and also by robins, which feed on them regularly and extensively in the fall, and by other birds, and probably by mice, for I sometimes see an old bird's nest half full of them. In the winter I surprise the partridge on the barberry bush, and also on the sumac, and see where they have hopped up to it, and I suspect that they eat the berries of both.

One would not expect the bayberry to be much sought after, yet it is said to be eaten by the yellow-rumped warbler, or *myrtle*-bird (which has got its name thence), the robin, hermit thrush, mockingbird; and Wilson, speaking of the white-bellied swallows at Great Egg Harbor at the end of summer, says that he saw them completely covering some of the myrtle bushes and that "for some time before their departure, they subsist principally on the myrtle berries (*Myrica cerifera*) and become extremely fat."

I know of but one fertile bayberry bush in this town, but I have found that its berries were all gone by the middle of October—probably eaten by birds, for, where abundant, a great part hold on till the next year.

The fruit of the tupelo (pepperidge, sour gum) is small, very acid, and has a large stone, and you would not think of tasting it a second time—yet it is singularly attractive to birds, especially robins. "So fond are they of gum berries," says Wilson, "that wherever there is one of these trees covered with fruit, and flocks of robins in the neighborhood, the sportsman need only take his stand near it, load, take aim, and fire; one flock succeeding another, with little interruption, almost the whole day: by this method prodigious slaughter has been made among them with little fatigue."

Other birds which are said to feed on them are the rose-breasted grosbeak (eagerly), pigeon woodpecker (plentifully), red-headed woodpecker, mockingbird, cherry-bird, and bluebird.

It is said in Loudon's *Arboretum* that "in Livonia, Sweden, and Kamtschatka, the berries of the mountain ash [the same we have introduced, though we have one of our own] are eaten, when ripe, as fruit." But I think that the climate there must have an ameliorating effect on them, or else the inhabitants are very hard pushed—though I know that there is nothing so crabbed but somebody will be found to eat it somewhere. They are exceedingly bitter and austere to my taste, and I do not see how the birds can eat them; but it is to be observed that they do not stand to chew them. However, I observe that the robins, cherry-birds, and purple finches have the same taste with the Livonians, and Evelyn says that the thrushes are so fond of them that as long as these trees last in your woods you will be sure of their company.

About the 20th of September—though they often begin before the berries are ripe—the trees which stand in front yards will be all alive with these birds, which have come after the fruit; nor is it only a transient bite which they take, for they do not stop till they have completely stripped them of their drooping orange clusters. It is as if a "bee" had assembled to do the most work in a short time, and in the merriest way—having just dispatched a similar business somewhere else. My neighbor complains that the birds first get most of his strawberries, at the same time that they are doing him some good, and finally when his mountain-ash berries get to be most ornamental to his front yard, they take every one of them in a few days.

It is not then a few seeds only that are dropped here and there, but the whole crop of some of the trees I have been speaking of, unless it is a very large one, is commonly dispersed far and wide by these agents.

Nevertheless, it chances that I have noticed but one mountain ash of any species (the American one is not indigenous in this town) which had been sown in this manner here. Yet where the soil and climate are suitable, this must be the way they are propagated.

The handsome but unpalatable fruit of the sassafras is so commonly devoured by birds that I can rarely find one ripe, and even the dry and repulsive fruit of the *Celtis* (hackberry) is said to be eaten by the pigeon and by the ivory-billed woodpecker.

In short, the seeds of trees or their pericarp are peculiarly the food of birds, rather than of quadrupeds, reptiles, or fishes. They can reach them most easily, and are fitted to disperse them the farthest.

About the 1st of September, if you would study the habits of birds, go where their food is—for example, to the wild black-cherry trees and elder bushes, the poke and mountain-ash trees. Excepting the whortleberries, which are past their prime and drying up, the wild cherries and elderberries are now the two prevailing wild fruits, and accordingly we find the berry-eating birds assembled where they grow, about the elderberries—the golden robins, bluebirds, and robins.

To the above list we may add, in their season, the fruit of the sumac, *Prinos*, *Viburnum*, thorn, rose-hips, shadbush, grape, *Amphicarpaea*, and checkerberry. Squirrels and mice also very commonly eat the above-named seeds of trees and shrubs. Charles Darwin says of the *Parus major* (of England) that he has "many times seen and heard it hammering the seeds of the yew." May not our chickadee, which is nearly allied to the former, feed on the seeds of our yew? Wilson says of the pokeberries, which are eaten by robins, "the juice of the berries is of a beautiful crimson, and

75

they are eaten in such quantities by these birds, that their whole stomachs are strongly tinged with the same red color"—which accident has sometimes saved the lives of the robins, since epicures feared that their flesh might be poisonous.

But what is more remarkable, even the skunk cabbage and arum berries are eaten by birds or quadrupeds.

About the middle of August, the small fruits of most plants are generally ripe or ripening, and this is coincident with the flying in flocks of such young birds now grown as feed on them.

Widely as it is dispersed, I do not know that I ever detected a seedling huckleberry. When I have examined the bushes of the common black huckleberry (*Gaylussacia resinosum*) in a thick pine wood thirty years old, I have found that they spread by vigorous runners just under the leaves, forking occasionally; and though the individual bushes were not more than eight or ten years old, the stock or runner was undoubtedly as old as the wood and was the relic of a flourishing huckleberry patch, which in one instance had grown along a wall in an open field. I sometimes traced the runner seven feet before it broke off, and it was undoubtedly much longer. There would be three or four bushes rising from it successively, which grew very feebly—not more than an inch in the last year—while the runner had grown from six to twelve inches at the end. The largest bushes still betrayed their origin in this runner by a curve at the base, for the end of the runner had turned upward to form the bush, while another shoot kept on horizontally.

A huckleberry bush in the open field appears to be in its prime at five or six years of age—and to live commonly ten or twelve.

The same was the case with the low blueberries (*Vaccinium vacillans* and *Vaccinium pennsylvanicum*), though on a smaller scale; and in one more open place I saw the former growing in rows several feet long, directly above the subterranean runners and indicating their position.

You will occasionally notice a young huckleberry bush growing lustily on the top of a high white-pine stump which has been sawed off, standing in the chink between the bark and the wood as if it had sprung from a seed which was left on the stump by a bird and was blown into this chink; but probably such bushes oftenest come from runners which find their way up from below. So with the *Pyrus arbutifolia* and so on. Plants of this order (*Ericaceae*) are said to be among the earliest fossil plants, and they are likely to be among the last to be found on the globe. The huckleberries form a humble and more or less dormant, but yet vivacious, forest under a forest, which bides its time.

Two or three years after a wood has been cut, you will commonly find an abundant crop of huckleberries and blueberries there, not to mention chokeberries, serviceberries, and so on. These have already been planted there by animals, just as I shall show that the little oaks are, or possibly some have survived there since the wood was cut before; for Nature keeps a supply of these important plants in her nursery under the larger woods, always ready for casualties, as fires, windfalls, and clearings by man.

I see the seeds of these and other berries left on the rocks in woods and pastures where birds have perched. They are constantly disseminating them in their season.

Probably no berries are more sought after by them. Wilson says that the cherry-bird makes an annual visit to the Alleghenies for them, and that in their season they form almost the whole fare of the summer redbird and scarlet tanager. To these we add the great crested flycatcher, small green-crested flycatcher, prairie hen, and turtledove—and we may also join with them the robin, brown thrasher, woodthrush, pigeon—and doubtless many other birds feed on them. George Emerson says that the low blueberry feeds immense flocks of wild pigeons.

The fox, too, eats huckleberries extensively; and I very often see their seeds mixed with the fur and bones of the animals which they have devoured. It chanced last September that in the only two instances in which I examined fox dung, on different days and in places far apart in the woods, it consisted chiefly of woodchuck's fur with a part of the lower jaw and incisor teeth, and huckleberry seeds with some whole huckleberries. Like ourselves, the fox likes two courses, woodchuck and huckleberries, at the same meal. Thus, it appears that Nature employs not only a great many birds but this restless ranger, the fox, to disperse the huckleberry. I frequently see also the seeds of other small fruits (perhaps rose-hips or winterberries) left in his excrement.

In like manner the high blueberry, chokeberry, and so on, are ready to spring up in swamps when they are cleared, but afterwards maples and so forth overshadow and kill them.

Going by a piece of rich, low ground last October, I observed an immense quantity of scarlet asparagus seeds, dotting the pale brown mist made by its withered branches and stems. There was at least an acre of the plant, and there must have been many bushels of the seed. This sight suggested how extensively the birds must spread it.

Examining, accordingly, an uncultivated and bushy hillside a dozen rods north and across a road, I saw numerous plants two or three feet high in the grass and bushes there, with already their own seed—which plants the birds must have formerly introduced there from the above-named patch. Also I find very small and slender wiry plants—thus planted, with the seed attached, in the remotest and wildest swamps in the town—a mile from the nearest house. They never come to anything in the latter case, and most would not know what they were.

For several years I have noticed small tomato plants growing in the woods in various places about Walden Pond, sometimes within hollow stumps, at least three-fourths of a mile from the nearest house or garden. The seeds may possibly have been carried there annually by picnic parties. Otherwise they must have been dropped by birds each year, for they do not bear fruit there. Yet I have not chanced to see the birds pecking at tomatoes in our gardens, nor have I ever seen seedling potato plants which were not sown by man, though they are a kindred plant and far more extensively cultivated. The goldfinch feeds on various seeds and has received various names accordingly. I know it chiefly as the thistle-bird, but I find that my neighbor who stores seeds calls it the lettuce-bird—and another knows it as the bird that gets his sunflower seeds, and still another, perchance, as the hemp-bird.

Consider how the apple tree has spread over the country, through the agency of cows and other quadrupeds, making almost impenetrable thickets in many places and yielding many new and superior varieties for the orchard.

Crows also feed on frozen-thawed apples extensively—and their crops will often be found full of their pulp. I have noticed that they even transport whole apples when in this state. One winter, observing under an oak on the snow and ice by the riverside some fragments of frozen-thawed apples, I looked further and detected two or three tracks of a crow and the droppings of several that must have been perched on the oak, but there were no tracks of squirrels or other animals there. Here and there was a perfectly round hole in the snow under the tree, and putting down my hand, I drew up an apple from under the snow at each hole. The nearest apple trees were thirty rods off across the river. The crows had evidently brought the frozen-thawed apples to this oak for security, and here eaten what they did not let fall on the snow.

Also the cherry-bird, catbird, and red-headed woodpecker eat apples and pears, especially the early and sweet ones. Wilson says of the latter bird that "when alarmed, he seizes a capital one [apple or pear] by striking his open bill deep into it, and bears it off to the woods," and Audubon has seen cherry-birds which, "though wounded and confined to a cage, have eaten apples until suffocation deprived them of life."

But I have elsewhere described the spread of the apple.

Even the pear has, to a considerable extent, introduced itself into our fields and woods, notwithstanding that so few have been cultivated. We do not often get one to grow in our gardens without we plant the seed at least, and know when we do it; so we may well be surprised on finding that they spread themselves at all. Thirty years ago there were very few cultivated pear trees in this township, and I rarely saw a pear at that date, still more rarely a pear seed. Yet Nature, being bent on spreading this tree, did secure some of the pears and seed, then and long before; for I knew a dozen large old trees growing wild at that date, and there were probably as many wild as cultivated ones in this town.

Great quantities of bass nuts are swept down the streams which the trees overhang in August and are carried in freshets still further inland, and they are even blown over the snow and ice to great distances. In Minnesota I have found them in the pouches of the gophers on the prairie.

One September I gathered some of the peculiarly formed nuts of the witch hazel, which grow in pretty clusters, clothed, as it were, in close-fitting buckskin, amid the yellowing leaves, and laid them in my chamber. The double-fruited stone splits and reveals the two shining black, oblong seeds. Three nights afterward, I heard at midnight a snapping sound and the fall of some small body on the floor from time to time. In the morning I found that it was produced by the witch-hazel nuts on my desk springing open and casting their hard and stony seeds across the chamber. They were thus shooting their shining black seeds about the room for several days. Apparently it is not when they first gape open that the seeds fly out, for I saw many if not most of them open already with seeds in them; but the seed appears to fit close to the shell at its base, even after the shell gapes above, and when I release one with my knife, it being still held by its base, it flies, as I have said. Its slippery base appears to be compressed by the un-yielding shell, which at length expels it, just as you can make one fly by pressing it and letting it slip from between your thumb and finger. Thus, it spreads itself by leaps ten or fifteen feet at a time.

Touch-me-not seed vessels, as all know, go off like pistols on the slightest touch, and so suddenly and energetically that they always startle you, though you are expecting it. They shoot their seed like shot. They even explode in my hat as I am bringing them home. De Candolle says that this *Impatiens fulva* is perfectly naturalized in England from America—escaped from gardens.

The seed of the sweet gale, which grows along the edges of brooks and rivers and in meadows, is transported by freshets. In midwinter I find an abundance of them frozen into the ice of the river meadows in windrows, just as they have been washed out by a freshet, and thus they may be planted somewhat in waving lines. In the spring I see the surface of the brooks, which they overhang, covered with their seeds as with a scum.

Exploded seed pod of touch-me-not

I frequently see the heads of the teasel, called abroad "fuller's thistle," floating in our river or washed up on the shore—having come from factories above; and thus the factories which use it may distribute its seeds from one to another by means of the streams which turn their machinery. It is not impertinent to add that it is said that the one who first cultivated the teasel extensively in this town obtained the seed—when it was not to be purchased, because the culture was monopolized—by sweeping a wagon which he had loaned to a teasel grower.

You may see, late in the fall, the tufts of indigo—now turned black—broken off and dropped exactly bottom up in woodland paths and in pastures, as if an industrious farmer or a simpler had been collecting it by handfuls and had dropped his parcel there. The account of it is that they grow up in tufts on benches, many stems close together, and their branches are so intersticed as not to be easily separated, so that the wind operates the more powerfully and breaks them all off together at the ground. And then, on account of their form, these parcels, after being blown about, are commonly left at last exactly bottom up. I see some such parcels with from three to fifteen or more stems within a diameter of four inches, looking exactly as if someone had plucked them and laid them together.

Also, at this season, you see the fly-away grass rolling over the pastures, or going over a wall or rock from time to time.

It is evident that the seeds of these plants may thus be extensively dispersed.

It is easy to see that the seeds of such plants as the pinweed and *Cistus*, which cover our dry fields and bear so abundantly, may be dispersed in various ways. I have seen one of the larger pinweeds growing out of the top of a pitch-pine stump, which yet preserved its form, a foot from the ground, with its roots reaching an inch or two into the decaying wood. The seeds in this case might have been blown there over the snow, when it was on a level with or deeper than the stump. So, as for grasses and weeds generally, Nature will ere long spread her white counterpane under them and catch their seeds, so that the sparrows can more readily detect them.

Fly-away grass seed

Then for that host of downy-seeded herbs whose seeds, as old Gerarde wrote, "are carried away with the wind."

About the 9th of May we begin to see the dandelion already gone to seed here and there in the green grass of some more sheltered and moist bank, when we are looking for the earliest flowers, perhaps before we have detected its rich yellow disk—that little seedy, spherical system which boys blow to see if their mothers want them. (If they blow off all the seeds at one puff, which they rarely do, then they are not wanted.) It is interesting as the first of that class of downy or fuzzy seeds so common in the fall. It is commonly the first of the many hints we get to be about our own tasks, which our Mother has set us, and bringing something to pass ourselves. We may depend on it that our Genius wants us and always will, till we can blow away the firmament itself at a puff. So much more surely and rapidly does Nature work than man.

By the 4th of June they are *generally* gone to seed in the rank grass. You see it dotted with a thousand downy spheres, and children now make ringlets of their crispy stems. [Half leaf of manuscript missing.] Its highest plot to plant the dandelion. Saint Pierre says truly, "It requires a tempest to carry the seed of the cedar to any considerable distance; but the breath of the zephyr is sufficient to resow those of the dandelion."

About the 20th of May I see the first mouse-ear going to seed, and beginning to be blown about the pastures and to whiten the grass together with bluets, and float on the surface of water. They have now lifted themselves much higher above the earth than where we sought for their first flowers. As Gerarde says of the allied English species, "These plants do grow upon sandy banks and untoiled places that lie open to the sun."

I mention these and the dandelions as being, together with the early willows and poplars, the earliest of those which have downy seeds—and excepting the elm, the very first of all to ripen their seeds. An allied plant, the low cudweed (*Gnaphalium uliginosum*), disperses its seeds by the low roadsides much later in the year.

De Candolle says that the *Antennaria margaritacea* (of the same genus with the mouse-ear), called American everlasting (in French, *immortelle*) and early planted in cemeteries in England, has escaped from gardens and cemeteries in England and fairly become naturalized.

The down and seeds of the *Krigia*, one of our earliest composite flowers, begin to fly about the 13th of June. I commonly observe its seeds before I do its flower, since it is open only in the forenoons, when it is not so convenient for most to go abroad.

Robin's plantain (*Erigeron bellidifolius*) is the first of its genus to go to seed, as to flower, with us.

A late American species of the same genus (*Erigeron canadensis*) has become a common weed in Europe and is found, according to De Candolle, as far as Kasan. Mrs. Lincoln says that "Linnaeus asserted that the *Erigeron canadensis* was introduced into Europe from America by seeds wafted across the Atlantic Ocean." But of course they would not wait for Columbus to show them the way. Another species, according to Gray, is native there.

Saint Pierre observes that "the maturity of most volatile seeds takes place toward the commencement of Autumn; and . . . then it is that we have the most violent gales of wind about the end of September or beginning of October, called the equinoctial winds."

I begin to see thistledown in the air about the 2d of August, and thenceforward till winter. We notice it chiefly in August and September.

What is called the Canada thistle is the earliest, and the goldfinch, or thistle-bird (*Carduelis tristis*), for he gets his name from his food (*carduus* being the Latin for "a thistle"), knows when it is ripe sooner than I. So soon as the heads begin to be dry, I see him pulling them to pieces, and scattering the down; for he sets it a-flying regularly every year all over the country, just as I do once in a long while.

The Romans had their *Carduelis*, or thistle-bird, also, which Pliny speaks of as the smallest of their birds—for eating thistle seeds is no modern or transient habit with this genus. The thistle seed would oftener remain attached to its receptacle till it decayed with moisture or fell directly to the ground beneath if this bird did not come like a midwife to release it—to launch it in the atmosphere and send it to seek its fortune, taking toll the while by swallowing a few seeds.

All children are inspired by a similar instinct and, judging from the results, probably for a similar purpose. They can hardly keep their hands off the opening thistle-head. Mudie, speaking of the food of the English goldfinch, observes that it is especially the winged seeds of those *Compositae* which "keep the air powdered all summer over with the excess of their pro-

84

ductiveness," and that of these "there is a constant succession all the year through, for the wind has not shaken the autumnal thistles bare by the time that the early groundsels are in flower; and to these the dandelion and many other species are soon added."

The thistles have a grayish white and a much coarser pappus than the milkweeds, and it begins to fly earlier. The first sight of it floating through the air is interesting and stimulating to me as an evidence of the lapse of the season, and I make a note of the first which I see annually.

It is remarkable how commonly you see the thistledown sailing low over water, and quite across such ponds as Walden and Fair Haven. For example, at five o'clock one afternoon last year just after rain, being on the middle of Walden, I saw many seedless thistledowns (sometimes they are seeded) sailing about a foot above the surface; yet there was little or no wind. It is as if they were attracted to the pond and there were a current just above the surface which commonly prevented their falling or rising while it drove them along. They are probably wafted to the water from the neighboring hollows and hillsides where they grow, because the currents of air tend to the opening above the water as their playground.

Here is a wise balloonist for you, crossing its Atlantic—perhaps going to plant a thistle seed on the other side; and if it comes down in a wilderness, it will be at home there.

Theophrastus, who lived 350 years before Christ, has this among his weather signs, that "when many thistledowns [*spinarum lanugines*, says the old translation] are borne dispersed over the sea, they announce that there will be a very high wind"; and Phillips, in his *History of Cultivated Vegetables*, says, "The shepherd when he sees the thistledown agitated without an appearance of wind,

'And shakes the forest leaf without a breath,'
drives his flocks to shelter and cries, Heaven protect yon vessel from the approaching tempest!"

Last August, being on Monadnock Mountain, I saw a thistledown, though without seed, floating just over the summit—though after a very careful search for nearly a week, I had not detected a thistle growing above the trees. It probably came up from the base of the hill, or the adjacent valleys, and it suggested how some plants peculiar to mountains, as the mountain goldenrod, may spread from one New England summit to another.

Pappus and achene of Canada thistle

I do not know how far this seed may be carried, but there is the fact that two of our commonest thistles (*Cirsium arvense* and *Cirsium lanceolatum*) have introduced themselves from Europe, probably stealing their passage across the Atlantic, and are now spread far over the northern states and Canada. The former, which by the way is called the *Canada* thistle, as if it were unquestionably American, is, as you know, one of the very worst and commonest pests in our new fields. You may ride for days together along roads which are densely lined and crowded with it. Thus, the words of Virgil are literally true applied to our country, for when men left off eating acorns here and the plow was introduced, the labors of the farmer commenced, and blight began to attack the grain and the noxious thistle to roughen all the fields:

segnisque horreret in arvis Carduus.

There is no mystery about the dispersion and propagation of the thistle—however abundant it may be—for its down sailing in the air is an unusual phenomenon observed by all, and it is one of the most fruitful as well as volatile of all plants.

One writer has calculated that the fifth year's crop from the single seed of a kind of thistle which he calls *Acanthium vulgare*, supposing all to grow, would amount to 7.962 trillions and upward; "a progeny," says he, "more than sufficient to stock not only the surface of the whole earth, but of all the planets in the solar system, so that no other vegetable could possibly grow, allowing but the space of one square foot for each plant." It is also said to spread extensively by the roots. The Canada thistle is a plant similar in its fecundity.

The pappus of the thistle is wonderfully elastic. I one day examined a lanceolate thistle which had been pressed and lain in my herbarium for a year, and when the papers were taken off, its head sprang up more than an inch, and the downy seeds began at once to fly off. Nothing but a constant pressure will retain them in an herbarium.

When crossing a hilltop in September or October, I often amuse myself with pulling to pieces and letting fly the withered and dry pasture thistle tops, and to my mind they carry as much weight as some larger bodies. When lately the comet was hovering in our northwest horizon, the thistle-down received the greater share of my attention. Perhaps one whose down is particularly spreading and open rises steadily from your hand, freighted with its seed, till it is several hundred feet high and then passes out of sight eastward. Was not here a hint to balloonists? Astronomers can calculate the orbit of that thistledown called the comet, conveying its nucleus, which may not be so solid as a thistle seed, somewhither; but what astronomer can calculate the orbit of your thistledown and tell where it will deposit its precious freight at last? It may still be travelling when you are sleeping.

The thistles which I see late in October commonly have their heads secured, which at least saves their down from so great a soaking by the autumn rains. But when I pull out the down, the seed is for the most part left in the receptacle, in regular order there like the pricks in a thimble, or set like cartridges in a circular and convex cartridge box, in hollow cylinders, which look like circles which have been crowded into more or less of a four-, five-, or six-sided form. I know of no object more unsightly to a careless glance than one of these drooping and half-empty thistle-heads. Yet if you examine it closely you will find that the perfectly dry and bristly involucre which hedges round the seed, so repulsive externally, is very neat and attractive within, as smooth and tender toward its charge as it is rough and prickly externally toward the foes that might do it injury. It is a hedge of imbricated, thin, and narrow leaflets of a light brown color, and beautifully glossy like silk—a most fit receptacle for the delicate downy parachutes of the seed—like a silk-lined cradle in which a prince is rocked.

The seeds are kept dry under this unsuspected satiny ceiling, whose old, weather-worn, and rough outside alone we see, like a mossy roof. Thus, that which seemed a mere brown and worn-out side of the summer, sinking into the earth of the roadside, turns out to be a precious casket.

Late in the fall I often meet with useless and barren thistledowns driving over the fields, all whose capital was long ago snapped up, perhaps by a hungry goldfinch. Not being detained nor steadied by any seed at the base, they are blown away at the first impulse and go rolling over all obstacles; they may indeed go fastest and farthest of all, but where they rest at last, not even a thistle springs up.

The fruitless enterprise of some persons who rush helter-skelter carrying out their crazy schemes, merely "putting it through," as the phrase is, when there is nothing there to be put through, reminds me of *these*. Such are busy merchants and brokers on 'change, doing business on credit, gambling in fancy stocks that have failed over and over again, and been assisted to get a-going again to no purpose. A great ado about nothing, all in my eye, with nothing to deposit, not of the slightest use to the great thistle tribe, not even tempting a jackass. When you right or extricate a ducking businessman (take him out of chancery) and set him before the wind again, it is worth the while to look and see if he has any seed of success under him. Such a one you may know afar. He floats more slowly and steadily, carrying weight—and of *his* enterprise, expect results.

Fireweed

By the middle of August the down of the fireweed (*Erecthites hieracifolia* and *Epilobium angustifolium*) begins to fly. However, those are not with very peculiar fitness called fireweeds, for they spring up in the same manner on new land when it is laid bare by whatever cause, hereabouts as often after a cutting as after a burning, though I will not deny that the ashes may be a good manure for them (and many other plants have the same habit). Their localities with us are recently cleared, gravelly, and bare spots in sproutlands. There are enough of these seeds in the air always ready to fall on and vegetate in such places. They may have been blown *into* the woods and settled there, when there was a lull, in the fall before the woods were cut or, for aught I know, preserved their vitality in the soil there for many years. Perhaps, moreover, these seeds are fitted to escape or resist fire, or even the wind which the fire creates may lift them again out of harm's way. I have seen the greatest quantities of *Epilobium* far in the wilderness of Maine, in places where there had been a burning or cutting, often in a dense mass an acre in extent, and easily distinguished when in flower by its pink color, though you are a mile off on a lake.

The *Erecthites hieracifolia* is the plant which is most commonly believed to be spontaneously generated, it not being noticed till a clearing is made (which is done by burning), and then it springs up densely; but as far as my observation goes, it is quite generally distributed through our woodlands, though it is comparatively rare and puny in the dense wood. It is like the thistle in its fruitfulness and volatility. Millions of these seeds may be blown along the very lane in which we are walking without our seeing one of them. A correspondent of the *Tribune*, writing from Chenango County, New York, in 1861, says that the fireweed was a great pest thereabouts some sixty years ago, wherever there had been a burning. "The down, or furze, from the blossom," says he, "being very fine, it was both choking and blinding to work among it [at logging time], and the next year the grain would sometimes be so full of it that we had to tie a veil over the face to thresh and clean it."

Why then suppose it to be spontaneously generated? I would ask those who still maintain this theory: If the fireweed is spontaneously generated, why is it not so produced in Europe as well as in America? Of course, the Canada thistle is spontaneously generated just as much, yet why was it not generated here until the seed had come from Europe? I have no doubt that the fireweed can be raised from the seed in corresponding places in Europe, if it is not already, and that it will spring up just as mysteriously there as it does here. But if it will grow thus *after* the seed has been carried thither, why should it not before, if the seed is unnecessary to its production?

Moreover, the greater part of that large family of weeds which spring up with the fireweed the next year after a cutting are perennials, and must already have lived one year in the woods before they were cut. If you had looked carefully, as I have done, you would have found their radicle leaves there. Such are several species of goldenrods and asters, *Epilobium*, thistles, and so on. But comparatively few of these live two years, or come to perfection unless the woods are cut.

Of the *Asclepias*, or milkweeds, which are very numerous and all American, four are common in this town—namely, the common, poke-leaved, wavy-leaved, and water milkweed. Their down is much finer and fairer than that of the thistle—and the first-named species, on account of the silkiness of its cotton, has been called by some the Virginian silk. Kalm said that the Canadians called it *le Cotonier* and that "the poor collect [its down] and fill their beds, especially their children's, with it instead of feathers." Alphonse De Candolle says that it has also been cultivated and its down used as fur or cotton, and it has been introduced in the south of Europe.

The earliest begins to fly about the 16th of September, and the *Asclepias cornuti* pods are in the midst of dispersing their seeds about the 20th or 25th of October. (I have seen one kind in the air in the spring.) Its pods are large, thick, and covered with soft prickles, and stand at various angles with the stem like a flourish. The wavy-leaved has slender pods. It is perfectly upright and five inches long. The water milkweed, whose down I begin to see about the 4th of October, has small, slender, straight, and pointed pods—perfectly upright—and large seeds with much margin or wing.

But to confine ourselves to the *Asclepias cornuti*. The pod, if you examine both inside and out, is a faery-like casket shape, somewhat like a canoe. As they dry, they turn upward, crack, and open by the seam along the convex or outer side—revealing the brown seeds with thin, silvery parachutes like the finest unsoiled silk closely compressed and arranged in an imbricated manner, and already right-side up. Some children call these manes of seed and silk fishes, and as they lie they somewhat resemble a plump, round, silvery fish with a brown head.

Densely packed in a little oblong chest armed with soft downy prickles and with a smooth, silky lining lie thus some two hundred (in one instance I counted 134, in another 270) of these pear-shaped seeds (or shaped like a steel-yard pine), which have derived their nutriment through a band of extremely fine silken threads attached by their extremities to the core. (The silk is moreover divided once or twice by the raised partitions of the core.)

At length, when the seeds are matured and cease to require nourishment from the parent plant, being weaned, and the pod with dryness and frost bursts, the pretty fishes loosen and lift their brown scales, somewhat bristling a little; the extremities of the silken threads detach themselves from the core and from being the conduits of nutriment to the seed, perchance to become the buoyant balloon which, like some spiders' webs, bears the seeds to new and distant fields. Far finer than the finest thread, they will soon serve merely to buoy up the full-fed seed.

The pods commonly burst after rain—opening on the underside, away from succeeding showers. The outer part of the down of the upper seeds is gradually blown loose, while they are still retained by the ends of the middle portion, in loops attached to the core. Perchance at the tops of some more open and drier pods is already a little flock of these loosened seeds and down, held by the converging tips of the down like meridians—just ready to float away when the wind rises, to be a vessel moored with long cables and lying in the stream, prepared to spread her sails and depart any moment. These may be blown about a long time, however, before a strong

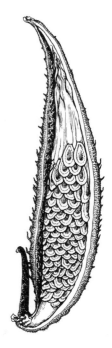

Ripening seeds
of milkweed pod
(cutaway view)

puff launches them away, and in the meanwhile they are expanding and drying their silk and becoming buoyant. These white tufts show afar as big as your fist. One of my neighbors says that the plant is now discounting.

The few seeds which I release soon come to earth, but probably if they waited for a stronger wind they would be carried far.

Others, again if you wait a while, are found open and empty, except of the brown core, and you may see what a delicate, smooth, white- or straw-colored lining this casket has.

If you sit at an open attic window toward the end of September, you will see many a milkweed down go sailing by on a level with you, though commonly it has lost its freight—notwithstanding that you may not know of any of these plants growing in your neighborhood.

On August 26th, 1860, I notice milkweed growing in hollows in the fields, as if the seed had settled there owing to the lull of the wind in such places.

Thus, the quietest behaved carries off the prize while exposed plains and hills send forth violent winds to hale the seed to them. The calm hollow, in which no wind blows, without effort receives and harbors it.

Returning one afternoon by way of Mount Misery from a walk through Conantum and over Lee's Bridge into Lincoln, I perceive in the little open meadow on Clematis Brook that the follicles of the *Asclepias cornuti* now point upward and are already bursting. When I release some seeds, the fine silky threads fly apart at once, opening with a spring—and then ray their relics out into a hemispherical form, each thread freeing itself from its neighbor, and all reflecting prismatic tints. These seeds are besides furnished with broad, thin margins or wings, which plainly keep them steady and prevent their whirling round. I let one go, and it rises slowly and uncertainly at first, now driven this way, then that, by invisible currents, and I fear it will make shipwreck against the neighboring wood. But no; as it approaches it, it surely rises above it, and then feeling the strong north wind, it is borne off rapidly in the opposite direction, over Deacon Farrar's woods, ever rising higher and higher, and tossing and heaved about with every fluctuation of the air, till at fifty rods off and one hundred feet above the earth, steering south—I lose sight of it.

I had watched it for the time with as much interest as his friends did Mr. Lauriat, disappearing in the skies. But not in this case is the return to earth fraught with danger, but toward night perchance, when the air is moist and still, it descries its promised land and settles gently down between the woods, where there is a lull of the wind, into some strange valley—it may be by some other brook like this—and its voyage is over. Yet it stoops to rise.

Thus, from generation to generation it goes bounding over lakes and woods and mountains. Think of the great variety of balloons which at this season are buoyed up by similar means! How many myriads go sailing away thus, high over hill and meadow and river, on various tacks until the wind lulls, to plant their race in new localities—who can tell how many miles away? I do not see but the seeds which are ripened in New England may plant themselves in Pennsylvania. At any rate, I am interested in the fate or success of every such venture which the autumn sends forth. And for this end these silken streamers have been perfecting themselves all summer, snugly packed in this light chest, a perfect adaptation to this end—a prophecy not only of the fall, but of future springs. Who could believe in prophecies of Daniel or of Miller that the world would end this summer, while one milkweed with faith matured its seeds?

I brought home two of these pods which were already bursting and amused myself from day to day with releasing the seeds and watching them rise slowly into the heavens till they were lost to my eye. No doubt the greater or less rapidity with which they rise would serve as a natural barometer to test the condition of the air.

Near the end of November I sometimes see the milkweed pods by the roadside yet but emptied of their silky contents, though we may have had snow. Thus, for months the gales are dispersing their seeds.

Similar to the milkweed pods are the very long and slender curved pods of the dog's-bane. The outside is a dull reddish or mahogany color, but the inside a polished pale brown. These open and release their downy seeds in a similar manner. I have seen one still closed near the end of April.

After the middle of September hard frosts put a period to many flowers and we begin to see their seeds only. By the 18th of September two or three kinds of *Hieracium* are already going to seed. Their little yellowish globes are characteristic of autumn in the woods. And ere long in all meadows the fall dandelion with its small spheres repeats the phenomena of May.

By the last of September the clematis begins to be feathered. A month later, when the leaves had mostly fallen, I have mistaken it, draping a low tree, for a tree full of white blossoms. It is said of the English species, in *The Journal of a Naturalist*, "I have often observed the long feathered part of the seed at the entrance of holes made by mice on the banks, and probably in hard seasons the seed may yield these creatures part of their supply."

The yet more brilliant and silvery *Andropogon scoparius* attracts our attention about the same time.

Almost all goldenrods are fuzzy about the 20th of October. Early in November many goldenrods and aster buds, which have been hoary for a month, are richly and exuberantly downy, their seed just on the point of falling or being blown away, before they are in the least weather-beaten. They are now puffed up to their utmost, clean and light. What masses of minute, thistle-like seeds graying the fields! So fine that when we jar the plant and set free a thousand, it is with great difficulty that we detect them in the air. You must be on the alert and look very sharp to see them before they settle to earth or, if the wind blows, are borne away. They are concealed not only by their size but by their color against the sky. They cover our clothes like dust. No wonder that they spread over all fields and far into the woods.

Many of these seeds and those of other *Compositae*, as the *Vernonia* and so on, hold on all winter and are dispersed in the spring.

There is a large class of plants (called *Adhaerentes* by Linnaeus) whose seeds, or fruit, are provided with small barbed spears, or hooks, or other contrivances by which they attach themselves to any passing body that touches them, and so get transported by it. The most common of these hereabouts are the different species of *Bidens* (bur marigold or beggarticks) and *Desmodium* (or tick trefoil); also the burdock, agrimony, *Circaea*, *Galium*, and so on.

Tick trefoil

> *Intereunt segetes, subit aspera sylva,*
> *lappaeque tribolique, interque nitentia culta*
> *infelix lolium et steriles dominantur avenae.*

> The crops perish, and up springs a rough forest
> Of burdocks and caltrops; and hurtful cockles and sterile oats reign
> In the cultivated fields.

The seed of the *Bidens*, of which we have five species, is shaped somewhat like a little flattish brown quiver, with from two to six downwardly barbed arrows projecting from it. The earliest ripen about October 2d. If in October you have occasion to pass through or along some half-dried pool, these seeds will often adhere to your clothes in surprising numbers. It is as if you had unconsciously made your way through the ranks of some countless but invisible Lilliputian army, which in their anger had discharged all their arrows and darts at you, though none of them reached higher than your legs. These bidents, tridents, quadridents, are shot into you till your clothes are all bristling with them, and as they are not to be brushed off with the hand, the neatest persons are fain to carry some of

95

them along with them. They are sometimes abundant as late as the middle of January.

It is remarkable that one species, the *Bidens beckii*, is with us confined to the river, growing only in the water and stretching in many places quite across it, so that it can rarely be brushed by a passing animal. Yet possibly a musquash or mink, a wading bird or moose or cow, or even a wading pickerel fisher of the old school, who does not mind if his clothes be wet (for Nature anticipated him as much as the moose), are the agents which transport it. It is to be noticed that this one has the greatest number of arrows in its quiver.

The seeds of the *Desmodium*, of which I find eight kinds in this town, are contained in jointed pods, which look like short chains of diamond-shaped, roundish, or triangular bodies and are densely covered with minute hooked hairs. The earliest ripen about August 31st.

Tick-trefoil pod

How surely the *Bidens* by the edge of the pool, and the *Desmodium* growing on some rough cliff, prophesy the coming of the traveller, brute or human, that will transport their seeds on his coat! I can hardly clamber along one of our cliffs in September in search of grapes without getting my clothes covered with *Desmodium* ticks (especially of the *Desmodium rotundifolium* and *paniculatum*). Though you were running for your life, they would have time to catch and cling to you—often the whole row of pods, like a piece of a very narrow saw blade with four or five great teeth. They will even fasten to your hand. They cling by the same instinct as babes to the mother's breast, craving a virgin soil—eager to descry new lands and seek their fortune in foreign parts; they steal a passage somewhere aboard of you, knowing that you will not put back into the same port. Instead of being caught and detained ourselves by bird-lime, we are compelled to catch these seeds and carry them with us. These almost invisible nets, as it were, are spread for us, and whole coveys of *Desmodium* and *Bidens* seeds steal transportation out of us.

You spend a long time picking them off, which it took a short time to attach. I have often found myself covered, as it were, with an imbricated scaly coat of the brown *Desmodium* seeds, a bristling *chevaux-de-frise* of beggar-ticks, and had to spend a quarter of an hour or more picking them off at some convenient place (perchance more convenient to them than to me) and so they got what they wanted—deposited in another place.

Thus, the most ragged and idle loafer or beggar may be of some use in the economy of Nature, if he will only keep moving.

One afternoon, having landed far down the river with a companion and walked about through a quantity of *Desmodium* (*marylandicum* or *rigidum*, which have roundish joints) by the shore there, we found our pantaloons covered with its seeds to a remarkable and amusing degree. These green scale-like seeds densely covering and greening our legs reminded me of the *lemma* on a ditch. It amounted to a kind of coat of mail. It was the event of our walk, and we were proud to wear this badge, regarding each other with a little envy from time to time, as if he were the most distinguished who had the most of them on his clothes. My companion betrayed a certain religion about it, for he said, reproving me, that he thought it would not be right to walk intentionally amid the *Desmodium* in order to get more of the ticks on us, nor yet to pick them off, but they must be carried about till they were rubbed off accidentally. The consequence was that when he reappeared for a walk a day or two after, his clothes were nearly as well covered as at first. I saw that Nature's design was furthered even by his superstition.

We often say that a person's clothes are old and seedy, which may mean that they are far gone and dilapidated like a plant that is gone to seed—or, possibly, that they are made untidy by many seeds adhering to them.

So with the fruit of the burdock, with which children are wont to build houses and barns without any mortar: both men and animals, apparently such as have shaggy coats, are employed in transporting them. I have even relieved a cat with a large mass of them which she could not get rid of, and I frequently see a cow with a bunch in the end of her whisking tail, with which, perhaps, she stings herself in her vain efforts to brush off imagined flies.

One January, when I returned from my walk through a deep and drifted snow, I found some of these dry burrs adhering to the lining of my coat, though I hardly knew where to find a plant at that season. Thus, even in the middle of the Great Snow, Nature does not forget these, her vegetable economies. By some of these modes this plant has introduced itself from Europe into America.

They who pick wool at the factories might tell us what they find in it. No doubt many a new weed is, at least transiently, introduced into our grounds with the wool waste used as manure. Wilson, the ornithologist, says that the cockle-bur (*Xanthium strumarium*) was so abundant in his day along the shores of the Ohio and Mississippi "as to render the wool of those sheep that pasture where it most abounds, scarcely worth the cleaning, covering them with one solid mass of burrs, wrought up and imbedded with the fleece"—and, according to Alphonse De Candolle, "the washing of wool from the east, has caused to appear in a locality near Montpellier, le pont Juvenal, a crowd of species [of plants even there] from Barbary, Syria, and Bessarabia, which, it is true, for the most part, have not endured in the country."

A few years ago I knew of but one place in the town where the hound's-tongue was naturalized. I put a handful of its nutlets into my pocket with my handkerchief, but it took me a long time to pick them out of the handkerchief when I got home, and I pulled out many threads in the process. I afterward spent twenty minutes in clearing myself of them after having brushed against the plant. But I do not mind such things; and so, the next spring, not intending any harm, I gave some of the above-named seeds, gathered the previous August, to a young lady who cultivates a flower garden, and to my sister, wishing to spread it, it is so rare. Their expectations were excited and kept on the *qui vive* for a long time, for it does not blossom till the second year. The flower and peculiar odor were sufficiently admired in due time; but suddenly a great hue and cry reached my ears, on account of its seeds adhering to the clothes of those who frequented these gardens. I learned that that young lady's mother, who one day took a turn in the garden in order to pluck a nose-gay, just before setting out on a journey, found that she had carried a surprising quantity of this seed to Boston on her dress, without knowing it—for the flowers that invite you to look at and pluck them have designs on you—and the railroad company charged nothing for freight. So this plant is in a fair way to be dispersed, and my purpose is accomplished. I shall not need to trouble myself further about it.

The civilized man transports more of these seeds than the savage does. Pickering, in his work on races, says that "the natives of Australia, being for the most part devoid of clothing, and possessing very few manufactures, have contributed perhaps less than any other branch of the human family to the dispersion of seeds and plants."

On October 13th, 1860, I find the shore of the river at Clamshell Hill quite greened with *Pontederia* seed which has been floated up and left there— mixed with the seed of the buttonbush; the slender bulbs of *Lysimachia*; and the round, green, leafy bush of the *Utricularia vulgaris*. Thus, probably, are all these dispersed. I see large masses of the last lodge against bridges and fences, with the conspicuous green leaf buds attached. They are dispersed in the fall and winter.

About the 1st of September I see the great peduncles of the *Peltandra*, one and a half to two feet long, curving downward along the riverside and in the meadows, with its globular mass of green fruit at the end, often two inches in diameter, looking like slung shot. This contains a mass of viscid seeds or nuts. The fruit curves downward so close to the ground that this part annually escapes the scythe, though the leaves are closely shorn, and thus the plant is preserved and propagated. Nature gives the mower the leaves but holds back the seeds, waiting for the floods to come to get them.

So too the yellow lily (*Nuphar advena*) is now curved back in the same manner, ripening its seed in the water and mud beneath the surface. This fruit is of an oblong conical form, and ribbed, with a sort of straight beak to it, [a] and is full of yellow seeds. [b] The white-lily fruit, having lost its blackened and decayed leaves, is of a handsome shallow, vase-like form. [c] The seeds are about a quarter as big as apple seeds, and of a similar color or rather more purplish. The white-lily seeds last longer and, when first taken out of the pods, which are now all withdrawn under water, will float—but as soon as the peculiar slimy or mucilaginous matter which envelops them is washed off, they sink to the bottom and plant themselves. Saint Pierre says that he is so entirely convinced of the perfect adaptation and harmony that reigns throughout all the works of Nature "as to conclude that the time when the seeds of aquatic plants drop is regulated, in most cases, by that of the overflowing of the rivers where they grow."

All these seeds must be the food of many creatures.

If you dig a pond anywhere in our fields you will soon have not only waterfowl, reptiles, and fishes in it, but also the usual water plants, as lilies and so on. You will no sooner have got your pond dug than Nature will begin to stock it. Though you may not see how or when the seed gets there, Nature sees to it. She directs all the energies of her Patent Office upon it, and the seeds begin to arrive.

In August 1855 I levelled for an artificial pond at our new cemetery, Sleepy Hollow. The pond had been dug gradually for three or four years past and was completed last year, 1859. It is now about a dozen rods long by five or six wide and two or three feet deep—with a bare, muddy, and sandy bottom. The water is supplied by deep and copious springs in the meadow. The outlet is a short, shallow ditch leading into a little wash, which empties into the river about half a mile off.

Last year I learned that many small pouts and some sizeable pickerel had already been caught in the pond—before it was done. They had undoubtedly come up from the river, slight and shallow as the connexion is, and this year—1860—I find several small patches of the *large* yellow and the *kalmiana* lily already established in the cemetery pond. Thus, in the midst of death we are in life. I think that these seeds have not been lying dormant in the mud, but that they have been brought up from the river, where they abound (or possibly from the larger ditches in the meadow a quarter of a mile nearer), by fishes, reptiles, or birds which feed on them. Wilson says that the seeds of the "spatterdock" and other aquatic plants are eaten by the great white heron, snowy heron, and the great blue heron (*Ardea herodias*). Turtles are also likely to eat the seeds, for I see them eating the decayed leaves. If there is any water communication, fishes will perhaps arrive before plants, and then use the aster plants for their food and shelter—for the former must multiply there till the surface is partially covered with pads. They may now lurk in safety behind these green blinds.

This water is otherwise as yet apparently clear of weeds.

On October 18th, 1860, I see spatterdock pads and *Pontederia* in that little pool at the south end of Beck Stow's. How did they get there? There is no stream in this case. (It was, perhaps, rather reptiles and birds than fishes, then.) *Indeed*, we might as well ask how they got anywhere, for all the pools and fields have been stocked thus, and we are not to suppose as many new creations as pools.

This suggests to inquire how any plant came where it is: how, for instance, the pools which were stocked with lilies before we were born or this town was settled, and ages ago, were restocked—as well as those which we dug. I think that we are warranted only in supposing that the former was stocked in the same way as the latter and that there was not a sudden new creation, at least since the first. Yet I have no doubt that peculiarities more or less considerable have thus been gradually produced in the lilies thus planted in various pools, in consequence of their various conditions, though they all came originally from one seed.

We find ourselves in a world that is already planted, but is also still being planted as at first. We say of some plants that they grow in wet places. The truth may be that their seeds are scattered almost everywhere, but in these places only do they succeed.

We see thus how the fossil lilies, if the geologist has detected any, were dispersed, as well as those which we carry in our hands to church. Unless you can show me the pool where the lily was created, I shall believe that the oldest of the fossil ones originated in their locality, in a similar manner to these at Beck Stow's.

The development theory implies a greater vital force in Nature, because it is more flexible and accommodating, and equivalent to a sort of constant new creation.

Darwin, in his *Origin of Species*, says: "I took in February, three table-spoonfuls of mud from three different points, beneath water, on the edge of a little pond; this mud, when dried, weighed only 6¾ ounces; I kept it covered up in my study for six months, pulling up and counting each plant as it grew; the plants were of many kinds and were altogether 537 in number; and yet the viscid mud was all contained in a breakfast cup! Considering these facts, I think it would be an inexplicable circumstance if water-birds did not transport the seeds of the fresh-water plants to vast distances," that is, on their feet and beaks.

You will not wonder if I make much of the seeds which are drifted by rivers and ponds, since larger seeds are known to be transported by currents across the widest oceans, and even formed islands in the sea to be stocked thus. Saint Pierre says:

It is a speculation well worthy of the attention of the philosophic mind, to trace those vegetable fleets sailing along, night and day, with the current of the rivulets, and arriving, undirected by any pilot, on unknown regions. There are some which, by the overflowing of the waters, now and then lose themselves in the plains. I have seen them sometimes, accumulated upon each other, in the bed of torrents, presenting around the pebbles where they had germinated, waves of verdure of the most beautiful sea-green. You would have thought that *Flora*, pursued by some river-god, had dropped her basket in the urn of that deity. Others, more fortunate, issuing from the sources of some stream, are caught by the current of the greater rivers, and conveyed away to embellish their distant banks with a verdure not their own.

There are some which cross the vast ocean; and, after a long navigation, are driven, by the very tempests, on the regions which they adorn and enrich. Such are the double cocoas of the Sechelles, or Mahé Islands, which the sea carries regularly every year a distance of four hundred leagues, and lands them on the coast of Malabar. The Indians, who inhabit it, were long under the persuasion that those unusual presents of the ocean must have been the produce of a palm tree that grew under its billows. They gave them the name of marine cocoa-nuts, and ascribed wonderful virtues to them. They set as high a value upon them as upon ambergris; and to such a pitch was this extravagance carried, that many of those fruits have been sold as high as a thousand crowns a piece. But the French having, some years ago, discovered the island of Mahé, which produces them, and which is situated in the fiftieth degree of south latitude, imported them in such quantities to India, that they sunk at once in value and in reputation. . . .

Alphonse De Candolle says that the coco de mer (*Laoidicea sechellarum*), "which has been carried in quantity for centuries from the Sechelle islands Prâlin and Ronde to the Maldive islands," has never established itself in the last. Saint Pierre also says:

The sea throws such quantities of fennel seed on the shores of Madeira that one of its bays has obtained the name of Funchal, or Fennel Bay.

It was by the course of those nautical seeds, too carelessly observed by modern seamen, that the savages formerly discovered the islands to windward of the countries which they inhabited. . . . By similar indications, Christopher Columbus acquired the assurance that another world existed. . . .

[The cocoa tree] never succeeds so well as in the sand on the seashore, and generally languishes in the interior of a country. . . .

The philosopher Francis Leguat and his unfortunate companions, who were, in the year 1690, the first inhabitants of the small island of Rodriguez, which lies a hundred leagues to the eastward of the Isle of France, found no cocoa trees in it. But precisely at the period of their short residence there, the sea threw upon the coast several cocoa-nuts in a state of germination; as if it had been the intention of Providence to induce them, by this useful and seasonable present, to remain on that island and to cultivate it.

One author has listed American fruits cast on the shore of Norway, some "so recent as to germinate. . . . These fruits are usually the *Cassia fistula*; *Anacardium*, or cashew nuts; *Cucurbitae lagenariae*, bottle gourds; pods of the *Mimosa scandens*, called cocoons in the West Indies; pods of the *Piscidia erythrina*, called dogwood tree by Sloane; and cocoa-nuts."

I do not always state the facts exactly in the order in which they were observed, but select out of my numerous observations extended over a series of years the most important ones, and describe them in a natural order.

One morning some five years ago, as I was on my way to survey a woodlot in the west part of Concord, and passing a tract in the woods where a peculiarly dense and exclusive white-pine wood had been cut a few years before, but was now occupied as exclusively with shrub oaks, my employer, an elderly man who had been buying and selling woodlots all his life, looking toward this lot, asked me that very common question, if I could tell him how it happened that when a pine wood was cut down an oak one commonly sprang up, and vice versa.

Now it happened that I had been attending to this subject and had even examined a portion of this very wood which remained uncut in order to learn the facts about it. Therefore, I assumed that I *could* tell—that it was no mystery to me. As I am not aware that this has been clearly shown by anyone, I shall lay the more stress on this point. First, as to the fact that pines are often or commonly succeeded by oaks, and vice versa, I could mention a great many instances of it, but it may suffice for the present to restate the case above referred to, reserving other examples for a different use.

The above-mentioned pine lot was as dense and exclusive a growth of pines as the town afforded, and well known as such to all acquainted with our woodlands, a dark and cavernous retreat for bluejays and red squirrels. Three or four years after the pines were cut, the same ground was occupied by an equally exclusive and almost equally dense growth of shrub oak. In the meanwhile, the lot, having been put up at auction, was readily bought by two of my neighbors unacquainted with woodlands, who considered only that oaks were oaks, and perhaps were imposed on by the reputation of the soil which had grown such pines; but the old farmer with whom I was riding, who had attended the auction with a view to purchasing, if the lot had not gone so high, declared that at this rate the purchasers, though young men, would not see any decent wood there as long as they lived—that their only recourse was to cut and burn, and start again. Nevertheless, *I* doubt if that would be the best course, after all. While clearing a line through shrub oaks which put his eyes out, he asked if I could tell him what shrub oak was made for.

Apparently there were only pines there before. They are cut off, and after a year or two you see oaks and other hardwoods springing up there, with scarcely a pine amid them, and the wonder commonly is how the seed could have lain in the ground so long without decaying. But the truth is that it has not lain in the ground so long, but is regularly planted each year by various quadrupeds and birds.

In this neighborhood, where oaks and pines are about equally dispersed, if you look through the thickest pine wood, even the seemingly unmixed pitch-pine ones, you will commonly detect many little oaks, birches, and other hardwoods, sprung from seeds carried into the thicket by squirrels and other animals, and also blown thither, but which are overshadowed and choked by the pines. The denser the evergreen wood, the more likely it is to be well planted with these seeds, because the planters incline

Shrub-oak acorns

105

to resort with their forage to the closest covert. They also carry it into birch and other woods. This planting is carried on annually, and the oldest seedlings annually die; but when the pines are cleared off, the oaks, having got just the start they want and now secured favorable conditions, immediately spring up to trees.

The shade of a dense pine wood is more unfavorable to the springing up of pines of the same species than of oaks within it, though the former may come up abundantly when the pines are cut, if there chance to be sound seed in the ground. But when you cut off a lot of hardwood, very often the little pines mixed with it have a similar start, for the squirrels have carried off the nuts to the pines, and not to the more open wood, and they commonly make pretty clean work of it; and moreover, if the wood was old, the sprouts will be feeble or entirely fail, to say nothing about the soil being, in a measure, exhausted for this kind of crop.

If a pine wood is surrounded by a white-oak one chiefly, white oaks may be expected to succeed when the pines are cut. If it is surrounded instead by an edging of shrub oaks, then you will probably have a dense shrub-oak thicket.

I have no time to go into details but will say, in a word, that while the wind is conveying the seeds of pines into hardwoods and open lands, the squirrels and other animals are conveying the seeds of oaks and walnuts into the pine woods, and thus a rotation of crops is kept up. I affirmed this confidently many years ago, and an occasional examination of dense pine woods confirmed me in my opinion. It has long been known to observers that squirrels bury nuts in the ground, but I am not aware that anyone has thus accounted for the regular succession of forests.

On the 24th of September in 1857, as I was paddling down the Assabet in this town, I saw a red squirrel run along the bank under some herbage, with something large in its mouth. It stopped near the foot of a hemlock, within a couple of rods of me, and, hastily pawing a hole with its forefeet,

dropped its booty into it, covered it up, and retreated part way up the trunk
of the tree. As I approached the shore to examine the deposit, the squirrel,
descending part way, betrayed no little anxiety about its treasure and made
two or three motions to recover it before it finally retreated. Digging there,
I found two green pignuts joined together, with the thick husks on, buried about an inch and a half under the reddish soil of decayed
hemlock leaves—just the right depth to plant it. In
short, this squirrel was then engaged in accom-
plishing two objects, to wit, laying up a store of winter
food for itself and planting a hickory wood for all creation.
If the squirrel was killed, or neglected its deposit, a hickory would spring
up. The nearest hickory tree was twenty rods distant. These nuts were
there still just fourteen days later, but were gone when I looked again, November 21st, or six weeks later still.

I have since examined more carefully several dense woods, which are
said to be, and are apparently, exclusively pine, and always with the same
result. For instance, I walked the same day to a small, but very dense and
handsome white-pine grove, about fifteen rods square, in the east part of
this town. The trees are large for Concord, being from ten to twenty inches
in diameter, and as exclusively pine as any wood that I know. Indeed, I selected this wood because I thought it the least likely to contain anything
else. It stands on an open plain or pasture, except that it adjoins another
small pine wood, which has a few little oaks in it on the southeast side. On
every other side, it was at least thirty rods from the nearest woods. Standing
on the edge of this grove and looking through it, for it is quite level and free
from underwood—for the most part bare, red-carpeted ground—you
would have said that there was not a hardwood tree in it, young or old. But
on looking carefully along over its floor I discovered, though it was not till
my eye had got used to the search, that alternating with thin ferns and
small blueberry bushes there was, not merely here and there, but as often

as every five feet and with a degree of regularity, a little oak, from three to twelve inches high, and in one place I found a green acorn dropped by the base of a pine.

I confess I was surprised to find my theory so perfectly proved in this case. One of the principal agents in this planting, the red squirrels, were all the while curiously inspecting me, while I was inspecting their plantation. Some of the little oaks had been browsed by cows, which resorted to this wood for shade.

Supposing this lot to be fifteen rods square, there were some twenty-five hundred oaks in it, or more than five times as many as pines, for there were not nearly five hundred pines there. This is only one of the thousand cases in which the proprietor and woodchopper tell you that there is not a single oak in the lot. So the tables were turned, and, as far as numbers were concerned, it would have been much truer to say that this was an exclusively oak wood and that there were no pines in it. Truly, appearances are deceptive. Moreover, I may as well state here that between these pines, which are about forty years old and had formed a vale of pine needles one to one and a half inches thick, there were no stumps of older pines, but old oak stumps were still very common. In short, they occupied the site of an oak wood and were preparing the way for another to succeed them.

Again I examined a pitch-pine lot in the west part of the town, which came up all together in 1826 on land which had been burned over. There was no other plant in it above the size of a shrub, and a casual observer would not have noticed anything except a few little white pines which had come up under the pitch pines, but the ground between the bases of the trees was apparently as bare and smooth as the original pasture. It is about as dense a pitch-pine grove as I know, for though it has been thoroughly turned up and is only a dozen or fifteen rods wide, you cannot see through it in some directions. It is twenty rods from the nearest wood and five times as far from any other, and yet, looking closely, I found it to be well planted with seedling oaks. Choosing hastily a spot where they appeared to be most numerous, I counted ten within fifteen square feet, but I could find only five pitch pines within an equal area; according to which there were twice as many oaks as pitch pines there.

In some cases I have found hundreds of these oak seedlings under only half a dozen pines.

At first thought, one would expect to find seedling oaks in the greatest abundance, if not exclusively, under and about seed-bearing oaks, that is, in oak woods; but when I looked for them there, they were obviously fewer and feebler than under pines.

Not being satisfied, however, with the kind of examination which I had already made of oak woods for this purpose, and not having come to any definite result, I resolved one afternoon that I would take my spade and get ten seedling oaks out of a purely oak—and then the same number out of a purely pine—wood and compare them, thinking that I could not fail to be the wiser for this in many respects.

I looked for trees, apparently seedlings one foot or less in height and convenient to dig up, and took the first I came to.

I first examined a small but dense wood of oak and hickory, hardly old enough to bear seeds, but adjacent to an older wood which did, yet after a careful search I had not found one young oak there.

I next went to an extensive wood of oak and pine and searched through the most exclusively oak portions of it. They were sprouts twenty-five or thirty years old, but there was generally a thin pine within two or three rods. There were many shrub oaks three or four feet high, but though I looked over three-quarters of an hour, I was discouraged, and I feared I should not have time to examine one pine. I found only three seedlings of the required kind.

However, remarking that it was all the same for my purpose whether I found the ten there or not, I then went to a young pitch- and white-pine wood which had sprung up in a pasture immediately adjacent to the last-named wood, and there were literally thousands of little seedling oaks

109

such as I was in search of, quite reddening the ground in some places, for it was October, and I immediately dug up ten of these. They no doubt sprang from acorns produced in the last-named wood.

I have now examined many dense pine woods, both pitch and white, and several oak woods in order to see how many and what kind of oak seedlings there were springing up in them, and I do not hesitate to say that seedlings under one foot high are *very* much more abundant under the pines than under the oaks. They prevail and are countless under the pines, while they are hard to find under the oaks, and what you do find have commonly (for whatever reason) very old and decayed roots, and feeble shoots from them.

Notwithstanding that the acorns are produced only by oaks and not by pines, the fact is that there are comparatively few seedling oaks (one foot or less in height) under the oaks but thousands under the pines. I would not undertake to get a hundred oaks of this size suitable to transplant under a dense and pure oak wood, but I could easily get thousands from under pines.

Indeed, it appears not to be known that the pine woods are a natural nursery of oaks, from whence we might easily transplant them to our grounds and thus save some of those which annually decay, so long as we let the pines stand. These oaks, at any rate, will bear exposure to the light, for such is their destiny.

This is the reason, then, why oaks and pines commonly grow together, or in the same region. If I am not mistaken, our oaks and pines (pitch and white) are nearly identical in their range. Or perhaps the former extend beyond the latter southward where there is less danger of frost, as the latter extend beyond the former northward where even their shelter cannot defend the oaks from the extreme cold. Perhaps the oak will be found to flourish best, and make the best wood, where the climate is so cold that it requires the shelter of the pines at first, yet not cold enough to kill it in spite of this defense. Nuttall, in his *North American Sylva*, says that "oaks ... are confined to the Northern Hemisphere. . . . The Old World contains sixty-three species, and North America, including New Spain, about seventy-four. Of these the United States possesses about thirty-seven, and New Spain the same number."

I have also noticed these little oaks abundant in birch woods, which afford a dense covert to jays, squirrels, and other animals which transport the acorns. In short, hereabouts a pine wood or even a birch wood is no sooner established than the squirrels and birds begin to plant acorns in it.

But it is remarkable that, for the most part, there are no seedling oaks in the midst of open grassy fields or pastures. Most kinds of acorns are but little likely to succeed if dropped there. Those springing up in such places appear to have been dropped or buried by birds and quadrupeds when on their way with them from one covert to another. For, depend on it, every such tree comes from a seed. When I examine these little oaks only two or three years old in native localities, I invariably find there the empty acorn from which they sprung.

So far from the seed having lain dormant in the soil since oaks grew there before, as many believe, it is well known that it is difficult to preserve the vitality of acorns long enough to transport them to Europe; and it is recommended in Loudon's *Arboretum*, as the safest course, to sprout them in pots on the voyage. The same authority states that "very few acorns of any species will germinate after having been kept a year," that beech mast "only retains its vital properties for one year," and the black walnut "seldom . . . more than six months after it has ripened." I have frequently found that in November almost every acorn left on the ground had sprouted. Cobbett says of the white oak that "if warm rains come in the month of November, which they very frequently do in America, the acorns still clinging to the tree actually begin to sprout before they are shaken down by the winds." On the 8th of October 1860, I found a great many white-oak acorns already sprouted, although they had not half fallen, and I could easily believe that they sometimes sprout before they fall. Yet it is stated by one botanical writer that "acorns that have lain for centuries, on being plowed up, have soon vegetated." It is remarkable how soon and unaccountably they decay. Many which I took from the tree and cut open, though they look sound without, are discolored and decaying on one side or throughout within, though there is no worm in them. What with frost, drought, moisture, and worms, the greater part are soon destroyed.

Mr. George B. Emerson, in his valuable *Report on the Trees and Shrubs of the State*, says of the pines: "The tenacity of life of the seeds is remarkable. They will remain for many years unchanged in the ground, protected by the coolness and deep shade of the forest above them. But when the forest is removed, and the warmth of the sun admitted, they immediately vegetate." Since he does not tell us on what observation his remark is founded, I must doubt its truth. Besides, the experience of nurserymen makes it the more questionable. According to Loudon, the vitality of the seed of very few of the *Coniferae* can be preserved more than three or four years by any *artificial* means known, though he says that the seeds of the *Pinus pinaster* often do not come up till the third year.

The stories of wheat raised from seed buried with an ancient Egyptian, and of raspberries raised from seed found in the stomach of a man in England who is supposed to have died sixteen or seventeen hundred years ago, are generally discredited simply because the evidence is not conclusive.

Several men of science, Dr. Carpenter among them, have used the statement that beach plums sprang up in sand dug up forty miles inland in Maine to prove that the seed had lain there a very long time, and some have inferred that the coast has receded so far. But it seems to me necessary to their argument to show, first, that beach plums grow only on a beach. Dr. Carpenter says it "had never before been seen, except immediately upon the seashore." They are not uncommon here in Concord, which is about half that distance from the shore, and I remember a dense patch a few miles north of us, twenty-five miles inland, from which the fruit was annually carried to market. How much further inland they grow I know not. Dr. Charles T. Jackson speaks of finding "beach plums" (perhaps they were this kind) more than a hundred miles inland in Maine. Moreover, the beach plum appears to prosper in sandy places, however far inland, and one of our patches grows on the only desert which we have. It chances that similar objections lie against all the more notorious instances of the kind on record.

Yet I am prepared to believe that some seeds, especially small ones, may retain their vitality for centuries under favorable circumstances. In the spring of 1859 the old Hunt House, so called, in this town, whose chimney bore the date 1703, was taken down. This stood on land which belonged to John Winthrop, the first governor of Massachusetts, and a part of the house was evidently much older than the above date and belonged to the Winthrop family. For many years I have ransacked this neighborhood for plants, and I consider myself familiar with its productions. Thinking of the seeds which are said to be sometimes dug up at an unusual depth in the earth, and thus to reproduce long-extinct plants, it occurred to me last fall that some new or rare plants might have sprung up in the cellar of this house, which had been covered from the light so long. Searching there on the 22d of September, I found, among other rank weeds, a species of nettle (*Urtica urens*) which I had not found before; dill, which I had not seen growing spontaneously; the Jerusalem oak (*Chenopodium botrys*), which I had seen wild in but one place; black night-shade (*Solanum nigrum*), which is quite rare hereabouts; and common tobacco, which, though it was often cultivated here in the last century, has for fifty years been an unknown plant in this town—and a few months before this, not even I had heard that one man, in the north part of the town, was cultivating a few plants for his own use. I have no doubt that some or all of these plants sprang from seeds which had long been buried under or about that house,

113

and that that tobacco is an additional evidence that the plant was formerly cultivated here. The cellar has been filled up this year, and four of those plants, including the tobacco, are now again extinct in that locality.

It is true, I have shown that the animals consume a great part of the seeds of trees, and so at least effectually prevent them becoming trees. But in all these cases, as I have said, the consumer is compelled to be at the same time the disperser and planter, and this is the tax which he pays to Nature. I think it is Linnaeus who says that while the swine is rooting for acorns he is planting acorns.

There are various other ways in which one kind of tree may succeed or supplant another. It may frequently happen that a fire runs through a young lot where mixed oaks and pines have succeeded to pines, and kills out every pine, while the oaks springing up again from the stumps, the forgetful or unobservant owner may be surprised to see an exclusively oak wood there.

Also, even the heavier seeds, as acorns and nuts, may be transported considerable distances by torrents. Chestnuts are frequently found in considerable heaps in the spring washed down the hills into the hollows by small torrents of melted snow or rain, and even thus they may be transported short distances.

Occasionally, when threading the woods in the fall, you will hear a sound as if someone had broken a twig and, looking up, see a jay pecking at an acorn, or you will see a flock of them at once about it in the top of an oak, and hear them break them off. They then fly to a suitable limb and, placing the acorn under one foot, hammer away at it busily, making a sound like a woodpecker's tapping, looking round from time to time to see if any foe is approaching, and soon reach the meat and nibble at it, holding up their heads to swallow, while they hold the remainder very firmly with their claws. Nevertheless, it often drops to the ground before the bird has done with it.

This same afternoon, when I had dug up my oak seedlings in the pine wood, I proceeded a little further to a white-pine wood which had sprung up in a pasture some twenty years ago. Here and there I found also numerous oak seedlings. As I was passing out of this, I saw a jay, which was screaming at me in the wood, fly to a large white oak which stood eight or ten rods from the edge of the wood in the pasture. It had no sooner alighted on the oak than it descended to the ground, picked up an acorn, and flew back into the pines with it near to me. This was evidently one, perhaps the principal, way in which that dense white-pine grove was stocked with the numerous little oaks which I saw beneath it.

Looking again more carefully, I found that the little oaks in that portion which was opposite to the large white oak were almost exclusively white oaks, and I am satisfied that by looking to see what oaks grow in the open land nearby or along the edge of a pine wood, I can tell surely what kinds of oaks I shall find in greatest abundance under the pines. What if the oaks are far off; think how quickly a jay can come and go, and how many times a day!

Just two days later, while sitting within the edge of another pine wood three miles from this, I saw a jay fly to a white oak half a dozen rods off in a pasture, and gathering an acorn from the ground, it flew into the tree with it; and placing it under its foot on a limb, it hammered away at it with its bill, with a rapid, but awkward see-saw or teetering motion—it had to lift its head so high to acquire the requisite momentum.

In short, this is a very common sight at this season (October). The jays keep up a very brisk communication now between the seed-bearing oaks and the pines. If I visit now one of the very few old oak woods left in this vicinity, the scream of the jays attracted thither by the acorns is frequently the only sound that greets me. And if I visit isolated white oaks in pastures, which I know to be peculiarly fruitful, the jays scold at me about almost every such tree, since I hinder their coming to it.

On the other hand, where will you look for a jay sooner, at any season, than in a dense pine thicket? It is there they commonly live and have their nests. I can confirm what William Bartram wrote to Wilson, the ornithologist:

The jay is one of the most useful agents in the economy of nature, for disseminating forest trees and other nuciferous and hard-seeded vegetables on which they feed. Their chief employment during the autumnal season is foraging to supply their winter stores. In performing this necessary duty they drop abundance of seed in their flight over fields, hedges, and by fences where they alight to deposit them in the postholes, &c. It is remarkable what numbers of young trees rise up in fields and pastures after a wet winter and spring. These birds alone are capable, in a few years' time, to replant all the cleared lands.

Much also is to be learned by examining the roots and the shoots of seedling oaks from various localities. The 17th of October last, I took up a red-oak seedling of that year, five inches high, in a mixed wood of oaks and pines. The great acorn lay on its side on the soil just under a loose covering of moist leaves where it was shaded and concealed. The part above ground, taking length and breadth together, was more bulky than the root. The root curved abruptly backward under the acorn, thus: [a] The great acorn was still so perfectly sound that I thought it had not only afforded a great part of the nourishment of the plant the first year, but must continue to furnish nourishment to it a part of next year.

On October 16th, 1860, I dug up four oak seedlings in Conant's pitch- and white-pine wood. The largest in the whole lot were about a foot high.

The first was a red or perhaps scarlet oak, apparently four years old. The acorn was about one inch below the surface of the leaves. It rose five inches above the leaves, and the root extended about one foot below the surface.

The second was a black oak, which rose six inches above the leaves (or eight, measured along the stem). This, too, was apparently four years old. It was much branched, and its tops had been cut off by rabbits last year. The root ran straight down about one inch, then nearly horizontally for five or six inches, and when I pulled it up, it broke off where less than an eighth of an inch thick, sixteen inches below the surface. It was a quarter of an inch in diameter at the surface, and nearly three-quarters of an inch in diameter five inches lower (measured along the root). At the same height above the surface, it was hardly one-fifth of an inch in diameter.

The third was a white oak, ten inches high, and apparently seven years old. It also had been browsed by a rabbit and had put out a new shoot accordingly. Two years' growth was buried in the leaves. The root was very similar both in direction and form to the last, only not quite so thick.

The fourth was a shrub oak, also quite similar to the others, though still less thick, and with two or more shoots from one stock.

In all these cases, or especially the first three, there was one main and unexpectedly great fusiform root, altogether out of proportion to the top, you would say. This was thickest at four or five inches below the surface and tapered both ways—but, of course, furthest and sharpest downward, with many fine, stringy fibers extending more or less horizontally on every side from it perhaps a foot. Just as a biennial plant devotes its energies the first year to producing a stock on which it can feed the next, so these little oaks, in their earliest years, are forming these great, thick, succulent, and vigorous roots on which they can draw when they are suddenly left to seek their fortunes in a sproutland.

Red-oak seedling

Anyone will be surprised on digging up some of these lusty oaken carrots for the first time, and it will strike him as a remarkable special provision for the succession of forest trees. This kind of root is peculiar to young oaks and is evidently designed as a resource when an accident happens to the part above ground. He will also be surprised at the firmness with which these short and feeble-looking twigs, not bigger round than a crow's quill, are set in the ground, for the roots do not run straight down like a carrot, but they slant off more or less horizontally from beneath the acorn two to six inches, yet commonly not straight, but with a half-turn or spiral, somewhat like a bit-stock whose handle is not over six inches one side of its point—and then, having acquired their greatest thickness, they descend straight downward. Thus side view: [a] or looking down on it: [b] Of twenty-two oak seedlings of various kinds which I brought home and examined at my leisure, the root of none ran directly and perpendicularly downward, but all turned to one side just under the acorn and ran more or less horizontally or aslant one to five inches, or say three inches on the average. Another, as you look down on it, has two turns [c] and three as you look from one side, so firmly is it rooted [d]—so that the twig must always part long before the root can be pulled up. Methinks they get the first horizontal turn from the manner in which the radicle is curved back under the acorn. The acorn is easily distinguished after the tree is five or six years old.

There was a marked difference between the seedlings found under oak woods and those found under pines. The former were not only very few, but much older, commonly, and more decayed, poor, and diseased root stocks; and the shoots from those were slender and feeble, and more or less prostrate under the leaves. In Warren's hill lot, the part exclusively oak, twenty or twenty-five years old, I found on October 17th plenty of little oaks less than a foot high; but, on examination, there were fewer manifestly seedling than in dense pines. They were oftenest shoots from the end of a horizontal twig running several feet under the leaves and leading to an old stub under the surface—probably older, larger, and more decayed seedlings. By "seedling" I mean a young oak which sprang from a seed, but of which the part above ground has never equalled in bulk the part beneath.

In the southeast part of Emerson's lot, chiefly oak, I examined two very slender oak shoots rising about eight inches above the leafy ground, which, traced downward, conducted me to a little stub which I mistook for a very old root or part of a larger tree; but digging it up, I found it to be a true seedling, of the usual fusiform but curved character, fifteen or eighteen inches long and at least seven-eighths of an inch thick, while the longest shoot was only one-eighth of an inch thick and ten inches high. This seedling had died down to the ground six years ago, and then these two slender shoots, such as you commonly see in old woods, had started. The root was probably ten years old when the seedling part died down and is now therefore some sixteen years old. Yet, as I say, the oak is only ten inches high. Thus it endures and gradually pines and dies.

As for those which I dug up: The afternoon referred to above, when I set out to get ten from an oak wood and as many from a pine wood, I carried them home and compared them at my leisure. There were, as I have said, three oak seedlings from the oak wood. One, the smallest, was like those in the pine woods, but the other two had singularly old, large, irregular, and twisted roots—were gnarled oblong knobs, as it were, with slender shoots having died down many times. You would think that you had come upon a dead but buried stump. The largest, for instance, was a red oak, with a slender shoot nine inches high and one-eighth of an inch thick at the ground, and apparently three years old. The root broke off where it was one-eighth of an inch thick, at about eighteen inches below the surface, and at three inches below the surface it was one and three-eighths inches thick. One was one inch; the other, being flattish, two or three of the side or horizontal fibers had developed into stout roots which ran quite horizontally twenty inches, and these broke off. They were apparently as long as the taproot. One of these at three inches below the surface was about half an inch thick and perfectly horizontal. The plant was thus fixed very firmly in the ground.

I counted the dead stubs or bases of shoots which had died down formerly, and there were several two or three times as large as the present one. If there was but one of these at a time and they decayed successively after living three years only (and they probably lived twice as long), then the root was thirty years old. But supposing that there were one and a half shoots at a time, it would then be about twenty years old. In short, I think that this root may have been as old as the large oaks around it, or some twenty-five years old.

From my experience, I should say that the short and slender twigs which rise from the ground in oak woods, and which are commonly referred to the roots of large trees, were really from these old roots of seedlings decaying in the ground.

There were nineteen seedlings from the pitch- and white-pine woods—including white, shrub, black, and perhaps red oaks—and the average height was seven inches; average length of roots, ten inches; thickness, where thickest, three-eighths of an inch. Quite a number were shrub oaks, which partly accounts for their slenderness, but the largest were not so stout as I had often dug up. The average age of the present shoot was four years, but more than half had died down once at least, so that they were really considerably older than at first appeared. There is in all cases at the surface of the ground, or head of the root, a ring of dormant buds ready to shoot up when an injury happens to the original shoot.

One shoot at least had been cut off, and so killed by a rabbit, a quite *common* occurrence.

Another evidence that few oaks spring up under an oak wood is found in the fact that in all *old* oak woods, as compared with younger ones, there is little or no underwood, but you walk freely in every direction, though in the midst of a dense wood.

The question that next arises is, Why are the oak seedlings in an oak wood so few, comparatively, and so diseased?

First: It is certain that, generally speaking, the soil under old oaks is more exhausted for oaks than under old pines. Carpenter, speaking of the injurious execretions of leaves, says that "few plants will grow in the soil formed by the leaves of the beech, and the oak . . . so completely impregnates the soil around its roots with tannin that few trees will grow in the spot from which it is rooted up." It evidently cannot be very injurious to pines.

Second: Seedling oaks under oaks would be least protected from frosts in the spring, just after leafing. Yet the sprouts prevail. It may be because acorns, little oaks, and squirrels all love warmth; and the ground does not freeze nearly so hard under dense pines as in a deciduous wood.

Third: Squirrels and jays resort to evergreens with their forage, and the oaks may not bear so many acorns, but that these creatures may carry off nearly all the sound ones.

These are some of the reasons that occur to me, but I do not quite understand it yet.

After some years the hardwoods, as I have said, evidently find such a locality unfavorable to their growth, the pines being allowed to stand. As an instance of this, I observed in the first pine wood above mentioned, a red maple twenty-five feet long which had been recently prostrated as if by the wind, though still covered with green leaves, the only maple in any position in the wood; and in a pitch- and white-pine grove growing over some twenty-five feet high, I observe that all the sugar maples planted with them are dying.

Wishing to know how long the oak seedlings lived in a dense pine wood, I examined the pitch pines by Thrush Alley, and I found that the oldest of them where the pines are thick were from eight to ten years old, though in little openings amid the pines only a rod across and where the pines were thinner, the oaks shot up higher and were becoming trees. The oldest I could find in Conant's strip of pitch and white pines was a black oak thirteen years old. But I saw none older under these and other dense pines, even when the pines were thirty years old, though I have no doubt that oaks began to grow there more than twenty years ago. Hence, they must have died, and I suppose that I could find their great roots dead and decaying in the soil, if I should dig for them.

At Meriam's much larger white-pine wood, which was quite open beneath, the oldest little oaks which I noticed were five years old and six inches high. I should say that they survived under a very dense pine wood only from six to ten years. But if you cut down the pines there, oaks begin to grow with great rapidity and take their places. For example, in order to ascertain the effect of cutting down the pines on the little oaks beneath, I visited on October 30th John Hosmer's pitch-pine wood, a part of which had been cut off the previous winter. In the cleared part of the wood they were manifestly springing up with new vigor.

Omitting such as were of the character of sprouts, though they had not been cut (that is, which had shot up from old roots to three feet high merely on account of the influx of light and air), I measured this year's growth of the first four oak seedlings under one foot in height, and found it to average five and a half inches. The average growth of the first four of the same kind amid the adjacent pines was one and a half inches. As may be seen, this was not nearly fair enough to the cleared part, for I should have included the higher shoots—many if not all of which, no doubt, were seedlings. But although these oaks almost invariably die if the pines are not cut down, it is probable that they do better for a few years under their shelter than they would anywhere else.

It is remarkable that the very extensive and thorough experiments of the English have at length led them to adopt a method of raising oaks almost precisely like this, which somewhat earlier had been adopted by Nature and her squirrels here, and which doubtless a thousand or two years ago she still practiced in their own island; they have simply rediscovered the value of pines as nurses for oaks. For many years they have been patiently and faithfully pursuing their experiments on a large scale, and returning gradually step by step to the method of Nature without knowing.

I find a very interesting and apparently complete account of these experiments in Loudon's *Arboretum*. They seem early and generally to have found out the importance of using trees of some kind as nurse plants for the young oaks, such is "the natural tenderness of the young shoots and leaves of the oak" with respect to frost. Speechly, the first writer on this subject, "found the birch the most suitable tree for shelter," and this, as we have seen, is one of those which Nature uses here. He "also found that sowing the poorer parts of the hills with furze was a very effective mode of sheltering the oak; for though, he says, 'it seems to choke and overgrow the oak for some time, yet after a few years we commonly find the best oak plants in the strongest beds of furze.' " Others used the Scotch pine, larch, and fir; but finally the Scotch pine, a tree very similar to our pitch pine, the most like our pines of any tree they have in England, was decided to be superior to all these for this purpose. I quote from Loudon what he describes "as the Ultimatum on the subject of planting and sheltering oaks"—an "abstract of the practice adopted by the government officers in the national forests" of England, prepared by Alexander Milne.

At first *some* oaks had been planted by themselves and others mixed with Scotch pines. But, says Mr. Milne:

In all cases where oaks were planted actually amongst the pines, and surrounded by them [though the soil might be inferior], the oaks were found to be much the best. . . . For several years past, the plan pursued has been to plant the enclosures with Scotch pines only . . . and when the pines have got to the height of five feet or six feet . . . then to put in good strong oak plants of about four or five years' growth, among the pines, not cutting away any pines at first, unless they happen to be so strong and thick as to overshadow the oaks. In about two years it becomes necessary to shred the branches of the pines, to give light and air to the oaks; and, in about two or three more years, to begin gradually to remove the pines altogether, taking out a certain number each year, so that, at the end of twenty or twenty-five years, not a single Scotch pine shall be left; although, for the first ten or twelve years, the plantation may have appeared to contain nothing else but pines. The advantage of this mode of planting has been found to be that the pines dry and ameliorate the soil, destroying the coarse grass and brambles which frequently choke and injure oaks; and that no mending over is necessary, as scarcely an oak so planted is found to fail.

Thus much the English planters have discovered by patient experiment, and, for aught I know, they have taken out a patent for it; but they appear not to have discovered that it was discovered before, and that they are merely adopting the method of Nature, which she long ago made patent to all. She is all the while planting the oaks amid the pines without our knowledge, and at last, instead of government officers, we send a party of wood-choppers to cut down the pines and so rescue an oak forest, at which we wonder, as if it had dropped from the skies.

Nay, so far are the English from realizing that they are not the original inventors, in this case, but that their "art and design" are the same which are practiced by "unassisted nature," that when, in the same essay in which the above extract was found, "Mr. Speechly observes that he found that the seedling oaks were not injured, but rather improved, by tall grass and large weeds growing among them," it is remarked that this "seems contrary to the nature of plants, and is certainly a practice that ought not to be generally followed, since these tall weeds and grass must prevent the sun and air from producing their full influence on the leaves of the seedling oaks. In this, as in similar cases," says this writer, and we cannot but be amazed by his remark, "it may be laid down as a principle, that, in all cultivation, every step in the process ought to be regulated according to art and design, and nothing whatever, or, at least, as little as possible, left to unassisted nature." He does not know that that "art" of which he speaks is the same which was practiced by the original inventor and planter of oak woods, so that his is at most only the rediscovery of a lost art.

It will be perceived that the age of the oaks at which the English begin to shred the pines and birches, and also at which they remove them altogether, corresponds remarkably well with what I find to be the age at which the oaks die if the pines are permitted to stand.

If anyone presumes that after all there cannot be so many acorns dropped or planted by animals amid the pines as we see oaks spring up there when the pines are cut, that is, enough to occupy the ground, I would suggest first that the number of acorns recommended to be planted on an acre by the English authorities varies from sixty to five hundred and averages about two hundred and forty, or one and a half to a rod, though probably not more than one to a rod will be left at last, and not nearly so many if they are designed to grow large.

In the densest old oak wood in this town I found, by counting a portion, that there were certainly not more than one hundred and eighty trees to an acre, or a fraction more than one to a square rod, and the trees generally owing to this density were not very large nor spreading. Whenever they were so, they took up far more room than this. Then let the reader consider that, according to our observation, the young oaks survive about ten years. There is allowed ten years for the animals to plant each such pine wood. So that if the tract contains one hundred square rods, it would be necessary only that they should plant ten acorns in a year, supposing all to succeed, in order that there might be as many as one oak to every square rod at the end of ten years. This, or anything like this, does not imply any very great activity among the planters. A striped squirrel could carry enough acorns for a year in his cheeks at one trip.

In short, we have seen that animals plant a great many more than this.

———

I went forth on the afternoon of October 17th expressly to ascertain how chestnuts are propagated. These trees have never been as common in this neighborhood as oaks and pines, that is, so generally dispersed; but though they have formed and still form extensive woods, they are confined to certain localities. Any dry woodland being cut, it is pretty certain that the ground will soon be covered again with oaks or pines, but it must be an unusual locality if we would expect a chestnut wood to spring up there.

Moreover, the chestnut timber hereabouts has rapidly disappeared within the last fifteen years, having been used extensively for railroad sleepers, as well as for rails, planks, and other purposes, so that it is now comparatively scarce and costly; and there is danger, if we do not take unusual care, that this tree will become extinct here.

The nearest chestnut wood at present is about a mile and a half southeast from the middle of Concord village. My way toward this lay at first across the open fields and meadows south of the village, and at the distance of about a mile I entered the extensive pine and oak wood, which half a mile eastward near the Lincoln line begins to contain a few chestnuts.

On entering the wood I began at once to look about carefully for oak seedlings or anything else of the kind, and directly, in a part of it almost exclusively oak, I was surprised to see a cluster of little chestnuts six inches high and close together. Working my hand underneath, I easily lifted them up with all their roots—four chestnut trees two years old, which had partially died down the first year, yet were quite flourishing, with the four great chestnuts from which they sprang still attached, but not the burr; and also four small acorns which had sent up puny little trees of the same age beneath the chestnuts, but it is remarkable that these were either dead or dying. These eight nuts all lay within a diameter of two inches, about an inch and a half beneath the present leafy surface, in a very loose soil of but half-decayed leaves. I have no doubt that they were buried there two falls ago by a squirrel, or possibly a mouse.

It is very rare that you distinguish a seedling chestnut in this neighborhood, and I do not *remember* that I had ever met with any of *this age* before, though it is very likely that I have. I had come forth on purpose to look for them, but did not expect to find them so soon. Such is the difference between looking for a thing and waiting for it to attract your attention. In the last case you are not interested at all about it, and probably will never see it.

Nevertheless, I was surprised at the sight of these chestnuts, for there are not to my knowledge, and I am thoroughly acquainted with that wood, any seed-bearing chestnut trees within about half a mile of that spot, and I should almost as soon have expected to find chestnuts in the artificial pine grove in my yard. And yet *it is possible* that within a very few years one or two pioneer seedlings may have borne their first burr much nearer than that. At any rate, no one acquainted with this lot, nor the proprietor of it, would have believed that a chestnut lay under the leaves in it, or within a long distance of it, and yet from what I saw then and afterwards, I have no doubt that there were hundreds such which were placed there by quadrupeds and birds.

These little chestnuts, as well as the three or four of the same age which I have examined since, have not the *great* roots which young oaks have.

As I proceeded onward over hill and dale through the mixed pine and oak woods toward Lincoln, with my eyes more widely open than ever, now *looking for* chestnuts and not waiting for them to call to me, I found many chestnut seedlings two or three years old, and some older and even ten feet high, scattered here and there but more numerous as I approached the chestnut woods. I should say that on an average there was one every half-dozen rods, made more distinct by their yellow leaves on the brown ground, which was the more surprising to me because I had not attended to the spread of the chestnut before, and every one of these came from a chestnut placed there by a quadruped or bird, which had brought it from further east, where alone it grew. And it is to be observed that these seedlings, like oaks, are the most numerous under the densest white pines, as that at Brister's Spring.

Several persons have expressed to me their surprise that they could not find a seedling chestnut to transplant. I myself, wishing to get a section of a chestnut seedling a dozen years old, spent the better part of two days walking rapidly through extensive chestnut woods without seeing one that I thought was a seedling. It is with them as with the young oaks: not only is a seedling more difficult to distinguish in a chestnut wood, but it is really far more rare there than in the adjacent mixed pine and oak woods. In this case I was compelled at last to return to our own mixed woods and cut down one of those which I have described above a quarter of a mile from a seed-bearing chestnut tree.

American chestnut burr

In short, after considerable experience in searching for these as well as seedling oaks, I have learned to neglect the chestnut and oak woods, and go only to the pines, or neighboring woods of a different species, for them. Only that course will pay.

You would say that the squirrels and so on went further for chestnuts than for acorns in proportion as they are a greater rarity. I suspect that a squirrel may sometimes convey them a quarter or half a mile. A squirrel goes a-chestnutting perhaps as far as the boys do, and when he gets there he does not have to shake or club the tree, or wait for frost to open the burrs, but he walks up to the burrs and cuts them off and strews the ground with them before they have opened. And the fewer they are in the wood, the more certain it is that he will appropriate every one; for it is no transient afternoon's picnic with him, but the pursuit of his life, a harvest that he gets as surely as the farmer his corn.

No doubt, as soon as a young chestnut fifteen or twenty feet high, far advanced by his agency beyond the chestnut woods into the pines and oaks, bears a single burr, which yet no man detects, a squirrel or bird is almost sure to gather it and plant it for that neighborhood, or still further forward—and thus the chestnut wood advances, and one kind of tree gradually succeeds to another.

Now it is important that the owners of these woodlots should know what is going on there and treat them and the squirrels accordingly. They little dream of it at present. They appreciate only some very gross results. They have never considered what is to be the future history of what they call their woodlots. They may have designs of their own on those acres, but they have not considered what Nature's design is. By a judicious letting Nature alone merely, we might recover our chestnut wood in the course of a century.

The jays scream and the red squirrels scold while you are clubbing and shaking the chestnut trees, for they are there on the same errand, and two of a trade never agree. I frequently see a red or gray squirrel cast down a green chestnut burr as I am going through the woods, and I used to think sometimes that they were cast to me. In fact, they are so busy about it in the midst of the chestnut season that you cannot stand long in the woods without hearing one fall. A sportsman told me that he had the day before, that was, in the middle of October, seen a green chestnut burr dropped on our great river meadow, fifty rods from the nearest wood and much farther from the nearest chestnut tree, and he could not tell how it came there.

Occasionally, when chestnutting in midwinter, I find thirty or forty nuts in a pile, left in its gallery just under the leaves by the common wood mouse (*Mus leucopus*), and another tells me that his boy found, one February, as much as a peck of chestnuts in different parcels within a short distance of one another, under the leaves, placed there, as he said, by the striped squirrel, which he saw eating them. Another tells me of finding nearly a bushel of chestnuts in a cleft in a rock when blasting for a ditch in the woods, a squirrel's deposit.

Yes, these dense and stretching oak forests, whose withered leaves now redden and rustle on the hills for many a New England mile, were all planted by the labor of animals. For after some weeks of close scrutiny I cannot avoid the conclusion that our modern oak woods sooner or later spring up from an acorn, not where it has fallen from the tree, for that is the exception, but where it has been dropped or placed by an animal.

Consider what a vast work these forest planters are doing! So far as our noblest hardwood forests are concerned, the animals, especially squirrels and jays, are our greatest and almost only benefactors. It is to them that we owe this gift. It is not in vain that a squirrel lives in almost every forest tree or hollow log or wall or heap of stones.

Thus, one would say that our oak forests, vast and indispensable as they are, were produced by a kind of accident, that is, by the failure of animals to reap the fruit of their labors. Yet who shall say that they have not a dim knowledge of the value of their labors?—that the squirrel when it plants an acorn, and the jay when it lets one slip from under its foot, has not sometimes a transient thought for its posterity, which at least consoles it for its loss?

But what is the character of our gratitude to these squirrels—to say nothing of the others—these planters of forests, these exported dukes of Athol of many generations, which have found out how high the oak will grow on many a mountain, how low in many a valley, and how far and wide on all our plains? Are they on our pension list? Have we in any way recognized their services? We regard them as vermin. The farmer knows only that they get his seed corn occasionally in the fields adjacent to his woodlot, and perchance encourages his boys to shoot them every May, furnishing powder and shot for this purpose, while perhaps they are planting the nobler oak-corn (acorn) in its place—while up-country they have squirrel hunts on a large scale every fall and kill many thousands in a few hours, and all the neighborhood rejoices. We should be more civilized as well as humane if we recognized once in a year by some symbolical ceremony the part which the squirrel plays in the economy of Nature.

The noblest trees, and those which it took the longest to produce, and which are the longest lived—as chestnuts, hickories, and oaks—are the first to become extinct under our present system and are the hardest to reproduce, and their place is taken by pines and birches, of feebler growth than the primitive pines and birches, for want of a change of soil. There is many a tract now bearing a poor and decaying crop of birches, or perhaps of oaks, dying when a quarter grown, and covered with fungi and excrescences, where for two hundred years grew oaks and chestnuts of the largest size.

The time will soon come, if it has not already, when we shall have to take special pains to secure and encourage the growth of white oaks, as we already must that of chestnuts, for the most part. These oaks will become so scattered that there will not be seed enough to seed the ground rapidly and completely.

The observations in the chestnut woods also suggest that you cannot raise one kind of wood alone in a country unless you are willing to plant it yourself. If no oaks grow within miles of your pines, then of course the ground under the pines will not be filled with little oaks, and you will have to plant them there—or put up with poor pines at last. Better have your wood of different kinds in narrow lots of fifty acres, and not one kind covering a township.

As for the planters of these oaks, I have not chanced to see squirrels actually planting or burying the acorns, though in the fall I very frequently, almost daily, see them transporting them, and where they have dropped them, and also where they have deposited them in holes—as does everyone who daily visits the woods. It is common to find several fresh acorns buried an inch or two deep under the grass or perhaps amid bushes just outside an oak wood when you are digging a ditch or the like. Almost every observant farmer finds one such deposit each year, and though at first it may seem to be the exception, if he compares notes with his neighbors, he will find it to be the rule. But it is to be observed that in order that an acorn may spring up and thrive in an evergreen wood, it does not require to be buried, but merely transported and dropped on the surface there. Every sound white-oak acorn that I could find on the 3d of December had sent down its radicle into the earth, though a great part in open pastures had already been killed. In the woods it will soon be more or less covered with leaves, under which it is kept moist and concealed.

In the fall I notice on the ground, either within or in the neighborhood of old oak woods on all sides of the town, stout oak twigs three or four inches long, bearing half a dozen empty acorn cups, which twigs have been gnawed off by squirrels, on both sides of the nuts, in order to make them more portable.

The squirrels have no notion of starving in a hard winter, and therefore they are unceasingly employed in the fall in foraging. Every thick wood, especially evergreens, is their storehouse against necessity, and they pack it as thickly as they can with nuts and seeds of all kinds. The squirrel which you see at this season running so glibly along the fence, with his tail waving over his head, frequently pausing on a post or stone, which you watch perhaps for twenty or thirty rods, has probably a nut or two in his mouth which he is carrying to yonder thickets.

This wonderful activity of the squirrels—in collecting and dispersing and planting nuts and acorns and so forth—every autumn is the more necessary, since the trees on whose fruit they mainly live are not annual plants like the wheat which supplies *our* staff of life. If the wheat crop fails this year, we have only to sow more the next year and reap a speedy harvest; but if the forests were to be planted only at intervals equal to the age of the trees, there would be danger, what with fires and blight and insects, of a sudden failure and famine. It is important that there be countless trees in every stage of growth, that there be an annual planting as of wheat. Consider the amount of work they have to do, the area to be planted.

But especially in the winter, the extent to which this transportation and planting of nuts is carried on is made apparent by the snow. In almost every wood you will see where the red or gray squirrels have pawed down through the snow in a hundred places, sometimes two feet deep, and almost always directly to a nut or a pine cone, as directly as if they had started from it and bored upward—which you and I could not have done. It would be difficult for us to find one before the snow falls. Commonly, no doubt, they had deposited them there in the fall. You wonder if they remember the locality of their deposit or discover it by the scent.

The red squirrel commonly has its winter abode in the earth under a thicket of evergreens, frequently under a small clump of evergreens in the midst of a deciduous wood. If there are any oak or nut trees which still retain their fruit standing at a distance without the wood, their paths frequently lead directly to and from them. We therefore need not suppose an oak standing here and there *in* the wood in order to seed it, but if a few stand within twenty or thirty rods of it, it is sufficient.

Having got this booty, they seek a dry place to open it, a fallen limb or a stump that rises above the snow, or the instep of the tree, or oftener still a lower dead stub projecting from the trunk of the tree, or the entrance to their holes. It is true, these cones and nuts are pretty black and commonly, for aught I can see, have only abortive or empty seeds at this season; yet they patiently strip them there and evidently find some good seed, and the snow is strewn with the empty and rejected ones, as well as the scales and shells.

The nuts thus left on the surface, or buried just beneath it, are placed in the most favorable circumstances for germinating. I have sometimes wondered how those which merely fell on the surface of the earth got planted; but by the end of December I find the chestnuts of the same year partially mixed with the mold, as it were, under the decaying and moldy leaves, where there is all the moisture and manure they want, for the nuts fall first. In a plentiful year, a large proportion of the nuts are thus covered loosely an inch deep and are, of course, somewhat concealed from squirrels. One winter, when the crop had been abundant, I got, with the aid of a rake, many quarts of these nuts as late as the 10th of January, and though some bought at the store the same day were more than half of them moldy, I did not find a single moldy one among these which I picked from under the wet and moldy leaves, where they had been snowed on once or twice. Nature knows how to pack them best. They were still plump and tender. Apparently they do not heat there, though wet. In the spring they were all sprouting.

Loudon says that "when the nut [of the common walnut of Europe (*Juglans regia*)] is to be preserved through the winter for the purpose of planting in the following spring, it should be laid in a rot heap as soon as gathered, with the husk on; and the heap should be turned over frequently in the course of the winter." Here again he is stealing Nature's thunder. How can a poor mortal do otherwise?—for it is she that finds fingers to steal with and the treasure to be stolen. In the planting of the seeds of most trees, the best gardeners do no more than follow Nature, though they may not know it. Generally, both large and small ones are most sure to germinate and succeed best when only beaten into the earth with the back of a spade and then covered with leaves or straw.

These results to which planters have arrived remind us of the experience of Kane and his companions at the North, who, when learning to live in that climate, were surprised to find themselves steadily adopting the customs of the natives, simply becoming Esquimaux. So, when we experiment in planting forests, we find ourselves at last doing as Nature does. Would it not be well to consult with Nature in the outset?—for she is the most extensive and experienced planter of us all, not excepting the dukes of Athol.

As soon as the snow melts, the squirrels can browse for acorns with yet more success. On March 25th, 1855, I see where the squirrels have fed extensively on the acorns now exposed by the melting of the snow. The ground is strewn with the freshly torn shells and nibbled meat in some places.

If one has not attended to the subject, he may think that the agency of the animals is not enough to account for the annual planting of such extreme tracts, just as we wonder where all the flies and other insects come from in the spring because we have not followed them into their winter quarters and counted them there. Yet it is certain that Nature does preserve and multiply the race of flies, to a great extent without a new creation, while we are inattentive and sleeping.

We must look where the animals are. Squirrels are to be found where their food is in its season. Plant a chestnut tree in your yard, and when it begins to bear, if it is on the outskirts of the village, it will be annually visited by squirrels from the woods at the season when its fruit is ripe. One who has half-tame red squirrels in an elm before his house observes that they regularly go off to the woods (chiefly pitch pine and shrub oak) behind his house about June and return in September when his butternuts are ripe. Do they not go for hazelnuts and pine seed? Another tells me of a gray squirrel which he had that would go off to the woods every summer and in the winter come back into his cage, where he whirled the wire cylinder.

Hereabouts nuts and pine cones imply the presence of squirrels, and squirrels imply nuts and pine cones. I visited last fall the three principal old oak woods in this vicinity, or that I know of within eight or ten miles, and found accidentally that these were such peculiar resorts for the gray squirrel that several with whom I talked supposed that I had come after these squirrels, and one was able to give me some information about the most distant and interesting wood because he had been accustomed to go there formerly to hunt gray squirrels. I saw their leafy nests in all those woods, though the only animal seen in the nearest wood was a red squirrel, and the only sound heard, the scream of jays—all which were doubtless attracted by the acorns. In fact, these woods are chiefly resorted to by those who hunt the gray squirrel, and not on account of their beauty. Moreover, two of these woods are great resorts for pigeons for the same reason, and I saw several pigeon places in them. One, indeed, by the confession of the owner, who is a great pigeon catcher, has been allowed to stand of late years on account of the food and shelter it affords to the pigeons.

 Although I have seen a squirrel planting hickory nuts, I have not been able to ascertain *with certainty* under what circumstances some young thickets of them in open land were planted.

It is remarkable how persistently Nature endeavors to keep the earth clothed with wood of some kind—how much vitality there is in the stumps and roots of some trees, though small and young. For instance, I examined this afternoon the little hickories on the bare slope of Smith's Hill, countless little hickories a foot high or a little more springing up every few feet. I have observed them for a dozen years past endeavoring to cover that pasture, otherwise perfectly bare, and have wondered how the seed came there; for it is not only a bare sward, but the middle of the field is necessarily remote from any seed-bearing trees. They extend over a space forty or fifty rods long, and are from one or two feet to six or more feet high, and in some places already form pretty dense thickets.

On examining closely, I find that they had often died or been cut down and had old roots. It being impossible to pull one up by the root, and difficult to examine the roots at all, I remembered that the upper part of this hill had been plowed up in the spring and that I should probably find such as had been eradicated cast out on one side of the field. It was exactly as I had anticipated: there were hundreds if not thousands of specimens, with the larger part of the root in each case. *These*, though on an average only one to three feet high, were two inches thick at the ground, and I judged that they might be fifteen years old. It must have been severe work for the oxen and plow to break up that land.

Selecting a large and healthy-looking one, I sawed it off and found it nearly dead. This growth was four years old. It had been cut down previously to a stub, which showed five rings more. I did not look beneath the surface to see how much older it might be. I now observed that the leading shoot, this year's growth of it, was perfectly withered and dead, apparently killed by the frost. The same was commonly the case except when the tree had got above a certain height.

At first I had hastily presumed that these hickories had been planted by squirrels in the open land, but now I began to inquire how long this had been open land. I do not know certainly. The old stumps are yet quite common, and I *presume* it is fifteen or twenty years since it was cleared. So I conclude that the nuts were probably planted here before the old wood was cut, and though they have been repeatedly cut down to keep the pasture clear and have been killed down by frost, yet such is their vitality, all these still remain. Nevertheless, a great many are quite feeble and dying in consequence of this treatment.

In an adjoining young wood of oaks, hickories, pines, and so forth, which were probably cut at the same time with the other, the hickories were three or four times as high as these. It *may* be that when these same trees were cut off on this spot and the land *cleared*, the pines and oaks even were exterminated with comparative ease, but the hickories, being tough and stubborn, did not give up the ground. I cannot as yet account for their existence in this place otherwise.

Again I examine this hill, and also Britton's Clearing, to see if I can find a seedling hickory under half a dozen years old. It is seventeen or eighteen years since the last tract was cleared, and within that time a peach orchard has been raised and has decayed there, and also an apple orchard has been raised, which is now going to ruin. I should say it had been cultivated within ten or twelve years at least. The little hickories are on the side and in the midst of these orchards. After searching long amid the very numerous young hickories in these two places, I fail to find one so recently planted as I sought (under half a dozen years old). I have not found *anywhere* a seedling with the seed attached. I find many at Smith's only one or two feet high, but they invariably have great roots, and old stubs which have died down are visible at or beneath the surface of the ground. It is very common, almost the rule, to find from one to three from one root, each one inch in diameter and two or three feet high, while the common stock beneath the ground is two inches in diameter. Accordingly, no man can pull one up by the roots, however short and slender it is above ground.

Nevertheless, pulling at one at Britton's which was two and a quarter feet high, it came up easily, to my surprise; but I found that it had broken square off just one foot below the surface where an inch and a half in diameter, being quite decayed there. It was three-quarters of an inch in diameter at the surface and increased regularly for five or six inches downward till it was one inch in diameter. There there was the stub of an old shoot, and the root was suddenly enlarged to about one and a half inches in diameter and held about the same to where it broke off. There was another stub about three inches above the ground, and the more recent growth above this was of about four years. This last had died, and this year two shoots had put out at six or eight inches above the ground and had grown two and four inches, respectively. Here, then, were evident at the very least four efforts to rise to a tree. The first stub was about the diameter of the whole tree at present above ground—

call it then	4 years
The second was at least (when it died)	2 years
The third, forming the present tree	4 years
The fourth, growth of this year	1 year
	11 years

This little hickory, two and a quarter feet high and three-quarters of an inch in diameter, standing in open land, was then at *least* eleven years old (there were at least eight rings above the first stub). What more the root would have revealed if I had dug it up, I do not know. The fact that the lowest observed stub was six inches below the surface, showing plainly to the eye that the earth had been heaped up about it, suggested that this root might have survived in the ground through a clearing and burning, and subsequent cultivation. What makes this the more likely is the fact that there are sprouts from several large chestnut stumps in the midst of the orchard, which, judging from their size, have probably been cut down once or twice since the tree was cut and which yet survive. What is true of these sprouts may be true of the hickory sprouts.

I do not think that a single hickory has been planted in either of these places for some years at least. Indeed, why should squirrels bring the nuts to these particular localities where other little hickories already stand?—which they must do, supposing them to be planted still and not to be all of one age.

There are a few hickories in the *open* land which I cultivated at Walden, and these may have been planted there by birds or squirrels since it was cleared; for, as I remember, it must be more than thirty-five years since there was wood there.

Also there is Fair Haven hillside. I remember when it was cleared some thirty-five years ago, and some twenty or twenty-five years ago pines began to spring up there. And I now see a good many hickories both within and *without* the pine, five feet high. I feel almost sure that *these cannot be* from stumps or old roots which have existed in the ground thirty-five years. How then did they come here; I mean those which keep in advance of the pines a rod or two, unlike oaks? Why do I never see those only two or three years old here? I am constrained to believe, nevertheless, that they were planted here by animals. If so, the walnut differs from the oak in the mode of its spreading, for I do not see oaks anywhere thus springing up in groves in grass ground or in advance of pines. Are animals more likely to plant walnuts in open land than acorns?—or is it that walnuts are more likely to live there when planted? Perchance acorns so planted fail to come up. I may be mistaken about those at Smith's Hill and Britton's after all.

On December 1st I examined the youngest in Fair Haven Hill to see how old they are. I sawed off three at two or three inches below the surface (and also higher up). These were about three feet high. The rings are very hard to discern, but I judge the very smallest of these (which is about one inch in diameter and three feet high) to be seven years old. The other two are probably older, yet not nearly so old as the pines, whose beginning I remember. It therefore must be that *these* hickories have sprung up from nuts within from seven to twenty-five years past. They are most numerous in openings four or five rods over (oaks would not be), amid the pines, and are also found many rods from the pines in the open pasture, and also especially along walls, though very far from other forest trees of any kind.

I infer, therefore, that animals plant them, and perhaps their growing along walls may be accounted for in part by the fact that the squirrels with nuts oftenest take that road. What is most remarkable is that they should be planted so often in open land, on a bare hillside, when oaks rarely are. How is this to be accounted for? It may be that they are more persistent at the root than oaks, and so at last succeed in becoming trees in these places where oaks fail. They may be more persevering. Perhaps also cattle do not browse and injure them so much as oaks.

Going from there to the hickories on Smith's Hill, I am somewhat inclined to return to my first opinion. But I still think that some of those outside hickories at Fair Haven Hill were planted within a dozen years in a manner in which oaks are not.

On December 3d I find no young hickories springing up on the open and quite *bare* side of Lee's Hill; yet if they do so elsewhere, why should they not here, where the nuts are so abundant? But *under* and about the hickory near the white oak on the north side of the hill, there are many small hickories two to four feet high amid the young birches and pines, the largest of which birches and pines have been lately cut down. I am inclined to think that both oaks and hickories are occasionally planted in open land a few rods beyond the edge of a pine or other wood, but that the hickory roots are more persistent under these circumstances and hence oftener succeed there. And now it occurs to me that perhaps there have been many little pines springing up on the side of Smith's Hill within a dozen years and that the hickory nuts were planted in and around these; but the pine being killed, the hickories have survived there. Yet I do not remember any such pines at Britton's, which I know so well.

One supposition I have not used: it is that walnuts planted in the woods may preserve their vitality a long time, and so come up many years after in *open* land!

It is wonderful how much these little hickories have endured and prevailed over. Though I searched the whole of Fair Haven hillside, not only for the smallest but the most perpendicular and soundest, each of the three that I sawed off had died down once *at least*, years ago, though it might not show any scar above ground. On digging, I found it an inch below the surface. Most of these small ones consist of several stems from one root, and they are often of such fantastic forms and so diseased that they seem to be wholly dead at a little distance. Some which have thus died down and sent up again two or more curving shoots are in the form of rude hooks and the like, and yet evidently many of them make erect, smooth, and sound trees at last—all defects smoothed over and obliterated.

There are many handsome young walnuts ten or twelve feet high scattered over the southeast slope of Annursnack, forming a very open grove. These trees, which spread almost as much as apple trees, are peculiar, sound, and vigorous, yet I have no doubt that they have had a similar history with those smaller ones I have described. (But I must inquire yet further into their history and how they came there.) The walnut may be twenty years old before it finally shoots up with accumulated impetus, rising above frost and other accidents, and fairly begins its existence as a young *tree*.

The three I dug up had great taproots considerably larger just beneath the surface than the stock above, and they were so firmly set in the ground that though the tree was scarcely an inch in diameter and you had dug round it to the depth of three or four inches, it was impossible to pull one up—yet I did not notice any side roots so high. They are iron trees—so rigid and so firm set are they.

There are those who write the lives of what they call *self-educated* men, and celebrate the *pursuit* of knowledge under difficulties. It will be very suggestive to such novices just to go and dig up a dozen seedling oaks and hickories, read their biographies, and see what they here contend with.

It is remarkable, with respect to hickories, that we often see these pretty dense groves of young trees, the size of hoop-poles, and yet rarely if ever nowadays meet with a dense wood of large hickory trees. We have no approach to a pure walnut wood of any size—or any *wood* at all. They seem to require *more* than oaks or other hardwoods, light and air and room to expand, before they can become even moderate-sized trees in great *numbers*. A dense thicket of a thousand or two little trees apparently becomes at last—a few scattered dozens of distinct trees in a pasture. Probably fires do often kill a great many of them. There were a great many in the open land about me when I first went to Walden, but on account of fires or frost or some other reason, there are very few there now. The pitch pines have done better.

It is also remarkable how walnuts love a hillside. Four of the five localities I have chanced to refer to *are* hillsides. Is it because of the light and air they get there? They spring up almost unaccountably in such places, as if they loved the prospect, or as if they had been ordered to occupy these posts.

In short, they who have not attended particularly to this subject are but little aware to what an extent quadrupeds and birds are employed, especially in the fall, in collecting, and so disseminating and planting, the seeds of trees. It is the most constant employment of the squirrels at that season, and you rarely meet with one that has not a nut in its mouth or is not just going to get one. As I walk amid hickories, even in August, I hear the sound of green pignuts falling from time to time, cut off by the chickadee over my head. Up-country they are obliged to make haste to gather their shag-barks on account of the squirrels. One squirrel hunter of this town told me that he knew of a walnut tree which bore particularly good nuts, but that on going to gather them one fall, he found that he had been anticipated by a family of a dozen red squirrels. He took out of the tree, which was hollow, one bushel and three pecks by measurement without the husks, and they supplied him and his family for the winter.

It would be easy to multiply instances of this kind. How commonly in the fall you see the cheek-pouches of the striped squirrel distended by a quantity of nuts! This species gets its scientific name *Tamias*, or "the steward," from its habit of storing up nuts and other seeds, as hazelnuts, acorns, walnuts, chestnuts, buckwheat, and so on. The red squirrels are said to collect nuts when the pericarp is still green and, covering a heap with leaves, wait till this opens, when they can transport them more easily. Look under a nut tree a month after the nuts have fallen and see what proportion of sound nuts to the abortive ones and shells you will find ordinarily. They have been already eaten, or dispersed far and wide. The ground looks like a platform before a grocery, where the gossips of the village sit and crack nuts and less savory jokes. You have come, you would say, after the feast was over, and are presented with the shells only.

Under such hickory trees as retain their nuts, the snow in midwinter will often be covered with the outer shells or husks rejected by the squirrels, while close to the base of the tree or of other trees in the neighborhood, where perhaps is a little bare ground, there will be a large collection of nutshells gnawed in two there by the squirrels in the course of the winter.

I am occasionally asked if I know what shrub oaks were made for. But worthless as the woodman regards it, it is to me one of the most interesting of trees and, like the white birch, is associated in my mind with New England. For whatever we have perceived to be in the slightest degree beautiful is of infinitely more value to us than what we have only as yet discovered to be useful and to serve our purpose.

Many of our dry plains and broad shelves, and little hollows high on the sides of our hills, are crowded with them from three to five feet high. About the 1st of October many leading shoots are perfectly bare of leaves, the effect of the frost; and the pretty fruit, varying in size, pointedness, and downiness, and now generally turned brown, with light converging meridional dark lines, is just ready to fall; and if you bend back the peduncles of these bare and frost-touched limbs, you find them just ready to come off, separating at the base of the peduncle, which remains attached to the fruit. Indeed, on some bushes one-half of the cups are already empty, but these generally bear the marks of squirrels' teeth (for they take the acorn out of the cup on the bush, leaving the cup there with a piece bit out of its edge), and probably but few acorns have fallen of themselves yet. The striped squirrels are very busy among them at this time, and this is about as great a height as they love to climb.

Though many twigs are bare of leaves, these clusters of brown fruit in their grayish brown cups are unnoticed and almost invisible, unless you are looking for them, above the ground which is strewn with their similarly colored leaves—that is, this leaf-strewn earth is of the same general gray brown color with the twigs and fruit, and you may brush against great wreathes of fruit without noticing them. You thus press through dense groves laden with this interesting fruit, each shrub seeming prettier than the last.

You also see where the squirrels have left their empty shells on rocks and stumps.

If you dig up old oak stumps in a young wood, even though they may be so completely decayed that only a hollow marks their site, and you do not find a particle that looks like decayed wood or bark even, and your spade meets with no resistance, you will commonly find perfectly open channels raying out from this hollow, with the pellicle of the root for a wall still, which for a hundred years the earth has learned to respect. These galleries are all underground runways of squirrels and mice, probably for many generations leading to their nests and granaries. The holes above lead to them. Every old stump, indeed, though it may be much more recent than this, is a very metropolis to them. And almost all holes in and about stumps have nutshells or nuts in them. Though you may not see a living creature in the woods, yet at the base of very many oaks will be a quantity of acorn shells.

The striped squirrels begin to eat the hazelnuts early in August, or about the time the flail begins to be heard, and you must gather those which are most expanded soon after the 20th of that month, if you would get them at all. Many a man who has observed these nuts peculiarly abundant has waited ten days before he went after them and then not found a dozen left.

Toward the end of August those bushes which grow along the walls and where squirrels abound will be all stripped by them while still green, and the ground will be strewn with their brown husks. Every nut that you can find left there will be a poor one, suggesting that they must have been very busy for a fortnight past climbing to the extremities of the slender twigs. Who witnesses the gathering of the hazelnuts—the hazel harvest? Yet what a busy and important season to the striped squirrel! Now, if ever, he needs to get a *bee*. Every nut that I could find left in that field (now hemlocks) was a poor one. By some frequented paths they did not get them so early.

When the bushes on the brink of the river are otherwise completely stripped, I sometimes find some clusters left hanging over the water, as if the squirrels had been unwilling to return there for them. I sometimes see a bird's nest in a thorn or other bush half full of acorn and hazelnut shells, where evidently some mouse or squirrel has left them.

How important the hazelnut to the ground squirrel! They grow along the walls where the squirrels have their homes. They are the oaks that grow before their doors. They have not far to go to their harvesting.

These bushes are generally stripped now, but isolated ones in the middle of the fields, away from the squirrel walks, are still full of burrs. The wall is both highway and rampart to these little beasts. They are almost inaccessible in their holes beneath it, and on either side of it spring up, also defended by the wall, the hazel bushes on whose fruit the squirrels in a great measure depend.

The squirrel lives in a hazel grove. There is not a hazel bush but some squirrel has his eye on its fruit, and he will be pretty sure to anticipate you; for you think of it only between whiles, but he thinks of it all the while. As we say, "The tools to those who can use them," so we may say, "The nuts to those who can get them."

I would not be surprised to find that they have an instinct which prompts them to plant hazelnuts—regularly.

They know better than to open an unsound nut, or at most they only peep into them. I see some on the walls with a little hole gnawed in them, enough to show that they are empty.

The same is true of other seeds, of which we make no account, as maple keys and so on. Indeed, almost every seed that falls to the earth is picked up by some animal or other, whose favorite, and perhaps peculiar, food it is. They are daily busy about it in the season, and the few seeds which escape are exceptions. There is at least a squirrel or mouse to a tree—and more, too, for their families are as large as ours—however quiet and uninhabited the place may seem when you are there. They do not stare at travellers. If you postpone your search but for a short time, you find yourself only gleaning after them. You may find several of their holes under every tree, if not within it. They ransack the woods. Though the seed may be almost microscopic, it is nuts to them. And this apparently is one of the principal ends which these seeds are intended to serve. These little creatures must live; and pray, what are they to eat—the gramnivorous ones—if not the fruits of the earth?

The common wild mouse (*Mus leucopus*), which runs all over the woods of North America, is seen carrying acorns and other seeds to its stores. You often find acorns and nuts tucked into the clefts of rocks. Exploring one of the old limestone quarries in the north part of Concord one November, I noticed in the side of an upright sliver of rock, where the limestone had formerly been blasted off, the bottom of the nearly perpendicular hole which had been drilled for that purpose, two or three inches deep and about two and a half feet from the ground, and in this I found two fresh chestnuts, a dozen or more pea-vine (*Amphicarpaea*) seeds, as many apparently of winterberry seeds, and several fresh barberry seeds, all bare seeds or without the pericarp, mixed with a little earth and rubbish.

What placed them there—squirrel, mouse, jay, or crow? At first I thought that a quadruped could hardly have reached this hole in the perpendicular side of a rock, but probably some rude kinds could easily; and it was a very snug place for such a deposit. I brought them all home in order to ascertain what the seeds were, and how they came there. Examining the chestnuts carefully in the evening, and wondering if so small a bird as a chickadee could transport one, I observed near the larger end of one some very fine scratches, which it seemed to me might have been made by the teeth of a very small animal while carrying it—certainly not by the bill of a bird, since they had pricked sharply into the shell, sucking it up one way. I then looked to see where the teeth of the other jaw had scratched it, but could discover no marks and was therefore still somewhat in doubt about it.

But an hour afterward I examined these scratches with a microscope, and then I saw plainly that they had been made by some fine and sharp cutting instrument like a pin, which was a little concave and had plowed under the surface of the shell a little, toward the larger end of the nut, raising it up. And, looking further, I now discovered on the same end at least two corresponding marks made by the lower incisors, plowing toward the first and about a quarter of an inch distant. These were scarcely obvious to the naked eye, but quite plain through the glass. I now had no doubt that they were made by the incisors of a mouse, and comparing them with the incisors of the common wild or deer mouse (*Mus leucopus*, whose skeleton I chanced to have), I found that one or two of the marks were exactly the middle of its two incisors combined, or about a twentieth of an inch, and that the others, though finer, might have been made by them; and the natural gape of the jaws corresponded. On one side at least it had taken fresh hold once or twice. I have but little doubt that these seeds were placed there by a deer mouse, our most common wood mouse.

The other chestnut, which had no marks on it, I suppose was carried by the stem end, which was now gone from both. There was no chestnut tree within twenty rods.

These seeds thus placed in this recess will help to account for chestnut trees, barberry bushes, and so on growing in chinks and clefts, where we do not see how the seeds could have fallen. There was earth enough even in this little hole to keep some very small plant alive.

I noticed the other day a young but sizeable huckleberry bush growing lustily on the top of a high white-pine stump which had been sawed off, in the chink between the bark and the wood, and I have no doubt that it sprang from a seed which had been left on the stump by a bird or other animal and had then been blown into this chink. Perhaps it had made its way up from beneath the bark.

The closely allied field mouse of Europe lays up acorns, nuts, grain, and so on. Pennant says, "The great damage done to our fields by the hogs rooting up the ground is chiefly owing to their search after the concealed hoards of the field mouse."

I learn from Bell's *British Quadrupeds*, and from Loudon, that when the experiment of planting acorns where they were to remain was tried on a very extensive scale, in the Forest of Dean and the New Forest, the field mouse (*Arvicola agrestis*) caused great deficiency by taking the acorns out of the holes, and much more by gnawing the plants after they had come up.

The depredators were caught by digging holes all over a forest of 3,200 acres, with smooth sides and broader at the bottom than at the top. Having got into them, they could not get out. As many as fifteen were taken in a hole in one night. Mr. Billington says, "We soon caught upward of 30,000 [in the Forest of Dean] that were paid for by number, as two persons were appointed to take an account of them and see them buried or made away with, to prevent imposition." Many also were killed in other ways and by birds and beasts of prey *after they were caught* in the holes. According to Bell, it was calculated that over 200,000 of them were destroyed by various means in these two forests. Even the musquash eats acorns and may help to disseminate them, especially the swamp white oak.

Birds too play their part in the dispersion of seeds. Saint Pierre says, "A bird of the Moluccas repeopled, with the nutmeg plant, the desert islands of that archipelago, in defiance of all the efforts of the Dutch, who destroy those trees in every place where they cannot be subservient to their own commerce."

Birds of the jay family—magpie, crow, raven, and so on—have been notorious from the remotest antiquity for gathering and hiding away in holes their food and other articles. Theophrastus in his *Causae Plantarum* (Origin of Plants), written in the fourth century B.C., speaks of the magpie (*Pica*) and other birds hiding acorns which they have dug up ("*Pica erim . . . glandes deforras sibi condit*," says his Latin translator). And Pliny says that the jackdaw (*Monedula*), "from its concealment of the seeds of plants in holes which serve as its storehouses," may have caused one tree to grow on another and so have suggested the art of grafting.

The English jay is called *Garrulus glandarius*, or the acorn jay. No doubt the acorns which we frequently see left sticking, often firmly wedged, in a crevice in the bark of an oak or other tree, were placed there by jays, chickadees, *possibly* nuthatches, and so on, to be held fast thus while they crack them with their bills. And probably some of those acorn shells which you see scattered about the base of trees in the woods, all of which we com-

149

monly refer to the squirrels, are such as have dropped from these crevices while the birds were pecking at them. I also find sometimes two or three acorns together hidden in the shallow hole made by a woodpecker in the upright trunk of a tree. Several times I have found kernels of corn tucked away in the crevices of the bark of trees or behind a lichen or other chinks in the very midst of our darkest and most remote woods, at least half a mile (sometimes a mile) from the nearest field, probably by the jay.

A neighbor tells me that he has been recently baiting the jays to his door with corn this winter that he might change their habits, and that he has been surprised to see one, after picking up the corn a while, fly into a tree nearby and deposit as many as a dozen grains successively in different crevices before it returned for more, showing that it could carry so many at once without swallowing them (past recovery).

I also observe that crows transport acorns, for seeing a large flock busy upon and under a white-oak tree which stood by itself on the top of a hill, and going to the place, I have found the acorns and their cups fully broken and the meat half consumed, and also left on the ground the large and heavy cups of a swamp white-oak acorn—a quarter of a mile from the nearest swamp white oak across the river. They also pluck and transport the same kind of acorns an equal distance in the winter and, alighting on other trees, drop the shells on the snow beneath, though I suspect that they find more animal than vegetable food in them then.

The pigeons depend much on acorns for food and can swallow one whole, and so may help to disperse them sometimes. They are glad to eat the half-decayed ones that are left on the ground in the spring. Evelyn says, "I am told that those small young acorns which we find in the stock-doves' craws are a delicious fare."

Nay, a trapper tells me that he once caught seven summer ducks by baiting his steel traps with acorns under water. They dove for them and were caught by the necks.

Indeed, to be convinced of the rapidity with which acorns are collected by quadrupeds and birds, you have only to compete with them for one season and see how alert you must be. The greater part are soon picked up.

Not only do animals thus systematically seek the fruit of trees, but according to Saint Pierre the fruits in some cases seek them—or meet them halfway. He states that "the lumpish cocoa-nut, as it falls from the height of the tree which bears it, makes the earth resound to a considerable distance. The black pods of the *Canneficier*, when ripe and agitated by the wind, produce, as they clash against each other, a sound resembling the tic-tac of a mill. When the grayish fruit of the *Genipa* of the Antilles comes to maturity and falls from the tree, it bounces on the ground with a noise like the report of a pistol. Upon this signal more than one guest, no doubt, resorts thither in quest of a repast. This fruit seems particularly destined to the use of the land crabs, which are eagerly fond of it, and very soon grow fat on this kind of food."

The consequence of all this activity of the animals and of the elements in transporting seeds is that almost every part of the earth's surface is filled with seeds or vivacious roots of seedlings of various kinds, and in some cases probably seeds are dug up from far below the surface which still retain their vitality. The very earth itself is a granary and a seminary, so that to some minds its surface is regarded as the cuticle of one great living creature.

Nature so fills the soil with seeds that I notice where travellers have turned off the road and made a new track for a short distance, the intermediate, narrow, and bare space is soon clothed with a little grove which just fills it.

Pines, being cut down, do not spring up from the roots. According to Herodotus, "Croesus . . . sent and commanded the Lampsacenians to release Miltiades; if not, he threatened that he would destroy them like a pine tree. The Lampsacenians, being in uncertainty in their interpreta-

151

tions, as to what was the meaning of the saying with which Croesus threatened them, that he would destroy them like a pine tree, at length, with some difficulty, one of the elders having discovered it, told the real truth, that the pine alone of all trees, when cut down, does not send forth any more shoots, but perishes entirely." There is, then, but one mode by which they are propagated by nature—that is, by the seed.

We have seen that very few young oaks and chestnuts (if not hickories) need the shelter of higher plants; but, on the other hand, young pitch and white pines thrive best in an open and sunny locality. The fact that the lower limbs of pines growing within a wood always die, leaving only a green spiring top, shows how much they depend on light and air. When dense, they are slender and tall; on the edge of the woods or in open lands, stout and spreading.

White pines are far more indifferent to shade than pitch. It is common enough to see groves of little white pines under full-grown pines and oaks, and indeed many get feeble ones to transplant from such localities, but you very rarely see many young pitch pines there. They evidently require more light and air.

As I was going through a pretty dense pitch-pine wood where there are only several white pines old enough to bear, and accordingly more than one thousand pitch-pine seeds to one white-pine one produced, I was surprised to find that there were countless little white pines springing up under the pitch pine (as well as many little oaks) and but very few or scarcely any little pitch pines, and they slender and sickly. There were at least one thousand white-pine seedlings to one pitch-pine seedling, or a similar proportion reversed.

Again, I examined a dense pitch-pine wood some thirty years old a dozen rods wide by three or four times as long, extending east and west. The western or quarter part of it contains not a single seed-bearing white pine, yet there are thousands of little white pines, and scarcely one little pitch pine within it. It is also, as usual, well stocked with minute oak seedlings. I did not have to hunt far to be satisfied that this was the source.

In short, the rule is, strange as it may seem, that under a dense pitch-pine wood, you will find few if any little pitch pines, but even though there may be no seed-bearing white pines in the wood, plenty of little white pines.

I have examined seventeen pitch-pine groves in this neighborhood for this purpose, and in thirteen instances this rule was well proved. In three of the others there were as many little pitch pines as white pines, but it was evidently because the wood was thin. There was but one decided exception, and then I looked only at *one* end of the wood.

I have obtained some hundreds of small white pines to set out under these pitch-pine woods, and another told me that wishing to get one hundred small white pines last summer to set about his house, he had found them all under his pitch-pine grove, where he might have got many more. The white pines will find their way up between the pitch pines, if they are not very large and exceedingly dense, but pitch pine will not commonly grow up under pitch pines. This is

Pitch-pine seedling

true today, and it was equally true two or three years ago. For instance, I know of one hillside where, judging from the annual rings of the stumps, a dense pitch-pine grove sprang up, and thirty or forty years later numerous white pines came up between them.

Hence, if you should cut the pitch pines, you would have next a white-pine wood, often quite a dense one, with perhaps some oaks in it. This is quite commonly done. For example, I examined last fall a dense pitch-pine wood some thirty-five years old, a part of which had been cut off the previous winter. The proprietor had cut off all the pitch pines and carefully left the white pines, now on an average five to eight feet high and forming already a pretty dense wood—a valuable woodland. Yet there were only three or four little pines old enough to bear seed, or as big as the pitch pines in the grove. The white pines were as thick as the pitch pines had been under which they sprang up. Thus, eight or ten years at least had been gained.

Exactly the same thing had been done in three out of the thirteen cases referred to above. The proprietors had taken advantage of this habit of the white pine, without knowing that it was its habit. Indeed, in some cases these white pines bid fair to supplant the pitch pines at last of their own force, they grew so well and steadily. Thus, as pines generally are pioneers to oaks, so the pitch pine is to some extent pioneer to the white pine. There are instances of this succession of white pines to pitch pines, but I am not aware that pitch pine ever succeeds at once to white pines.

But though the little pitch pines are *comparatively* so rare under a dense pitch-pine wood, you will almost invariably find them springing up abundantly along its edge on the open side. Though within the wood there may be one hundred little white pines to one little pitch pine, yet commonly along the open edge of the wood the relative proportion is reversed, and you find there one hundred little pitch pines to one little white pine, so much do they love the sun.

It is mainly the little pitch pines that spread so fast into the pasture, then, and perchance have already extended the wood a dozen rods into the grass. This spreading is commonly not at all into the adjacent woods, but only into the open land.

In the case of an artificial white-pine wood which I examined, a narrow strip half a dozen rods wide set out some twenty-five years ago, the seeds of pitch pines had blown through it and come up abundantly in the open land on the outside, though not a single one, nor a white pine, had come up under the white pines.

When a pitch-pine wood is cut, that fringe or edging of little pitch pines which commonly surrounds it on the open sides may remain to grow up and in a measure represent it. I often see where a large pitch-pine wood has recently been cut, and not a tree of that kind remains there; but in the open pasture on one side is a little grove which had spread from them. In short, this is the way these trees commonly spread.

In my classification of our woodlands, I call those *new woods* which have sprung up on land which has been cultivated or cleared long enough to kill all the roots in it, though the present growth may be different from that which came up soon after the clearing was abandoned. It happens that almost all the new woods that I remember are pine or birch. (Maple I have not attended to so particularly.) These also come up on land which was *never* cultivated, and in woodlands.

The woods which also spring up where there were no trees before are chiefly pine, birch, and maple; and accordingly you may see spaces of bare sward between the trees for many years. But oaks in masses are not seen springing up thus with the old sod between them. They form a sproutland, or stand amid the stumps of a recent pine lot.

I am not sure but that our most exclusively pine woods are such as have recently sprung up in open land. And *generally* where pines most prevail in our woods, there probably, at the date of their springing up, the earth was most bare.

How commonly you see pitch pines, white pines, and birches filling up a pasture, and when they are a dozen or fifteen years old, shrub and other oaks beginning to show themselves, enclosing apple trees and walls and fences gradually, and so changing the whole aspect of the region. These trees do not cover the whole surface equally as yet, but are grouped very agreeably after natural laws which they obey. You remember perhaps that fifteen years ago there was not a single forest tree, nor a germinating seed of one, in this pasture, and now it is a pretty dense forest ten feet high. The cow paths, the hollow where you slid in winter, the rocks, are fast being enveloped and becoming rabbit walks and hollows and rocks in the woods.

This, as I have said, is particularly true of the pitch pine. If you look from a hilltop over our forest, you will perceive commonly that the white pine is much the most dispersed and oftener forms mixed woods with oak and so on, and frequently grows in straight or meandering lines (it may be on a ridge, in the midst of the forest, occasionally swelling into a dense grove), even as the explorers report it to grow in the primitive woods of

155

Maine. It also grows oftener in low ground which has never been re-deemed than the pitch pine does.

The pitch pines with the short and crispy plumes *commonly* occupy a dry soil, a plain, or the brow of a low hill where the *Cladonia* lichen flour-ish, often the site of an old grain field or pasture, and are much the most exclusive; for being a new wood, oaks and so on have had no opportunity to grow up there if they would.

If you enter the densest pitch-pine groves, the pasture is still betrayed under the trees by the firmer smooth and sward-like surface, there being fewer leaves and less of leafy mold formed; by the patches of green moss and of whitish *Cladonia* peeping out here and there; by the birches it may be already decaying, which (I think) do not spring up in an old wood; per-haps by an old apple tree enclosed—and sometimes you may even feel with your feet, if you do not see, the ancient cow paths of the pasture. In several of these *new* woods, both pitch pine and also birch, I see the old corn hills still very distinctly in their rows, and in some instances in this neighborhood these were the work of our predecessors, the Indians. In short, I do not know a single *dense* pitch-pine wood—and I have exam-ined and can enumerate more than forty such in this town—which did not evidently spring up in open land.

I have even examined, among the rest, the site of such a grove now in the midst of the woods cut a dozen or fifteen years ago and still indicated by its stumps amid the shrub oaks and other trees which have succeeded it. I in-ferred from that crowd of stumps that it had originated in open land, but I soon found an evidence that it had or had been just such another *new wood*, as one which sprang from it and still stands on the north side—that all along the lower edge at least, where the abrupt descent begins, though in the midst of the woods, there were many long heaps of stones which were tipped over the edge of the bank where it was formerly plowed and cultivated.

The nearest *approach* to a dense pine wood springing up on land not bare that I have yet observed was a case where they were coming in quite numerously, together with shrub and other oaks and birches, where pitch pines had been cut. But I was not surprised at this, for the soil being exceedingly sandy and barren, the shrub oaks which had prevailed in it at first had failed to cover it, and the pitch-pine seed from a few seed-bearing trees that were left could still catch there.

So when for any reason, as sometimes on account of frost or fire, a lot which has been cut off remains comparatively bare for several years, or perhaps becomes more or less grassy, both pitch and white pines may catch there thickly.

One will naturally inquire, "Where then did the pitch pine stand before the white man came—if there were any *dense* groves of it then? Who cleared the land for its seedlings to spring up in? Is it, perhaps, proportionally a more common tree now, being better able to survive cultivation and maintain its ground?"

It is commonly referred to very poor and sandy land. The expression "a pitch-pine plain" is but another name for such a soil. Does it not answer Linnaeus's sixteenth kind of soil: "*Sylvae umbrosae terra sabulosa sterili refertae*"? Yet we find it growing on the best land also. It grows both in the sand and in the swamp, and its growing chiefly in the sand is an evidence not so much that it prefers such a locality as that other trees have excluded it from better soil. It is not peculiar to the pitch-pine plains, for if you cut down the pines, they will probably be succeeded by oaks there.

Who knows but the fires or clearings of the Indians may have originated many of these bare plains, and so account for the presence of these trees there? We know that they not only annually burned the forest to expedite their hunting, but regularly cleared extensive tracts for cultivation, and these were always level tracts and, where the soil was light, such as they could turn over with their rude implements. When the thin soil was exhausted in one place, they resorted to another.

Such was the land which they are known to have cultivated extensively in this town. It is in such places chiefly that you find their relics in any part of the country. They did not cultivate such soil as our maple swamps occupy, though we do, nor such a succession of hills and dales as our oak woods so commonly cover. I know of no tree so likely to spread rapidly over such areas when abandoned by the aborigines as the pitch pine, and next the birch and white pine. It will be seen, then, that, generally speaking, pitch pines will not spring up numerously within a wood, though they may take advantage of any thinness or openings, and most of the large pitch pines we see within the woods are probably as old as the wood itself, having come up with it. Hence, I infer that pitch pines will not often, or at once, succeed when oaks are cut, though if anything occurs to keep that ground bare and open, they may gradually cover it.

Also the young *white* pines which spring up in pastures, in open and sunny places, are much the thickest and stoutest, as all who dig up pines to transplant know. They have also a yellowish hue, like the pitch pines, betraying the sun. You can easily tell how much they have been exposed by their density and color and stoutness. But unlike the pitch pine, the white pine very generally springs in the midst of the woods and survives, if it does not flourish, in much denser parts of it—though it is quite a different-looking plant there. Not only do the little white pines under a dense pitch-pine wood so greatly outnumber the little pitch pines there, though there may be few or no seed-bearing white pines in it, but I *suspect* that you will find more little white pines in such a wood than you will in a *white*-pine wood of *equal* density, notwithstanding that such an abundance of seed is produced in the latter place. However, I have examined only three dense white-pine groves—namely, that beyond the F. Wheeler artificial, Tarbell's Swamp *dense*, and by J. P. Blood's Cold Hole—and this suggests that pitch pines must possess other advantages over white pines as nurses for white pines than simple shade or shelter, since these are common to both.

What I have said about young pitch pines in an old pitch-pine wood thriving first or only on the edge or in the opening is true, though to a less extent, of young white pines in a white-pine wood. In a *dense* white-pine wood you will see few if any little *white* pines springing up beneath, but plenty of them under its edge and in the open spaces within it.

For example, I examined a white-pine wood by J. P. Blood's Cold Hole. Within half a dozen years a perfectly open pasture came up within a rod of it on the north side, and now, though the fence has been removed, the different condition and history of the ground is very apparent from the growth and aspect of the white pines. On the one side is the dense pine wood with no little ones under it; on the other, only a rod off, is a dense thicket of vigorous little pines only two or three feet high, bounded by a perfectly straight line on the wood side, showing where the fence stood as truly as a surveyor could find it. And yet the pines have not been interfered with, unless by cattle, on the north side of the fence!

In another case, when a road runs parallel with and close to the edge of a large wood, chiefly white pine, there being no fence on the inside, I see that there are no little white pines in the wood where it is dense; but one rod off across the road, there is a dense row of them exactly under the fence, concealing the lower rail for many rods, they having been prevented from spreading further by the plow. On the Marlborough road I see many little white pines sprung up along the edge of a dense oak wood, but scarcely one within it, for they too want light and air, though not so much as the pitch pines.

Yet, as I have said, within a white-pine wood, wherever it is more open from any cause, you will see a great many little white pines springing up; though they are thin and feeble comparatively, yet most of them will perhaps come to be trees. White pines will spring up in the more open parts, especially hollows, of a white-pine wood—even under pines, though they are thin and feeble—just in proportion to the density of the overshadowing pines. But where the large trees are quite dense, they will not grow at all. So also white pines will come up in the more open parts of any wood— as, for instance, where there has been a slight cutting.

I also see where they have come up quite numerously in a young oak woodland and are evidently half a dozen years at least younger than the oaks. One had apparently blown for a considerable distance.

I frequently see them springing up in a sproutland where other trees have failed to fill it up for some years. Accordingly, extensive and dense *white*-pine woods are not nearly so common in this town as the same kind of pitch-pine woods are. They are more likely to have oaks in them.

In the three oldest oak woods which I visited last fall (Wetherbee's, Blood's, and Inches), which have never been cut over, I saw how the white pine succeeded to the oak naturally, that it introduced itself into primitive woods of average density.

At Wetherbee's, there are many slender white pines straggling into the oak wood, all under its shade, though there is only one large one.

At Blood's, many white pines some twenty years old are distributed throughout the lot, and I have no doubt if let alone this would in a hundred years look more like a white-pine wood than an oak one.

At Inches also, I noticed many young white pines of various sizes, twenty feet high or more, springing up in the more open or thinner parts and dells; but there, indeed, there were considerable tracts of large white pine, as well as pine and oak mixed, especially on the hills. The smaller ones are not high enough to be seen at a distance or from hills. They are not now dense except in more open places, but come up stragglingly every two or three rods, tall and slender trees making little show. If the oaks were cut off, there would very soon be a dense white-pine wood here. As it is, the natural succession is rapidly going on. You occasionally see a massive old oak prostrate and decaying, and its place is evidently supplied by a pine, not an oak. If entirely let alone, this which is now an oak wood will become a white-pine wood.

Hence, we see how the character of a primitive oak wood may gradually change from oak to pine, the oaks gradually and successively decaying and not being replaced by oaks but by pines. Perhaps this is the way that a natural succession takes place. Oak seedlings do not so readily spring up and thrive under a mixed pine and oak wood as pines do, in the more open parts, and thus as the oaks decay, they are replaced by pines rather than by oaks.

In all these three old oak woods, I saw that a natural succession was already beginning, and the white pines were preparing to take the place of the oaks. At any rate, in all these old oak woods, if the oaks should be cut, no sprouts would come up from the stumps. It is by seeds only that a growth can be renewed, then, and it should be a different growth from the last. If the proprietors contemplate removing the oaks, they should be careful to favor the growth of the pines there, already so forwardly coming in.

We have seen how the white pine succeeds to pitch pine quite commonly, just as oaks succeed to pines generally. So it will succeed to white pine (or itself) when a white-pine wood which is more or less open, and hence contains plenty of little pines, is cut, though there will probably be oaks mixed with them in that case unless the little pines are thick and considerably grown. So it may succeed to an oak wood in which it has already sprung up thickly, especially to an old oak wood whose stumps fail to send up sprouts. It may spring up as soon as such an oak wood is cut, the ground being bare, but this depends on circumstances.

For instance, I examined last fall a small sproutland about a dozen rods square where large pines and oaks were cut off the previous winter. It had been apparently about two-thirds white pine and one-third oak. I counted at once twenty or more seedling white pines of that year an inch high on the bare spots, but not a single oak seedling of that age. According to my observation, white pines and white oaks do not bear much seed except at intervals of several years, and during the last half-dozen years there has not been an abundant crop of both kinds the same year. The previous year white-pine seed had been very abundant, but there had been scarcely any white-oak seed.

This shows how much the species of the succeeding forest may depend on whether this or that kind of tree was fertile or not the year before it was cut. If that wood had been cut and that ground left in exactly the same condition at any time for four or five years previously, white pines would not have sprung there in this manner because there would have been no seed. The time may come when the proprietor will take these things into consideration before he cuts off a woodlot.

White pines may also, in course of time, take the place of an old oak wood.

There are many ways in which a mixed wood is produced. First, though the oak seedlings die at last under dense pines, yet in parts where they are thin or in openings and on their edges, they shoot up more or less rapidly and become trees. Or when you thin out a pine wood, the oaks, which otherwise would die, spring up here and there; or when you thin an oak wood, the pines plant themselves in it and grow up in like manner. If the pines are quite small and far apart, fewer acorns will be planted amid them, it is true, but more will come to trees.

A fire may run over a mixed wood of pines, birches, maples, and oaks ten to twenty feet high and entirely kill all the pines, while the hardwoods shoot up again rapidly from the root and are nearly as high as ever in a few years. Or if, in the natural course of events, a fire does not occur, the soil may at last be exhausted for pines; but there are always the oaks, ready to take advantage of the least feebleness and yielding of the pines.

Under a large and open white-pine wood you will often see thousands of little white pines, as well as many little oak seedlings—whence you may have a mixed wood. After oaks have once got established, it must be hard to get them out without clearing the land. But after a *dense* pine wood, you are more likely to have oaks chiefly. A pure oak wood *may* be obtained by cutting off at once and clearing a pure and dense pine wood, and it may still succeed from the sprouts, when the same oak wood is cut off.

Pines are continually stealing into oaks and oaks into pines, where, respectively, they are not too dense or where they are burned or otherwise thinned, and so mixed woods may arise. When a pitch-pine wood is cut off, leaving the little white pines which have sprung up beneath it, often many little oaks, birches, and so on mingle with the last, especially where the white pines are not too high and dense—and hence a mixed wood. When the oaks and birches and so forth on very poor land fail to cover the soil for many years after pitch pines have been cut, pitch pines may come in again to mingle with them. If you expect oaks to succeed a dense and purely oak wood, you must depend almost entirely on sprouts. Yet they will succeed abundantly to pine where there is not an oak stump for them to sprout from. If you cut a dense mixed wood of pine and oak in which no little pines have sown themselves, it is evident that a wood exclusively of oak sprouts may succeed.

As a consequence of the different manner in which trees which have winged seeds and those which have not are planted—the former being blown sometimes all together in one direction, the latter being dispersed irregularly by animals—I observed that the former (pines, white birches, red maples, alders, and so on) often grow in more or less regular rounded or oval or conical patches, as the seeds fell, while oaks, chestnuts, hickories, and so on merely form woods of greater or less extent, whether pure or mixed, and of irregular boundaries—unless they have derived an oval or conical form from undisturbed pine groves in which they were planted.

For instance, take this young white-pine wood, half a dozen years old, which has sprung up in a pasture adjacent to a grove of oaks and pines mixed. It has the form of a broad crescent or half-moon, with its diameter resting in the old wood, opposite to where a large white pine stands. It is true most such groves are early squared by our plows and fences; for in this sense we square the circle every day in our rude practice, whatever we may do in mathematics. These seeds will often fall in like manner in an oak sproutland or even an old wood. Indeed, standing on a hilltop, I think that

I can distinguish, in distant woods of pine and oak mixed, these more or less rounded and regular masses of pines a dozen or more rods in width—the white pine in the forests of Maine is said by explorers for lumber to grow in "veins" and "communities"—while it is the oak most commonly that fills up the irregular spaces and crevices between, beside occupying extensive spaces by itself.

It happens that as the pines themselves, not to mention their fruit, have a more regularly and solidly conical outline than deciduous trees, so with the groves which they form. It frequently happens in settled countries like this that the new community of pines, sprung from seeds blown off from an older one, is very youthful compared with the trees it sprang from, because many successive crops of trees or seeds have been cut or plowed up before the owner allowed Nature to have her way. Naturally, the pines spread more steadily and with no such abrupt descents. In the wild woods, at least, there are commonly only fires and insects or blight, and not the axe and plow and cattle, to interrupt the regular progress of things.

Our woodlots, of course, have a history, and we may often recover it for a hundred years back, though we *do* not. A small pine lot may be a side of such an oval as I have described, or a half or a square in the inside with all the curving sides sheared off by fences. Yet if we attended more to the history of our woodlots, we should manage them more wisely.

I observed today on the edge of Loring's woodlot, where his shrub oaks bounded on a neighbor's small but dense pitch pines, that the line of separation was remarkably straight and distinct, neither a shrub oak nor a pine passing its limit. A pine wood had stood where the oaks were, and an open field in which young pines came up had bounded them. In running the boundaries of lots, I am often enabled to take my course quite accurately from this manifest line of separation, where there is no fence answering to a line on the plan. In one instance, for an observation of ten rods I was enabled to strike a bound eighty rods distant.

Many a man's field has a dense border of pitch pines which strayed into it when the adjacent woods were of that species, though they are now hardwood.

This afternoon, in the middle of October, as I am walking across the fields in the outskirts of the town, I observe at a distance an oak woodlot some twenty years old with a dense, narrow edging of pitch pines about a rod and a half wide and twenty-five or thirty years old along its whole southern side, which is straight and thirty or forty rods long, and next to it is an open field or pasture. It presents a very singular appearance because the oak wood is broad and has no pines within it, while the narrow edging is perfectly straight and dense and pure pine, so that from that side the whole wood appears to be pine. It is, beside, the more remarkable at this season, because the oak is all red and yellow and the pine all green. I understand it and read its history easily before I get to it. I find, as I expected, a fence separating the pines from the oaks, and that they belong to different owners.

I also find, as I expected, that eighteen or twenty years ago a pitch-pine wood had stood where the oaks are and was then cut down, for there are their old stumps in great numbers. But before they were cut, their seeds were blown into the neighbor's field, and the little pines came up all along its edge; and they grew so thickly and so fast that this neighbor refrained at last from plowing them up or cutting them off for just this rod and a half in width, where they were thickest. Moreover, though there are no seed-bearing oaks mixed with these pines, the whole surface even of this narrow strip is, as usual, completely stocked with little seedling oaks less than a foot high.

This is the history of countless woodlots hereabouts, and broad ones too. But, I ask, if the neighbor so often lets this narrow edging grow up, why not oftener, by the same rule, let them spread over the whole of his field? When at length he sees how they have grown, does he not often regret that he did not do so? Or why be dependent, even to this extent, on these windfalls from our neighbor's trees, or on accident? Why not control our own woods and destiny more?

There are many such problems in forest geometry to be solved. For example, the same afternoon and almost within sight of the above-mentioned lot, I read, still farther back in forest history, a more varied story.

After crossing a barren field, I come to a green strip of dense pitch and white pine some thirty or forty rods long by four wide, and thirty years old. This is bounded on the east by an extensive red- and yellow-oak woodlot, generally about fifteen years old. And on the west, between the pines and the perfectly open and recently cultivated field, is a strip three rods wide of both white and pitch pines four to ten feet high which have sprung up in the grass—which I had not distinguished from the old wood at first.

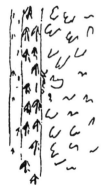

Given these facts—to find the wall. If you think a moment, you will know without my telling you that it is between the large pine wood and the oak.

Fifteen years ago there was a large pine wood where the oak wood now is, for looking there I find it stops under the oaks, and west of this, reaching up to the wall, an open field belonging to another man. But long before this the seeds of the pines had blown over the wall and taken so well in the open land that for four rods in width it was suffered to grow, or rather may be said to have defended itself, and crowded the former back.

When fifteen years ago the old pine wood was cut by its owner, his neighbor was not ready to cut his younger one. This is now thirty years old and for many years has been endeavoring to spread into the open land by its side, as its parents did. But for a long time the proprietor, not taking the hint, blind to his own interest, plowed quite up to the edge of the wood, as I noticed, and got a few beans for his pains. But the pines, which he did not plant, grew while he slept; and at length one spring he gave up the contest and concluded at last to plow only within three rods of the wood, the little pines were so thick and promising. He concluded not to cut his own fingers any more, that is, not further than up to the last joint, and hence this second strip of little pines. They would have covered the half, or perhaps the whole, of his barren field before this if he had let them.

Examining this pine wood carefully, I found that the strip of little pines, yet far apart, contained also a little white birch, much sweet fern, and thin open sod, but scarcely any oak seedlings, and those very small. The strip of large pines contained countless oak seedlings—white, red, black, and shrub oak; many little pines of both kinds; a little wild cherry; white birch; and some hazel and high blueberry. While the pines were blowing into the pasture from this narrow edging, the animals were planting the acorns under the pines. Even pine woods as small as this smallest, if they are dense, are thus perfectly equipped.

Thus, this double forest was advancing to conquer new (or old) lands, the pines sending forward their children on the wings of the wind, while already the oak seedlings from the oak wood behind had established themselves beneath the pines, preparing to supplant them. The pines are the vanguard—they with their children before them stand up to fire, while the little oaks kneel behind and between them. The pine is the pioneer, the oak the more permanent settler who buys out the other's improvements. As I have shown, two or three pines will run swiftly forward a quarter of a mile into a plain, which is their favorite field of battle, taking advantage of the least shelter, as a rock or fence, that may be there, and entrench themselves behind it, and through a glass you may see their plumes waving there. Or, as we have seen, they will cross a broad river without a bridge and swiftly climb a steep hill beyond, like Zouaves, and permanently occupy it, regardless of heat and cold.

Pines take the first and longest strides. Oaks march deliberately in the rear. In this case, the pines are the light infantry, supplying the scouts and skirmishers of the army; the oaks are the grenadiers, heavy paced and strong, that form the solid phalanx.

The geologists tell us that the coniferous trees are older, as they are lower in the order of development, than oaks.

There was, even under these dark and dense pines thirty years old, a pretty thick bed of blueberry and huckleberry bushes ten feet in width next the wall (where also stones have been cast from the field), the relic of a still denser and higher one that grew there when it was an open field. The farmer had thus been driven back three times: first by the blueberry hedge, second by the pines of thirty years ago, and third by the young pines that sprang from these. Thus, a woodlot had been forced upon him; and yet, perhaps, he will talk about it as a creation of his own.

It chanced that there were two proprietors within half a mile who had done exactly the same thing, that is, had a woodlot that was forced on them, and I have no doubt that there are several more exactly similar cases within the circle of which that half-mile is the diameter.

But I have not done with the last-named woodlot yet.

Sudbury River in Concord

A few days later I examined more carefully the young oak wood east of the wall, and I found not only the stumps of the pines which were cut when it sprang up some fifteen years ago and which were then about forty years old, as appeared plainly from their annual rings—but, to my surprise, the stumps in great numbers, now much decayed, of an old oak wood which stood there and was cut between fifty and sixty years ago. Thus, I distinguished three successions of trees, and, I may say, five generations— namely: first, the old oaks of fifty or sixty years ago; second, the pines which succeeded and were cut fifteen years ago; third, the pines now thirty years old west of the wall which came from the seed of these; fourth, the strip of little pines west of the last; and fifth, the oak seedlings under the little pines.

I frequently find in numbers in our forests the stumps of oaks which were cut at the very beginning of this century or at the end of the last, while a forest the third in succession, including them, waves over them. No doubt we may thus in many cases behold the stumps, at least, of trees which stood here before the white man came, and in this case we have one advantage over the geologist, for we can not only detect the *order* of events but often the time during which they elapsed by counting the rings on the stumps.

Thus you can unroll the rotten papyrus on which the history of the Concord forest is written.

I frequently see an old and tall pine wood standing in the midst of a younger but more extensive oak wood, it being merely a remnant of an extensive pine wood which once occupied the whole tract—but having a different owner, or for some other reason, it has not been cut.

Sometimes also I see these pines, of the same age, reappear at half a mile distant, the intermediate pines having been cut for thirty or forty years, and oaks having taken their places; or the distant second growth of pines, especially if they stand on the land of another than he who owns the oaks, may, as we have seen, be a generation smaller and have sprung from the pines that stood where the oaks do. In the grandfather's day, perhaps, it was chiefly oak or pine for three-fourths of a mile, but now the necessities or whims of John and Sally and Jonas, to whom it has descended, have disturbed its uniformity, so it is alternate pine and oak.

At this season of the year, when each leaf acquires its peculiar color, Nature prints this history distinctly—as it were, an illuminated edition—and we can read it from afar. Every oak and hickory and birch and aspen, sprinkled amid the pines, tells its tale a mile off, and you have not to go laboriously through the wood examining the bark and leaves. These facts would therefore be best illustrated by colors.

The history of a woodlot is often, if not commonly, *here* a history of cross-purposes, of steady and consistent endeavor on the part of Nature, of interference and blundering with a glimmering of intelligence at the eleventh hour on the part of the proprietor. The latter often treats his woodlot as a certain Irishman I heard of drove a horse—that is, by standing before him and beating him in the face all the way across a field.

Cattle have a remarkable propensity to dive into young evergreen trees and gore them, as it were, breaking them down and often destroying them completely when they are six or eight feet high even. I do not know what their object is, unless to scratch their heads on them. For this purpose, by their density and rigidity, they appear to be peculiarly agreeable to them. From thus being rudely trimmed and barked with their horns, I often see hundreds which have been thus broken down within a short distance, and they will go a good deal out of their way to get at one.

A passing cow once entered my front-yard gate, attracted by an arborvitae which I had recently set out and, trying her head on it, in an instant, and before I could reach her, broke it off within a foot of the ground, so that I thought it was spoiled. However, it survived this accident, and the numerous low boughs which spread over the ground gradually erected themselves around the center, so that instead of one slender spring stem, I have now half a dozen forming one dense tree of a beautiful and perfectly regular conical form. A neighbor who has some of these trees trimmed off in the usual stiff manner, which did not content him, lately took the pains to come to me and ask how I had treated my arbor-vitae to produce such a result. I told him that all he had to do was to leave his gate open at the season when cattle are driven up-country. The white pine, which is so common and so tender, suffers the most.

So universal is this propensity that you would think that they owed the pines a spite; or perchance, knowing that their own existence depends on keeping the land in grass, they instinctively attack the encroaching pines as enemies which are invading their pastures. It is natural enough that there should be an everlasting feud between the cow and the pine. No doubt most of the large white pines in pastures which branch close to the ground, their branches curving out and upward, harp-wise, without one erect leading shoot, were broken down when young by cows.

In some unremembered gale the winged seeds of the white pine are gently wafted to their resting places, and a few years afterward we begin to see the landscape dotted there with their cheerful green fires and are pleased to wind our way amid them.

But I often notice how recklessly the proprietor treats this godsend, the gift of a forest which has thus sprung up in some starved pasture—allowing his cattle to break them down, rub most of them out of existence; and not till they are higher than his head does he recognize them for trees at all, and at the eleventh hour, after many years' growth has been lost, surround them with a fence. Not till they are too stout for his bushwhack, till regard for his axle-tree compels him to turn out for them, does he begin to respect them and conclude that a pine forest will be a profitable investment. No wonder that he is sometimes surprised to see them there after such treatment—no wonder that he sometimes thinks they sprang from nothing—as he has done all that he could to make nothing of them.

What shall we say to that management that halts between two courses?

Does neither this nor that but botches both? I see many a pasture over which the pitch or white pine are spreading, where the bushwhack is from time to time used with a show of vigor, and I despair of my trees (I say *mine*, for the owner evidently does not mean that they shall be his); and yet this questionable work is so poorly done that those very fields grow steadily greener and more forest-like from year to year, in spite of cows and bushwhack, till at length the farmer gives up the contest from sheer weariness and finds himself the owner of a woodlot (which he does not deserve).

Now whether a woodlot or pasture is most profitable for him, I will not undertake to say, but I am certain that a woodlot and pasture combined is not profitable.

The custom with us is to let the pines spread into the pasture, and at the same time to let the cattle wander there and contend with the former for the possession of the ground, from time to time coming to the aid of the cattle with a bushwhack. But when, after some fifteen or twenty years, the pines have fairly prevailed over us both, though they have suffered terribly and the ground is strewn with their dead, we then suddenly turn about, coming to the aid of the pines with a whip, and drive the cattle out. They shall no longer be allowed to scratch their heads on them, and we fence them in. This is the actual history of a great many of our woodlots. While the English have taken great pains to learn how to create forests, this is peculiarly our mode. It is plain that we have thus both poor pastures and poor forests.

It chances that I came out to this distant part of the town this October afternoon not to look into the history of these woodlots, which chanced to detain me and which I have described, but to examine the site of a dense white-pine wood which was cut off the previous winter and see how the little oaks, with which I knew the ground must be filled there, looked now.

To my surprise and chagrin, I find that the fellow who calls himself its owner has burned it all over and sowed winter rye there! He no doubt means to let it grow up again in a year or two, but he thought it would be clear gain if he could extract a little rye from it in the meanwhile. What a fool! Here Nature had got everything ready for this emergency, kept them ready for many years—oaks half a dozen years old with fusiform roots full charged and tops already pointing skyward, only waiting to be touched off by the sun—and he thought he knew better and would get a little rye out of it first, which he could feel at once between his fingers, and so he burned it and dragged his harrow over it.

He has got his dollars for the pine timber, and now he wishes to get his bushels of grain and finger the dollars that they will bring—and then, Nature, you may have your way again. A greediness that defeats its own ends, for Nature cannot now pursue the way she had entered upon. As if oaks would bide his time or come at his bidding! Or as if he preferred to have a pine or a birch wood here, possibly thirty or fifty years hence, rather than an oak wood at once.

After a year or two he lets it alone. It is a bare field, or possibly a few oak seedlings survive this treatment, but further than this oaks cannot spring up here, for they must be preceded by pines. Pines and birches may, however, if there are seeds ready to be blown hither; but it may take a long while, and moreover the land is "pine-sick."

So he trifles with Nature. I am chagrined for him. That he should call himself an agriculturalist! He needs to have a guardian placed over him. Let us purchase a mass for his soul.

Forest wardens should be appointed by the town—overseers of poor husbandmen.

If a man is rich and strong anywhere,
it must be on his native soil.
Here I have been these forty years
of learning the language of these fields
that I may better express myself.

Other Late Natural History Writings

Wild Fruits

Agrestem tenui meditabor arundine musam
I am going to play a rustic strain on my slender reed,
non injussa cano.
but I trust that I do not sing unbidden things.

This selection is the beginning of a book-length manuscript that Thoreau wrote during the summer of 1860 and the winter of 1860–61. He set the manuscript aside in late February or early March 1861 so that he could work full time on The Dispersion of Seeds.

Throughout the 1850s Thoreau had noted in his journal the dates on which plants in Concord reached certain stages of development (leafing, flowering, ripening, and so on). Late in the decade he occasionally compiled lists of these phenomena, which totaled several dozen pages. Beginning in 1860 he assembled hundreds of pages of these lists and used them as the source for large charts or "calendars" on which he cross-listed plants with the dates they attained a specific stage of development. By averaging eight to ten years of data, he was able to determine the approximate date a certain plant would reach each developmental stage.

In Wild Fruits *he presents the plants "in the order in which they are first observed"; that is, in the order the plants ripen. He began, after an introductory section, with the samarae of the elm, which ripens on 10 May, and ended with the cone of the pitch pine, which ripens on 16 November. By the time he set aside* Wild Fruits, *he had completed a first draft of almost 300 pages and had written 112 pages of a second draft; he stopped after completing a section on black huckleberries, which follows the final section (on the low blueberry) in this selection.*

Wild Fruits, *like* The Dispersion of Seeds, *is important for many reasons, not the least of which is that it demonstrates how a major American author at the height of his career succeeded in making science and literature mutually enriching, rather than mutually exclusive, pursuits.*

MANY public speakers are accustomed, as I think foolishly, to talk about what they call *little things* in a patronizing way sometimes, advising, perhaps, that they be not wholly neglected; but in making this distinction they really use no juster measure than a ten-foot pole and their own ignorance. According to this rule, a small potato is a little thing, a big one a great thing. A hogshead full of anything, the big cheese which it took so many oxen to draw, a national salute, a state-muster, a fat ox, the horse Columbus, or Mr. Blank, the Ossian Boy—there is no danger that anybody will call these *little things*. A cartwheel is a great thing, a snowflake a little thing. The *Wellingtonia gigantea*, the famous California tree, is a great thing, the seed from which it sprang a little thing. Scarcely one traveller has noticed the seed at all, and so with all the seeds or origins of things. But Pliny said, "*In minimus Natura praestat*"—Nature excels in the least things.

In this country a political speech, whether by Mr. Seward or Caleb Cushing, is a great thing, a ray of light a little thing. It would be felt to be a greater national calamity if you should take six inches from the corporeal bulk of one or two gentlemen in Congress than if you should take a yard from their wisdom and manhood.

I have noticed that whatever is thought to be covered by the word "education"—whether reading, writing, or 'rithmetic—is a great thing, but almost all that constitutes education is a little thing in the estimation of such speakers as I refer to. In short, whatever they know and care but *little* about is a little thing, and accordingly almost everything good or great is little in their sense and is very slow to grow any bigger.

When the husk gets separated from the kernel, almost all men run after the husk and pay their respects to that. It is only the husk of Christianity that is so bruited and wide spread in this world; the kernel is still the very least and rarest of all things. There is not a single church founded on it. To obey the higher law is generally considered the last manifestation of littleness.

I have observed that many English naturalists have a pitiful habit of speaking of their proper pursuit as a sort of trifling or waste of time—a mere interruption to more important employments and "severer studies," for which they must ask pardon of the reader—as if they would have you believe that all the rest of their lives was consecrated to some truly great and serious enterprise. But it happens that we never hear more of this, as we certainly should if it were only some great public or philanthropic service, and therefore conclude that they have been engaged in the heroic and magnanimous enterprise of feeding, clothing, housing, and warming themselves and their dependents, the chief value of all which was that it enabled them to pursue just these studies of which they speak so slightingly. The "severe study" they refer to was keeping their accounts. Comparatively speaking, what they call their graver pursuits and severer studies was the real trifling and misspense of life, and were they such fools as not to know it? It is, in effect at least, mere cant. All mankind have depended on them for this intellectual food.

Most of us are still related to our native fields as the navigator to undiscovered islands in the sea. We can any afternoon discover a new fruit there, which will surprise us by its beauty or sweetness. So long as I saw in my walks one or two kinds of berries whose names I did not know, the proportion of the unknown seemed indefinitely, if not infinitely, great.

As I sail the unexplored sea of Concord, many a dell and swamp and wooded hill is my Ceram and Amboyna. Famous fruits imported from the east or south—and sold in our markets, as oranges, lemons, pine-apples, and bananas—do not concern me so much as many an unnoticed wild berry whose beauty annually lends a charm to some wild walk, or which I have found to be palatable to an outdoor taste. We cultivate imported shrubs in our front yards for the beauty of their berries, while at least equally beautiful berries grow unregarded by us in the surrounding fields.

The tropical fruits are for those who dwell within the tropics. Their fairest and sweetest parts cannot be imported. Brought here, they chiefly concern those whose walks are through the marketplace. It is not the orange of Cuba but rather the checkerberry of the neighboring pasture that most delights the eye and the palate of the New England child. For it is not the foreignness or size or nutritive qualities of a fruit that determine its absolute value.

We do not think much of table fruits. They are especially for aldermen and epicures. They do not feed the imagination as these wild fruits do, but it would starve on them. The bitter-sweet of a white-oak acorn which you nibble in a bleak November walk over the tawny earth is more to me than a slice of imported pine-apple. The South may keep her pine-apples, and we will be content with our strawberries, which are, as it were, pine-apples with "going a-strawberrying" stirred into them, infinitely enhancing their flavor. What are all the oranges imported into England to the hips and haws in her hedges? She could easily spare the one, but not the other. Ask Wordsworth, or any of her poets who knows, which is the most to him.

The value of these wild fruits is not in the mere possession or eating of them, but in the sight and enjoyment of them. The very derivation of the word "fruit" would suggest this. It is from the Latin *fructus*, meaning "that which is used or enjoyed." If it were not so, then going a-berrying and going to market would be nearly synonymous experiences. Of course, it is the spirit in which you do a thing which makes it interesting, whether it is sweeping a room or pulling turnips. Peaches are unquestionably a very beautiful and palatable fruit, but the gathering of them for the market is not nearly so interesting to the imaginations of men as the gathering of huckleberries for your own use.

A man fits out a ship at a great expense and sends it to the West Indies with a crew of men and boys, and after six months or a year, it comes back with a load of pine-apples; now, if no more gets accomplished than the speculator commonly aims at, if it simply turns out what is called a successful venture, I am less interested in this expedition than in some child's first excursions a-huckleberrying, in which it is introduced into a new world, experiences a new development, though it brings home only a gill of berries in its basket. I know that the newspapers and the politicians declare otherwise—other arrivals are reported and other prices quoted by them—but that does not alter the fact. Then I think that the fruit of the latter's expedition was finer than that of the former. It was a more fruitful expedition. What the editors and politicians lay so much stress upon is comparatively moonshine.

The value of any experience is measured, of course, not by the amount of money, but the amount of development we get out of it. If a New England boy's dealings with oranges and pine-apples have had more to do with his development than picking huckleberries or pulling turnips have, then he naturally and rightly thinks more of the former; otherwise not. No, it is not those far-fetched fruits which the speculator imports that concern us chiefly, but rather those which you have fetched yourself in the hold of a basket, from some far hill or swamp, journeying all the long afternoon, the first of the season, consigned to your friends at home.

Commonly, the less you get, the happier and the richer you are. The rich man's son gets cocoa-nuts and the poor man's pignuts; but the worst of it is that the former never gets the cream of the cocoa-nut, as the latter does the cream of the pignut. That on which commerce seizes is always the very coarsest part of a fruit—the mere bark and rind, in fact, for her hands are very clumsy. This is what fills the holds of ships, is exported and imported, pays duties, and is finally sold in the shops.

It is a grand fact that you cannot make the fairer fruits or parts of fruits matter of commerce, that is, you cannot buy the highest use and enjoyment of them. You cannot buy that pleasure which it yields to him who truly plucks it. You cannot buy a good appetite even. In short, you may buy a servant or slave, but you cannot buy a friend.

The mass of men are very easily imposed on. They have their runways in which they always travel and are sure to fall into any pit or trap which is set there. Whatever business a great many grown-up boys are seriously engaged in is considered respectable, and great even, and as such is sure of the recognition of the churchman and statesman. What, for instance, are the blue juniper berries in the pasture, considered as mere objects of beauty, to church or state? Some cow-boy may appreciate them—indeed, all who really live in the country do—but they do not receive the protection of any community; anybody may grab up all that exist; but as an article of commerce, they command the attention of the civilized world. Go to the English government, which of course represents the people, and ask, "What is the use of juniper berries?"—and it will answer, "To flavor gin with." I read that "several hundred tons of them are imported annually from the Continent" into England for this purpose; "but even this quantity," says my author, "is quite insufficient to meet the enormous consumption of the fiery liquid, and the deficiency is made up by spirits of turpentine." This is not the *use*, but the gross abuse, of juniper berries, with which an enlightened government, if ever there shall be one, will have nothing to do. The cow-boy is better informed than the government. Let us make distinctions and call things by their right names.

Do not think, then, that the fruits of New England are mean and insignificant while those of some foreign land are noble and memorable. Our own, whatever they may be, are far more important to us than any others can be. They educate us and fit us to live here in New England. Better for us is the wild strawberry than the pine-apple, the wild apple than the orange, the chestnut and pignut than the cocoa-nut and almond, and not on account of their flavor merely, but the part they play in our education.

If it is of low tastes only that you speak, then we will quote to you the saying of Cyrus, the Persian king, that "it is not given to the same land to produce excellent fruits and men valiant in war."

I mention these phenomena in the order in which they are first observed.

Before the 10th of May, the winged seeds or samarae of the *elms* give them a leafy appearance, or as if covered with little hops, before the leaf buds are opened. This must be the earliest of our trees and shrubs to go to seed. It is so early that most mistake the fruit before it falls for leaves, and we owe to it the first deepening of the shadows in our streets.

About the same time, we begin to see a *dandelion* gone to seed here and there in the greener grass of some more sheltered and moist bank, perhaps before we had detected its rich yellow disk—that little seedy spherical system which boys are wont to blow to see if their mothers want them. If they can blow off all the seeds at one puff, then their mothers do not want them. It is interesting as the first of that class of fuzzy or downy seeds so common in the fall. It is commonly the first of the many hints we get to be about our own tasks, those our Mother has set us, and bringing something to pass ourselves. So much more surely and rapidly does Nature work than man. By the 4th of June they are generally gone to seed in the rank grass. You see it dotted with a thousand downy spheres, and children now make ringlets of their crispy stems.

By the 13th of May the earliest *willows* (*Salix discolor*) about warm edges of woods show great green wands a foot or two long, consisting of curved worm-like catkins three inches long. Like the fruit of the elm, they form conspicuous masses of green before the leaves are noticeable, and some have now begun to burst and show their down—and thus it is the next of our trees and shrubs to shed its seeds after the elm.

Three or four days later the *Salix humilis* and the smallest of our willows, *Salix tristis*, commonly on higher and drier ground than the ash and the early aspen, *begin* to show their down. The *Salix tristis* is generally gone to seed by the 7th of June.

As early as the 14th of May, such as frequent the riverside pluck and eat the inner leaf of the *sweet flag* and detect small critchicrotches, which are the green fruit and flower buds. The old herbalist Gerarde thus describes them: "The flower is a long thing resembling the cat-tails which grow on hazel; it is about the thickness of an ordinary reed, some inch and a half long, of a greenish yellow color, curiously checkered, as if it were wrought with a needle with green and yellow silk intermixt."

By the 25th of May this bud, before it has blossomed and while yet tender, is in condition to be eaten and would help to sustain a famished traveller. I often turn aside my boat to pluck it, passing through a dense bed of flags recently risen above the surface. The inmost tender leaf near the base of the plant is quite palatable, as children know. They love it as much as the musquash does. Early in June I see them going a-flagging even a mile or two and returning with large bundles for the sake of this blade, which they extract at their leisure. After the middle of June, the critchicrotch, going to seed, becomes unfit to eat.

How agreeable and surprising the peculiar fragrance of the sweet flag when you first bruise it in the spring! That this plant alone should have extracted this odor surely for so many ages from the moist earth!

Gerarde says that the Tartars hold the root "in such esteem that they will not drink water (which is their usual drink) unless they have just steeped some of this root therein."

Sir John Richardson tells us that "the Cree name of this plant is *watchuske-mitsu-in*, or 'that which the muskrat eats,' " and that the Indians of British America use the root of this plant as a cure for colic: "About the size of a small pea of the root, dried before the fire or in the sun, is a dose for an adult. . . . When administered to children, the root is rasped, and the filings swallowed in a glass of water." Who has not when a child had this same remedy administered to him for that complaint—though the medicine came recommended by a lump of sugar, which the Cree boys did not get—which perhaps was longest in use thus by the Indians. Thus, we begin our summer like the musquash. We take our first course at the same table with him. These are his greens, while we are also looking for dandelions. He is so much like us; we are so much like him.

About the 20th of May I see the first *mouse-ear* going to seed and beginning to be blown about the pastures and whiten the grass, together with bluets, and float on the surface of water. They have now lifted themselves much higher above the earth than when we sought for their first flowers. As Gerarde says of the allied English species, "These plants do grow upon sandy banks and untoiled places that be open to the sun."

I begin to see the *white-maple keys* on the water as early as the 28th of May. Gerarde's account of the seeds of the "great maple" of European mountains applies to these. Having described the flowers, he says, "After them cometh up long fruit fastened together by couples, one right against another, with kernels bumping out near to the place in which they are combined; in all the other parts flat and thin like unto parchment, or resembling the innermost wings of grasshoppers."

About the 20th the similar large green keys of our white maple are conspicuous. They are nearly two inches long and half an inch wide, with waved inner edges to the wings, like green moths ready to bear off their seeds. By the 6th of June they are about half fallen, and I notice that their fall takes place about the time that the great emperor moth (*Attaeus cecro-*

pia) comes out of its chrysalis, and it is sometimes found in the morning wrecked on the surface of the river amid them.

The *red-maple keys* are not half so large as the white, but many times as beautiful. You notice the little fruit just formed early in May, while some trees are still in flower. As it increases in size, the maple tops acquire a browner red, almost a birch red. About the middle of May, the red maples along the edges of swamps, their fruit being nearly ripe, are among the most beautiful objects in the landscape, and more interesting than when in flower, especially if seen in a favorable light.

I stand now on a knoll in the midst of a swamp and observe a young red maple at its base a few rods off on one side with respect to the sun. The keys are high colored, a sort of pink scarlet, and hang down three inches or more. Masses of these double samarae with their peduncles gracefully rising a little before they curve downward, and only a little darker shade than the fruit, are unequally dispersed along the branches and trembling in the wind.

Like the flower of the shadbush, this handsome fruit is seen for the most part against bare twigs, it is so much in advance of its own and of other leaves. It is fairly ripe about the 1st of June, and much of it is conspicuously light colored instead of scarlet. It is in the midst of its fall about the 7th of June. By the 1st of June most trees have bloomed and are forming their fruit. Green berries also begin to be noticed.

The *strawberry* is our first edible fruit to ripen. I begin to find them as early as the 3d of June, but commonly about the 10th, or before the cultivated kinds are offered. They are in their prime the last of June. In meadows they are a week later, and they linger there till late in July.

Even old Tusser, who confines himself mostly to the coarser parts of husbandry, sings in his homely strain under "September":

Wife, into the garden, and set me a plot,
    with strawberry roots, of the best to be got:
Such growing abroad, among thorns in the wood,
    well chosen and pricked, prove excellent good.

The old herbalist Gerarde, writing before 1599, gives us this lively account of the English strawberry, which is sufficiently applicable to our own. He says:

The strawberry hath leaves spread upon the ground, somewhat snipt about the edges, three set together upon one slender footstalk, like the trefoil, green on the upper side and on the nether side more white; among which rise up slender stems, whereon do grow small flowers, consisting of five little white leaves, the middle part somewhat yellow, after which cometh the fruit, not unlike to the mulberry, or rather the raspis, red of color, having the taste of wine, the inner pulp or substance whereof is moist and white, in which is contained little seeds. The root is threaddy of long continuance, sending forth many strings, which disperse themselves far abroad, whereby it greatly increaseth.

Of the fruit he adds, "The nourishment which they yield is little, thin and waterish, and if they happen to putrify in the stomach, their nourishment is naught."

By the 30th of May I notice the green fruit, and two or three days later, as I am walking, perhaps, over the southerly slope of some dry and bare hill, or where there are bare and sheltered spaces between the bushes, it occurs to me that strawberries have possibly set; and looking carefully in the most favorable places, just beneath the top of the hill, I discover the reddening fruit, and at length, on the very driest and sunniest spot or brow, two or three berries which I am forward to call ripe, though generally only their sunny cheek is red. Or else, I notice one half-turned on the sand of the railroad causeway, or even on sand thrown out of a ditch in a meadow.

187

They are at first hard to detect in such places amid the red lower leaves, as if Nature meant thus to conceal the fruit, especially if your mind is unprepared for it. The plant is so humble that it is an unnoticed carpet. No edible wild fruit, except the bog cranberry (*Vacciniae oxycoccus*), and that requires to be cooked, lies so close to the ground as these earliest upland strawberries. Hence, Virgil with propriety refers to the strawberry as *"humi nascentia fraga"*—"strawberries growing on the ground."

What flavor can be more agreeable to our palates than that of this little fruit, which thus, as it were, exudes from the earth at the very beginning of the summer, without any care of ours? What beautiful and palatable bread! I make haste to pluck and eat this first fruit of the year, though they are green on the underside, somewhat acid as yet, and a little gritty from lying so low. I taste a little strawberry-flavored earth with them. I get enough to redden my fingers and lips at least.

The next day, perhaps, I get two or three handfuls of ripe berries, or such as I am willing to call ripe, in a similar locality, the largest and sweetest where the vines hang over the sand; and at the same time, commonly, I get my first smelling, aye, even tasting, of that remarkable bug (one of the *Scutellaridae*) which we are wont to say tastes exactly as a certain domestic bug smells—and thus I am set up for the season. This bug, as you know, "has only to pass over a fruit to impart to it" its peculiar odor. Like the dog in the manger, he spoils a whole mouthful for you, without enjoying them himself. It is wonderful by what affinity this fellow can find out the first strawberry.

You seek the early strawberry on any of the most favorable exposures, as the sides of little knolls or swells (protuberances or warts on the slopes of the hills), or in and near those little sandy hollows where cows have pawed in past years, when they were first turned out to pasture, settling the question of superiority and which should lead the herd. Sometimes the berries have been dusted by their recent conflicts.

I perceive from time to time in the spring, and have long kept a record of it, an indescribably sweet fragrance, which I cannot trace to any particular source. It is perchance that sweet scent of the earth of which the ancients speak. Though I have not detected the flower that emits it, this appears to be its fruit. It is natural that the first fruit which the earth bears should emit and be, as it were, a concentration and embodiment of that vernal fragrance with which the air has lately teemed. Strawberries are the manna found, ere long, where that fragrance has been. Are not the juices of each fruit distilled from the air?

This is one of the fruits as remarkable for its fragrance as its flavor, and it is said to have got its Latin name *fraga* from this fact. Its fragrance, like that of the checkerberry, is a very prevalent one. Wilted young twigs of several evergreens, especially the fir-balsam, smell very much like it.

Only one in a hundred know where to look for these early strawberries. It is, as it were, a sort of Indian knowledge acquired by secret tradition. I know well what has called that apprentice who has just crossed my path to the hillsides this Sunday morning. In whatever factory or chamber he has his dwelling place, he is as sure to be by the side of the first strawberry when it reddens as that domestic smelling bug that I spoke of, though he lies concealed all the rest of the year. It is an instinct with him. But the rest of mankind have not dreamed of such things as yet. The few wild strawberries that we have will have come and gone before the mass know it.

I do not think much of strawberries in gardens, nor in market baskets, nor in quart boxes, raised and sold by your excellent hard-fisted neighbor. It is those little natural beds or patches of them on the dry hillsides that interest me most, though I may get but a handful at first, where, however, the fruit sometimes reddens the ground and the otherwise barren soil is all beaded with them—not weeded or watered or manured by a hired gardener. The berries monopolize the lean sward now for a dozen feet together, being the most luxuriant growth it supports, but they soon dry up unless there is a great deal of rain.

Sometimes it is under different circumstances that I get my first taste of strawberries. Being overtaken by a thundershower as I am paddling up the river, I run my boat ashore where there is a hard sloping bank, turn it over, and take shelter under it. There I lie for an hour in close contact with the earth, and in a fair way to find out what it produces. As soon as the rain begins to hold up, I scramble out, straighten my legs, and stumble at once on a little patch of strawberries within a rod, the sward all red with them, and these I pluck while the last drops are thinly falling.

But it is not without some misgivings that we accept this gift. The middle of June is past, and it is dry and hazy weather. We are getting deeper into the mists of earth; we live in a grosser element, further from heaven these days, methinks. Even the birds sing with less vigor and vivacity. The season of hope and promise is passed, and already the season of small fruits has arrived. We are a little saddened because we begin to see the interval between our hopes and their fulfillment. The prospect of the heavens is taken away by the haze, and we are presented with a few small berries.

I find beds of large and lusty strawberry plants in sproutlands, but they appear to run to leaves and bear very little fruit, having spent themselves in leaves by the time the dry weather comes. It is those earlier and more stunted plants which grow on dry uplands that bear the early fruit formed before the drought.

In many meadows, also, you find dense beds of rank leaves without fruit, yet some meadows produce both leaves and fruit, and these are they whose clusters are handsomest. In July these ranker meadow strawberries are ripe, and they tempt many to trample the high grass in search of them. They would not be suspected for aught that appears above, but you spread aside the tall grass and find them deep in little cavities at its roots, in the shade, when elsewhere they are dried up.

But commonly it is only a taste that we get hereabouts, and then proceed on our way with reddened and fragrant fingers till that stain gets washed off at the next spring. The walker in this neighborhood does well if he gets two or three handfuls of this fruit in a year, and he is fain to mix some green ones and leaves with them, making a sort of salad, while he *remembers* the flavor of the ripe ones. But it is not so up-country. There they are prosaically abundant, for this plant loves a cool region. It is said to be "a native of the Alps and the forests of Gaul," but to have been "unknown to the Greeks." A hundred miles north from here, in New Hampshire, I have found them in profusion by the roadside, and in the grass and about the stumps on the adjacent hillsides in newly cleared land everywhere. You can hardly believe with what vigor they grow and bear there. They are not far off, commonly, from where trout lurk, for they love the same sort of air and water, and the same hut commonly offers the traveller amid the New Hampshire mountains strawberries and trout rods. In the vicinity of Bangor, as I am told, they are found at the roots of grass where it is up to your knees, and they are smelled before they are seen, in hot weather. Also on mountains whence you see the Penobscot fifteen miles off and the white sails of a hundred schooners flapping. There, sometimes, where silver spoons and saucers are scarce but everything else is plentiful, they empty countless quarts into a milk pan, stir in cream and sugar, while the party sits around with each a big spoon.

Hearne, in his *Journey to the Northern Ocean*, says that "strawberries [the *Oteagh-minick* of the Indians is so called because it in some measure resembles a heart], and those of a considerable size and excellent flavor, are found as far north as Churchill River," especially where the ground has been burned over. According to Sir John Franklin, the Cree name is *Otei-meena*; and Tanner says that the Chippeway name is *O-da-e-min*—all evidently the same word, as they have the same meaning. Tanner says that the Chippeways frequently dream of going to the other world, but when one gets to "the great strawberry, at which the *Ie-bi-ug* (or spirits of the dead) repast themselves on their journey," and takes up the spoon, to separate a part of it, he finds it turned to rock, the soft red sand rock which is said to prevail about Lake Superior. The Dakotahs call June *Wazuste-casa-wi*, "the moon when the strawberry is red."

191

From William Wood's *New England's Prospect*, printed about 1633, it would appear that strawberries were much more abundant and large here before they were impoverished or cornered up by cultivation. "Some," as he says, "being two inches about; one may gather half a bushel in a forenoon."

They are the first blush of a country, its morning red, a sort of ambrosial food which grows only on Olympian soil.

Roger Williams says, in his *Key*, "One of the chiefest doctors of England was wont to say that God could have made, but God never did make, a better berry. In some parts, where the natives have planted, I have many times seen as many as would fill a good ship, within a few miles' compass. The Indians bruise them in a mortar, and mix them with meal, and make strawberry bread . . . having no other food for many days."

Boucher, in his *Natural History of New France*, printed in 1664, tells us that the land is filled with an incredible and inexhaustible quantity of raspberries and strawberries; and in Loskiel's *History of the Mission of the United Brethren among the Indians of North America, especially the Delawares* (1794), it is said, "Strawberries grow so large and in such abundance that whole plains are covered with them as with a fine scarlet cloth." In the year 1808 a Mr. Peters, a southerner, wrote to a Philadelphia society to confirm the statement that a tract of forest containing some eight hundred acres somewhere in Virginia, as it appears, having been burned in the last century, strawberries come up profusely. "The old neighbors," says he, "dwelt much on the exuberant plenty, and general cover of the strawberries; which, they said, could be scented, when perfectly ripe, from a great distance. Some of them described the vast surface and waste of flowers, when the plants bloomed in a style that, if the fact had not been well attested, would have appeared fiction. This inimitable gala dress of nature, and the immense number of bees, with their busy hum, frequenting the blossoms and fruit, with the rugged and diversified mountains on the borders [of the tract], would have furnished a scene of pastoral imagery, for poetic description."

The historians of New Hampshire towns tell us that "strawberries are less abundant than in former days, when the land was first cultivated." In fact, hereabouts the strawberries and cream of the county are gone. That ineffable fragrance which gives to this berry its Latin name can never exhale from our manured fields. If we would behold this concentrated perfume and fruit of virgin and untoiled regions in perfection, we must go to the cool banks of the North, where perhaps the parhelion scatters the seeds of it, to the prairies of the Assineboin, where by its abundance it is said to tinge the feet of the prairie horses and the buffaloes, or to Lapland, where, as one reads, the gray rocks that rise above the lowly houses of the Laps "blush literally crimson with the wild strawberries—those wondrous strawberries that spring up everywhere in Lapland, whose profusion is such that they stain the hoofs of the reindeer, and the sledge of the traveller, yet are so delicate and matchless in flower, that the czar himself sends for them, by *estaffettes*, all the long way to his summer palace of *Tsazkoy Chèlè*." In Lapland, that twilight region, where you would not expect that the sun had power enough to paint a strawberry red, still less mature it! But let us not call this by the mean name of "strawberry" any longer, because in Ireland or England they spread straw under their garden kinds. It is not that to the Laplander or the Chippewayan—better call it by the Indian name of heart-berry, for it is indeed a crimson heart which we eat at the beginning of summer to make us brave, or all the rest of the year, as Nature is.

You occasionally find afar ripe ones of a second crop in November, a slight evening red, answering to that morning one.

Wild raspberries begin to be ripe by the 25th of June, and last into August, being at their height about the 15th of July.

193

The sight of these light red berries on a comparatively large and leafy bush—as, perchance, winding our way through the little groves which they make, we pluck the fruit dripping with rain—surprises us while it reminds us of the progress of the year.

This seems to me one of the simplest, most innocent, and ethereal of fruits. One European species is well named "I dream." Hereabouts it grows chiefly in open swamps, though also on hilltops, but rarely bears enough fruit to be of much account. In wet summers, however, like those of 1859 and 1860, it bears quite abundantly in some places in this neighborhood and is gathered for the table.

Like the strawberry, it loves a new country, or one recently burned or cleared, where the soil is still moist, and it was far more common here formerly.

Both Indians and whites, ancients and moderns, have turned aside to pluck this little fruit. The English botanist Lindley says: "I have before me three plants of raspberries, raised from seeds which were taken from the stomach of a man whose skeleton was found thirty feet below the surface of the earth [in England]. He had been buried with some coins of the emperor Hadrian, and it is therefore probable that the seeds were 1,600 to 1,700 years old." The correctness of this statement has, however, been questioned.

I sometimes see a few berries still fresh in the swamps in the middle of September, and I have heard of a second crop being found in some localities much later in the fall.

Pliny, after observing how the European species at length bends down and takes root at the extremity, so that it would occupy all places if it were not for cultivation, says that therefore "men seem to have been made to take care of the earth," and, alas, that "thus a thing most noxious and to be execrated has taught us the art of multiplying by layers and quicksets."

———

I see the *red mulberry* ripe the 28th of June, and still a few the 26th of July. I know of one or two trees in the fields, but they have probably spread from cultivation. Pliny says of mulberry trees: "They are among the latest to blossom, but among the first to ripen their fruit. Ripe, they stain the hands with their juice; sour, they take out the stain. Art has effected least of all in this tree—whether in its names [that is, varieties], or by grafting, or by any other mode, except in the size of the fruit," which appears to be true still.

Early in July the early blueberry, raspberry, and thimbleberry are all beginning to be ripe together.

Black thimbleberries begin June 28th and last through July, being at their height about the 15th of July. I notice the green ones by the 19th of June. They grow along walls where the mowers pluck the fruit at the end of each swath, and in sproutlands.

This is an honest and homely berry, without much flavor, but wholesome and firm. I used to have a pleasant time when young, ranging the wall-sides for them, competing with the birds, gathering the large black and blackening ones, and stringing them on herd's-grass culms, the most convenient way of bringing them home if you have no dish.

They commonly begin to dry up by the middle of July. I have seen a second crop of large and perfectly ripe berries, with others still unripe, as late as the 8th of October, when there had been an abundance of rain the previous six weeks.

Some ten days later comes the *high blueberry*, swamp blueberry, or bilberry. We have two common varieties: the blue and the late black (*Vaccinium corymbosum* and its variant, *atrococcum*). The latter, which is the least common, is small and black, without bloom, more acid, and a day or two earlier than the other, as early or earlier than the thimbleberry, beginning the 1st of July, and *both* last till September. I notice the green berries by the 30th of May, and between the 1st and 5th of July begin to see a few ripe ones. They are at their height from the 1st to the 5th of August.

They are said to be found as far north as Newfoundland and Quebec. They grow in swamps, or if they are very wet, about their edges, and about the edges of ponds, and occasionally you meet with a bush even on a hillside. It loves the water so much that though it may grow about the edge of a pond with steep and hard shores, like Walden and Goose Pond, it is confined strictly to the shoreline, and it will not bear well except in seasons when the water is high. By the sight of these bushes, as of buttonbushes and some others, in a hollow, you may know when you have got down to the water level. Let the ground in the woods sink to a certain depth so that water or considerable moisture is reached, and sphagnum and other water plants spring up there; and if man does not interfere, a dense hedge of high-blueberry bushes will commonly spring up all around the edge, curving over it, or perhaps will extend through it, and this whether it is a mere hollow a rod across or a swamp of a hundred acres.

This is the commonest stout shrub of our swamps, of which I have been compelled to cut down not a few when running lines on a survey or in low woods. When I see their dense curving tops ahead, I expect a wet foot. The flowers have an agreeable, sweet, and berry-promising fragrance, and a handful of them plucked and eaten have a sub-acid taste, agreeable to some palates. The fruit has a singularly cool and refreshing, slightly acid flavor; yet the botanist Pursh says of his (*Vaccinium corymbosum*, which must be another kind) simply, "berries black, insipid." In the Duc d' Aremberg's garden at Enghien, it is said to be "cultivated in the peat border for its fruit, which is used like that of the cranberry"—so slow are they to find out what it is good for! Rarely I find some which have a peculiar and decided bitter taste, which makes them almost inedible. They are of various sizes, colors, and flavors, but I prefer the large and more acid blue ones with a bloom. These embody for me the essence and flavor of the swamp.

When they are thick and large, bending the bushes with their weight, few fruits are so handsome a sight.

Some growing sparingly on recent shoots are half an inch or more in diameter, or nearly as big as cranberries. I should not dare to say now how many quarts I once picked from a single bush which I actually climbed.

These are not all that tempt most into the swamp. Annually we go on a pilgrimage to these sacred places, in spite of dogwood and bilberry bumps. There are Beck Stow's, and Gowing's, and the Damon Meadows, and Charles Miles's, and many others, which all have heard of, and there is many a preserve concealed in the midst of the woods known only to a few.

I remember years ago breaking through a thick oak wood east of the Great Fields and descending into a long, narrow, and winding blueberry swamp which I did not know existed there. A deep, withdrawn meadow sunk low amid the forest, filled with green waving sedge three feet high, and low andromeda, and hardhack, for the most part dry to the feet then, though with a bottom of unfathomed mud, not penetrable except in midsummer or midwinter, and with no print of man or beast in it that I could detect. Over this meadow the marsh-hawk circled undisturbed, and she probably had her nest in it, for flying over the wood she had long since easily discovered it. It was dotted with islands of blueberry bushes and surrounded by a dense hedge of them, mingled with the pannicled andromeda, high chokeberry, wild holly with its beautiful crimson berries, and so on, these being the front rank to a higher wood. Great blueberries, as big as old-fashioned bullets, alternated, or were closely intermingled, with the crimson hollyberries and black chokeberries, in singular contrast yet harmony, and you hardly knew why you selected those only to eat, leaving the others to the birds.

From this meadow I entered southward by a passage hardly a foot wide, stooping close to the ground and brushing off the berries with my pack, into another yet larger swamp or meadow of a similar character; for it was a twin meadow.

Thus hedged about, it is only in some late year that you stumble on some of these places in your neighborhood and stand surprised on the edge of a blueberry preserve, as retired and novel as if it were a thousand miles removed from your ordinary walks, as far off as Persia from Concord.

The timid or ill-shod confine themselves to the land side where they get comparatively few berries and many scratches, but the more adventurous—making their way through the open swamp which the bushes overhang, wading amid the water andromeda and sphagnum, where the surface quakes for a rod around, and wetting their feet at least with the contents of many an upset and rent pitcher plant—obtain access to the great drooping clusters which no hand has disturbed. There is no wilder and richer sight than is afforded from such a point of view of the edge of a blueberry swamp, when various wild berries are intermixed.

There was Charles Miles's Swamp also, where you might get more than the value of the berries, in the beauty of the spruce trees with which it was beset, though not the less wildly rich and beautiful the cool blueberries hung high over your head there. I remember years ago picking blueberries in that swamp, before it began to be *redeemed*, when from its very depths I could hear the trembling strains of Mr. Miles's bass viol, from the unseen house, for he was a famous timist and held the choir to harmony on the sabbath. I am not sure but some echo of those strains "touched my trembling ears" and reminded me about those times, what true fame was, for it did not seem a "mortal soil" where I stood.

Thus, any summer, after spending the forenoon in your chamber reading or writing, in the afternoon you walk forth into the fields and woods and turn aside, if you please, into some rich withdrawn and untrodden swamp, and find there bilberries large and fair awaiting you in inexhaustible abundance. This is your real garden. Perhaps (as at Martial Miles's Swamp) you press your way through thickets of chokeberry bushes higher than your head, with many of their lower leaves already red, attenuating with young birch; raspberries; andromeda, high and low; and great, dense, flat beds of the evergreen swamp blackberry (*Rabus sempervi-rens*)—and ever and anon you come to a cool opening in which stands an island or two of great dark green high-blueberry bushes, dotted with the big cool berries. Or they rise far above your head in the shade of the swamp, retaining their freshness and coolness a long time, little blue sacks full of swampy nectar and ambrosia commingled, whose bonds you burst by the pressure of your teeth. This reminds me that according to Gerarde, whortleberries are "called in Low Dutch *Crakebesien*, because they make a certain crack whilst they be broken between the teeth."

Some large swamps consist almost exclusively of blueberry bushes growing in large clumps, whose spreading tops are closely intermingled above the countless narrow winding paths, or such they *seem*, which separate their bases, forming thus a perfect labyrinth to which there is no clue, but you must steer by the sun; paths which can be convenient only to rabbits, where you make your way with difficulty, stooping low and straddling from tussock to tussock in order to keep out of water, guided perhaps by the accidental rattling of your companion's tin pail.

The gray blueberry bushes, venerable as oaks—why is not their fruit poisonous? It has the wildest flavor of any of the huckleberry tribe that I pluck. It is like eating a poisonous berry which your nature makes harmless. I derive some of the same pleasure from it as if I were eating the arum berries and musquash root with impunity, as if I were a Mithridates among the berries.

Sometimes copious rains early in August will cause those masses of small green berries, of which commonly but few get ripe, to swell and ripen every one, so that their harvest fulfills the promise of their spring, even in swamps where a fortnight before you had despaired of them, and nobody can believe what sights you have seen.

Here they hang for many weeks unchanged, in dense clusters, half a dozen berries touching each other, black, blue, and intermediate colors. But our appreciation of their flavor commonly prevents our observing their beauty, though we admire the color of the hollyberries, which are their neighbors. If they were poisonous, we should hear more of their beauty to the eye.

They hang on into September. Once, when Walden Pond was high, I found perfectly fresh high blueberries overhanging the south side of the pond, which together form a heap, on the 15th of September, and there are many still green among them, though in swamps they are all shrivelled. Commonly they begin to wilt after the middle of August, though they may still be pretty thick, lose their raciness, or wild and sprightly taste, and acquire a dead and flat one.

I sometimes see a variety two or three feet high with large, rather oblong, black berries, with little or no bloom, narrow leaves, and a conspicuous calyx, which appears to be intermediate between this and the *Vaccinium vacillans* or *Vaccinium pennsylvanicum*.

Many swamps in this neighborhood are considered quite valuable for the blueberries, they being made private property, and I have heard of damages being allowed by referees on account of blueberry bushes that were burned. I believe that the most peculiar dish made with these berries is the "blueberry hollow," which is a pudding with a distinct crust enclosing the berries, and the same disposition is made of blackberries.

When their leaves have fallen, they are scraggy, gray, dead-looking bushes, and the oldest have quite a venerable appearance; indeed, they are much older than you would suspect; for since they grow on the edges of swamps and ponds, and on islets in swamps, they frequently escape being cut with the wood and so are older than one growth of wood. There are many growing quite on the edge of Goose Pond, occupying a strip only some three or four feet wide entirely around it, between the steep hillside and the pond, which have accordingly escaped being cut. This is the whole extent of their territory there, not one growing above or below this line.

They are a kind of eyelashes to the pond. They have all the appearance of age, being gray and covered with lichens, commonly crooked, zigzag, and intertwisted with their neighbors, so that when you have cut one off, it is hard to extract it from the mass.

The winter season, when you can stand on the ice, is a good time to examine them. They bend over nearly to the ice, literally bowed with the weight of many winters' snows, yet with lusty young shoots running up perpendicularly by their sides, like erect young men destined to perpetuate the family, by the side of their stooping sires. They have a gray, flat, scaly bark split into long, fine, closely adhering scales, the inner bark being dull reddish.

I find that many of these bushes have attained half the age of man. On one, which measured eight and a half inches in circumference at the butt, I counted pretty accurately forty-two rings. From another I cut a straight and round club four feet long and six and a half inches in circumference at the smaller end, a heavy and close-grained wood, and nobody could tell me what it was.

But the largest and handsomest that I ever saw is on what I call Sassafras Island in Flint's Pond. It, in fact, makes a small tree or clump of trees, about ten feet high and spreading the same or more, and is perfectly sound and vigorous. It divides at six inches above the ground into five stems, which, at the height of three feet, measure respectively eleven, eleven and a half, eleven, eight, and six and a half inches in circumference, or an average nine and a half inches; and near the ground, where they form one solid trunk, they are thirty-one inches in circumference, or more than ten inches in diameter; but probably they have grown together there—indeed, they look as if they had sprung from the different seeds of one berry. The branches spread a little as they rise in their usual zigzag and half-spiral manner, one sometimes resting in the forks of its neighbor, and the finely divided reddish bark is at intervals handsomely clothed with large yellow and gray lichens (the prevailing ones being *Parmelia caperata* and *saxatilis*, the sulfur and rock lichens), which extend quite around them. Next the ground, the bank is quite reddish. The top, which is spreading, is somewhat flattish or corymbose, consisting of a great many fine twigs, which give it a thick and dark appearance against the sky even in winter, compared with the more open portion beneath. In these fine twiggy tops the catbird oftenest builds her nest, and the black snake loves to rest, with or without a view to the young birds. Judging from those whose rings I have counted, the largest of these stems must be about fifty years old.

I climbed up this tree and found a comfortable seat with my feet four feet from the ground, and there was room for three or four persons more there, but unfortunately it was not the season for berries.

This blueberry grove must be well known to the partridges. No doubt they distinguish its peculiar tops from afar and launch themselves in bullet-like flight toward it. In fact, I noticed in the ice the tracks of them which had been there to feed on its large red buds during a previous thaw.

These have not been cut because they stand on that rather inaccessible little island; above there is little woodbine, and therefore they have attained their full size. Perhaps yet larger ones were to be seen here before the whites came to cut down the woods. They are often older than many whole orchards of cultivated fruit trees and may have borne fruit before the writer was born.

About the same time, the late or second kind of *low blueberry*, the common low blueberry (*Vaccinium vacillans*), the firm berry which is generally found with huckleberries on a bush of the same size, begins to be ripe. This is an upright, slender shrub with a few long wand-like branches, with green bark and crimson-colored recent shoots and glaucous green leaves. The flowers have a considerably rosy tinge of a delicate tint. They grow either on open hillsides or pastures, or in sproutlands, or in thin woods, and are from one and a half to two feet high.

This glaucous-leaved bush ripens its fruit somewhat in advance of huckleberries, and it is sweeter than they (if not than the fruit of any of our *Vaccineae*). Both this and the high blueberry are more densely flowered than our other whortleberries, and accordingly the berries are not scattered like huckleberries, but in dense clusters, raceme-like, so that you can strip off a handful at once, of various sizes and qualities. At first you find the ripest ones, not on the very top, nor on the lower slopes, but in the brows, or what is called the "pitch" of a hill, or the southeast or southerly side where they get the most light and heat.

This is the only kind of low blueberry known to many who are belated in their observations and expeditions. The earlier low blueberry, which we might for convenience call bluets (*Vaccinium pennsylvanicum*) (which we now presume to be a little in the rear and out of bearing), is mountain- and spring-like with its fine light-blue bloom—very handsome and simple and ambrosial, to be sure, but, we must admit, soft and rather thin and tasteless. But the second kind is more like solid food, hard and bread-like, though at the same time more earthy.

Some years they are particularly large, as well as abundant. By the 20th of August they begin to be a little wilted, though still good, when huckleberries are getting to be suspected. By the 1st of September they are more or less shrivelled and, if it is a wet season, spoiling; but otherwise they are half dried, many as hard as if dried on a pan; yet they are still very sweet and good, and not wormy like huckleberries. This is a great recommendation, and you can accordingly pluck and eat with confidence that they are still vegetable food. They are often very abundant in this state when there has been a drought. I gather them sometimes as late as the middle of September, quite sound, in fact, after all the rest of the plant has turned to a deep crimson, which is its autumnal tint. These almost spicy lingering clusters of blueberries contrast strangely with the bright leaves.

Weeds and Grasses

This brief selection contains material that Thoreau almost certainly planned to revise for use in the section on shrubs, weeds, and grasses in The Dispersion of Seeds *(page 80, line 12 to page 82, line 16). The first portion of the selection is little more than extracts from Thoreau's reading. The final paragraph, on the other hand, reads as though Thoreau planned to use it near the end of the section on grasses, but he left no explicit indication of his intention. He used the sentence referring to Darwin on De Candolle's remark about winged seeds in* The Dispersion of Seeds *(page 25, lines 11–13). This fragment is interesting because it provides a glimpse of Thoreau transmuting raw sources into literary art.*

Pickering, in his work on races, says, "I found two weeds growing abundantly around the Chinook villages, *Polygonum aviculare* and *Chenopodium album*, and Mr. Brackenridge met with a third, *Plantago major*, in the secluded district of Gray's Harbor."

Plants recently introduced into Northwest America: *Anthemis cotula*, *Amaranthus*, and *Capsella* at Fort Colville; *Sonchus oleraceus* at Fort Nisqually; *Campanula* and *Polygonum persicaria* in Oregon; *Mullugo verticillata*.

Found by Cook and Foster in New Zealand: *Sonchus oleraceus* (of aboriginal introduction—one of the first to extend itself over new countries where it gets a foothold), *Sicyos angulatus*, *Calystegia sepium*.

Of European introduction: *Sicyos angulatus* at Hawaiian Islands and *Portulaca oleracea*, *Sonchus oleraceus* in Peru, Patagonia, and so forth.

Introduced plants of Egypt: *Polygonum circularia*, *Chenopodium album*, *Urtica dioica*, *Urtica urens*, *Lamium amplexicaule*, *Arenaria sulra*, *Stellaria media*, *Polygonum persicaria*.

In Darwin's *Origin of Species*: "In the last edition of Dr. Asa Gray's *Manual of the Flora of the Northern United States*, 260 naturalised plants are enumerated, and these belong to 162 genera. We thus see that these naturalised plants are of a highly diversified nature. They differ, moreover, to a large extent from the indigenes, for out of the 162 genera, no less than 100 genera are not there indigenous."

The same says, "Alphonse De Candolle has remarked that winged seeds are never found in fruits which do not open."

Darwin, in his *Voyage Round the World*, speaks of the cardoon (*Cynara carduculus*), introduced from Europe and now very common in Buenos Ayres—and spread across the continent. In Banda Oriental alone, says he, "very many (probably several hundred) square miles are covered by one mass of these prickly plants, and are impenetrable by man or beast. Over the undulating plains, where these great beds occur, nothing can now live. . . . I doubt whether any case is on record of an invasion on so grand a scale of one plant over the aborigines."

Darwin, who speaks of a difference between the country about Montevideo and some other places, attributed it to the manuring and grazing of cattle, and refers to Atwater as saying that the same thing is observed on the prairies of North America, "where coarse grass, between five and six feet high, when grazed by cattle, changes into common pasture land."

Carpenter in his *Vegetable Physiology* says:

It seems a remarkable fact that those plants of the grass tribe, the seeds of which furnish food for man, follow him like the domestic animals. The reason is that none of the corn plants can bear seeds that will yield a large quantity of flour without a good supply of phosphate of magnesia and ammonia. Hence, these plants grow only in a soil which contains these ingredients, in addition to the silex and potash already mentioned; and no soil is richer in them than those where men and animals dwell together; since these substances are largely contained in the animal body, and are set free in their excretions during life and by their general decay after death.

I notice in the excrement of cattle kernels of grain on which the crows and doves feed, and which probably preserve their vitality and help to disseminate their food.

If, after all, anyone doubts if I have shown him seeds enough to account for the army of weeds which springs up annually by the wayside and elsewhere, let him consider how far a few seeds go, or rather how little bulky they are—how many green gardens, not to say fields, in this town may be traced annually to two or three shallow boxes of garden seeds, and they not half emptied, which a travelling Shaker left at the stores. Why, you could almost put them whole into your coat pockets. Of some seeds you can hardly get little enough. How much surface, think you, would a gill of turnip seed plant if it were economically expended?

Forest Trees

*Prompted, no doubt, by his own observations of forest-tree succession, Thoreau
began researching the subject to determine what had been said by earlier writers. Exactly when he conducted his research is unclear, although the paper type
suggests that he wrote these paragraphs during or after the early fall of 1860.
Two drafts are extant, but in neither did Thoreau indicate where—or even if—
he planned to use the material in* The Dispersion of Seeds. *This selection,
which contains the results of his background research, shows the care and thor-
oughness of Thoreau's approach to plant succession.*

ALL that I have met with of importance on the subject of the succession
of forest trees is contained in a few numbers of the *Memoirs of the
Philadelphia Society for Promoting Agriculture*, which appeared about 1808,
and in an article by John William Dawson of Picton in the *Edinburgh New
Philosophical Journal* for April 1847.

The four expert writers on this subject in the former journal are a Mr.
Peters, apparently the first to treat of it, a Mr. Mease, a Mr. Adlum, and a
Mr. Caldwell. They refer to Hearne's *Journey to the Northern Ocean*, where
it is stated that as far north as Churchill River, both on the coasts and in the
interior, "after the ground, or more properly the underwood and moss,
have been set on fire, [not only strawberry, but] raspberry bushes and hips
have shot up in great numbers on spots where nothing of the kind had ever

been seen before." Hearne, I find, thinks that not only the sun was admitted, but the soil loosened by heat, so that the plants already rooted could shoot up.

They quote from Cartwright's *Journal of Transactions at Labrador* that "if through the carelessness of those who make fires in the woods, or by lightning, the old spruce woods are burnt, Indian tea is generally the first thing which comes up; currants follow next, and after them birch."

In the *Memoirs of the Philadelphia Society for Promoting Agriculture*, Peters in 1808 writes to confirm Hearne with regard to strawberries, which come up where a large tract of pine timber was burned.

In the same *Memoirs*, Mr. Adlum of Maryland says that "the white ash and wild cherry" were in his day the trees which came up after wind-falls on the New York side of Pennsylvania.

These men believed in "a rotation or succession of forest trees."

Mease refers to "the production of white clover, without seed being sown, upon the wretched, poverty-struck heath and moss ground of Scotland, merely from the influence of lime spread on the surface."

Peters is reminded by Adlum that in a forest in Lycoming County, "the old decayed timber, long blown down or fallen with age, was of an entirely different species from that standing."

Peters uses "pine-sick" as a country phrase for soil where pines did not succeed pines.

Caldwell writes to Peters that after the woods were cut, fireweed came up, and after them "it never failed to produce, during the second or third summer, a crop of white clover, although not a sprig of that vegetable grew within many miles of the place." Caldwell also refers to the Duxbury pines and believes that "these plants are a new and spontaneous production," and not introduced by man or animals.

But the most sensible paper which I find is Mr. Dawson's "On the Destruction and Partial Reproduction of Forests in British North America." He says, "In general the deciduous or hardwood trees prevail on intervale ground, fertile uplands, and the flanks and summits of slaty and trappean hills; while swamps, the less fertile and lightest upland soils, and granitic hills, are chiefly occupied by coniferous trees."

He quotes Mr. Titus Smith of Nova Scotia as saying:

If an acre or two be cut down in the midst of a forest, and then neglected, it will soon be occupied by a growth similar to that which was cut down; but when all the timber, on tracts of great size, is killed by fires, except certain parts of swamps, a very different growth springs up; at first a great number of herbs and shrubs which did not grow on the land when covered by living wood. The turfy coat, filled with the decaying fibres of the roots of the trees and plants of the forest, now all killed by the fire, becomes a kind of hot-bed, and seeds which had lain dormant for centuries, spring up and flourish in the mellow soil. On the most barren portions, the blueberry appears almost everywhere; great fields of red raspberries and fire weed or French willow, spring up along the edges of the beech and hemlock land, and abundance of red-berried elder and wild red cherry appear soon after. But in a few years, the raspberries and most of the herbage disappear, and are followed by a growth of firs, white and yellow birch, and poplar. When a succession of fires has occurred, small shrubs occupy the barren, the kalmia, or sheep's poison, being the most abundant, and in the course of ten or twelve years, form so much turf, that a thicket of small alder begins to grow, under the shelter of which fir, spruce, hacmatac (larch), and white birch spring up. When the ground is thoroughly shaded by a thicket twenty feet high, the species which originally occupied the ground begins to prevail, and suffocate the wood which sheltered it; and within sixty years, the land will generally be covered with a young growth of the same kind that it produced of old.

Dawson takes the above for granted and enlarges upon it.

He says first come up a *Trillium* and *fern*, whose roots survive the fire. Then the *Epilobium*, *Solidagos*, *asters*, *ferns*, *Lycopodia*, and *mosses*, whose seeds float in the air. *Then* small fruits dropped by birds.

"The pine woods of Miramichi destroyed by the great fire [1825] above referred to, have been followed by a second growth, principally composed of white birch, poplar, and wild cherry."

"The second growth almost always includes many trees similar to those which preceded it, and when the smaller trees have attained their full height, these and other trees capable of attaining a greater magnitude, overtop them and finally cause their death. The forest has then attained its last stage, that of perfect renovation. The cause of the last part of the process evidently is, that in an old forest, trees of the largest size and longest life have a tendency to prevail, to the exclusion of others." But, as he observes, man interferes with this renovation.

Henry David Thoreau, 1817–1862

(From the Dunshee ambrotype taken August 1861)

A Thoreau Chronology

1817   Born 12 July in Concord, Massachusetts, to John and Cynthia (Dunbar) Thoreau.

1828–33   Attended Concord Academy.

1833–37   Attended Harvard College.

1837   Taught briefly at Concord Center School (public).

1838–41   Conducted a private school in Concord with his elder brother John.

1839   Went on boating excursion on Concord and Merrimack rivers with his brother John.

1840   Poems and essays published in *Dial*.

1841–43   Lived with Ralph Waldo Emerson and his family in Concord.

1842   Brother John died suddenly of lockjaw; "Natural History of Massachusetts" published.

1843   "A Walk to Wachusett" and "A Winter Walk" published; tutored William Emerson's children on Staten Island, New York.

1844   Accidentally set fire to woods in Concord with Edward Hoar.

1845–47   Lived in small house on shore of Walden Pond.

1846   Traveled to Maine woods; spent one night in jail for refusing to pay poll tax.

1847–48   Lived in Emerson household while Ralph Waldo Emerson lectured in England.

1848   Began career as professional lecturer; "Ktaadn and the Maine Woods" published.

1849   *A Week on the Concord and Merrimack Rivers* and "Resistance to Civil Government" published; traveled to Cape Cod; sister Helen died, apparently of tuberculosis.

1850   Traveled to Cape Cod and Quebec.

1853   Traveled to Maine woods; portions of "A Yankee in Canada" published.

1854   *Walden; or, Life in the Woods* and "Slavery in Massachusetts" published.

1855   Portions of "Cape Cod" published; traveled to Cape Cod.

1856   Surveyed Eagleswood Community near Perth Amboy, New Jersey.
       May–June: Wrote passages in journal explicitly about succession of forest trees.
       November: Discussed spontaneous generation of plants with Horace Greeley.

1857   Traveled to Cape Cod and Maine woods; "Chesuncook" published.

1858   Traveled to White Mountains in New Hampshire.

1859   Father, John, died; "A Plea for Capt. John Brown" published.

1860   *1 January*: Discussed Darwin's *On the Origin of Species* (published in London, 24 November 1859) with friends.
       February: Read and copied extracts from *On the Origin of Species*.
       20 September: Delivered "The Succession of Forest Trees" before Middlesex Agricultural Society.
       29 September: Sent "The Succession of Forest Trees" to Horace Greeley, editor of *New-York Weekly Tribune*.
       8 October: "The Succession of Forest Trees" published in *New-York Weekly Tribune*.
       October–November: Visited local woodlots almost daily; drafted many passages in journal later used in *The Dispersion of Seeds*; began expanding "The Succession of Forest Trees" into *The Dispersion of Seeds*.
       December: Worked on *Wild Fruits* manuscript.
       3 December: While researching tree growth, contracted a severe cold, which rapidly worsened into bronchitis and kept him housebound.

11 December: Delivered last lecture, "Autumnal Tints," in Waterbury, Connecticut.

30 December: Responded to Horace Greeley's letter of 13 December about spontaneous generation of plants.

1861 *January–February*: Continued work on *Wild Fruits* manuscript.

2 February: Letter of 30 December 1860 to Greeley denying possibility of spontaneous generation published in *New-York Weekly Tribune*.

March–early May: Worked on *The Dispersion of Seeds*.

12 May–14 July: Traveled to Minnesota with Horace Mann, Jr., in effort to regain health.

1862 Prepared earlier lecture-essays for publication in anticipation of death. Died 6 May in Concord, Massachusetts.

Editor's Notes

Henry D. Thoreau was a meticulous, well-organized writer. When he ceased working on his late natural history manuscripts in early May 1861, exactly a year before his death, they were doubtless in perfect order. Since his death, however, the manuscripts have passed through many hands and have lost their original order. Indeed, several manuscript leaves (no one knows how many) have been lost altogether. This regrettable circumstance, and the difficulties inherent in generating reliable texts from works-in-progress generally, have hitherto prevented these extraordinary works from reaching the public.

Of the three book-length projects that Thoreau worked on in his last years but did not live to complete—*The Dispersion of Seeds*, *Wild Fruits*, and *Moonlight*—the first is by far the most finished. The scope of *Wild Fruits* was so ambitious that Thoreau can be said only to have begun that work, although he did complete a rudimentary first draft and start a second draft. Unfortunately, his *Moonlight* manuscripts have been so widely scattered that it is difficult to comment on them with any authority.

This volume presents a clear reading text of *The Dispersion of Seeds* and a representative selection from *Wild Fruits* so that the significance of Thoreau's late natural history writings may be appreciated by his large and growing audience of general readers, by scientists and environmentalists, by historians of science, and by students of American literature. For ease of reading, I have regularized the idiosyncrasies of Thoreau's manuscripts. For instance, I have silently (1) expanded his contractions and abbreviations, including his ampersands; (2) written

217

words for his numerals, except dates and numerals where they appear in sources from which he quoted; (3) used ellipses within quotations where he employed a series of asterisks or dashes; (4) italicized his foreign quotations, book titles, and foreign words, including Latin names for plants and animals; (5) corrected his misspellings when they were in none of the lexicons he is known to have used; and (6) supplied articles and prepositions he inadvertently left out of a few sentences. (Readers interested in a detailed treatment of my editorial procedures and decisions can consult my doctoral dissertation, "A Textual Study of Thoreau's *Dispersion of Seeds* Manuscripts," University of Connecticut, 1993.)

I explain more substantive editorial intrusions in the following notes, which are keyed to pages and lines in the text. In the notes I have tried to cite the editions that Thoreau himself consulted; rather than giving page numbers, I have in some cases cited book, chapter, section, and so on, in order that readers can more conveniently locate the material in other editions. I also quote in the notes all of Thoreau's interlined comments and certain on-line remarks that he seems to have written for himself as reminders. Finally, except to indicate where Thoreau's drawings were inserted in his manuscripts and to mark two fairly obvious editorial intrusions—both mentioned in the notes (page 48, line 2, and page 83, line 3)—square brackets in the text are Thoreau's own.

Title page of "The Dispersion of Seeds"
(Courtesy of Berg Collection, New York Public Library)

Index for two portions of "The Dispersion of Seeds"
(Courtesy of Berg Collection, New York Public Library)

Transcript of index on facing page

Thoreau used this index (written sideways on the leaf, with the top line along the right edge) to order his topics in *The Dispersion of Seeds* on pages 24–39 and 82–95 of the present volume. The numerals to the left of the citations represent the order of topics for his first draft; those to the right represent the order of topics for his second draft, published herein. Corresponding page numbers in the present volume are supplied in square brackets along the right margin.

1) Beauty of *wht* p. fruit	6	[p. 34]
7) Pigeons eat	(8	[p. 37]
2) P. pine cones grow how—pine apples	(1	[pp. 24–27]
p p. blown over snow		
4	(2	[pp. 27–28]
How *far* latter blows		
How pine woods spring up		
5	(4	[pp. 33–34]
from smallest		
same of *wht* pines		
3	(7	[pp. 34–37]
Natures geologic pace—		
8) Pleasant to observe growth in wood	(5	[p. 33]
6) Squirrels eat p p. cones (2 places	(3	[pp. 28–33]
(3 Gather *wht* p. cones	9	[pp. 38–39]

[WRITTEN VERTICALLY IN RIGHT MARGIN:]

2/7 Downy seeded plants — Dandelion — mouse ear (St. Pierre   [pp. 82–95]
extracts on *mt* plants)   Thistle down   —Fireweed
G. rods   Milk weed — Dogs bane pod

Chart of "Leafing of Trees & Shrubs"
(The Pierpont Morgan Library, New York. MA 610)

Page 23, title. The Dispersion of Seeds} This title is Thoreau's. Sources for *The Dispersion of Seeds* consist of three hundred eight manuscript pages, nine sentences from Thoreau's essay "The Succession of Forest Trees" as printed in the *New-York Weekly Tribune* on 8 October 1860, and thirty-two sentences from the slightly truncated reprinting of the essay in *Eighth Annual Report... of the Massachusetts Board of Agriculture... for 1860* (Boston: William White, Printer to the State, 1861), pp. 11–23. Of the three hundred eight manuscript pages, two are in the Rare Books Collection at the Wilson Library, University of North Carolina at Chapel Hill; one is in the Rare Books and Manuscripts Collection at the John Hay Library, Brown University; one is in Special Collections at the Samuel Paley Library, Temple University; and the remaining three hundred four are in a folder labeled "Dispersion of Seeds" at the Henry W. and Albert A. Berg Collection of the New York Public Library, paged with accession numbers 1, 3–48, 67–95, 139–47, 148A–B, 149–212, 214–32, 244–45, 257–81, 282A–B, 283–308, 310–38, 351–56, 358–85, 385A–B, 386–99.

Page 23, lines 1–7. Pliny... considered inauspicious."} Pliny the Elder, *The Natural History of Pliny*, trans. John Bostock and H. T. Riley, 6 vols. (London: H. G. Bohn, 1855–57), bk. 16, ch. 45.

Page 23, line 5. [*Ulmus campestris* ... England]} This interpolation is Thoreau's, as are the square brackets; it is based on John Claudius Loudon's remark that *Ulmus campestris* "does indeed produce seeds occasionally, though rarely, in England" (*Arboretum et Fruticetum Britannicum; or, The Trees and Shrubs of Britain*... 2d ed., 8 vols. [London: The Author, 1844], 3:1374).

Page 24, line 4. planted by Nature.} After "Nature," the MS continues without deletion "—deferring, however, to speak of oaks, chestnuts, and hickories for the present." As this phrase indicates, Thoreau began his first draft of *The Dispersion of Seeds* with a discussion of hardwoods. He began his second draft (published here), however, with a discussion of the pitch pine, so the phrase about oaks, chestnuts, and hickories has been editorially deleted.

Page 24, lines 21–28. It is related... an apple.'"} Thoreau's source is Loudon, *Arboretum et Fruticetum Britannicum*, 4:2112. He has translated some of Loudon's Latin. Ediles, according to the *Oxford English Dictionary* (OED), were Roman magistrates "who had the superintendence of public buildings, shows, police, and other municipal functions."

Page 25, line 6. its prickly shield.} Thoreau interlined in the MS at this point "count seventy-seven *good* in one."

Page 25, lines 11–13. Darwin ... do not open.} Charles Darwin, *On the Origin of Species by Means of Natural Selection, or The Preservation of Favored Races in the Struggle for Life* (New York: D. Appleton, 1860), p. 146.

Page 25, line 30. little to one side} MS reads "little one side."

Page 26, lines 15–19. Michaux ... for several years."} François André Michaux, *The North American Sylva, or A Description of the Forest Trees of the United States, Canada, and Nova Scotia ... to Which Is Added a Description of the Most Useful of the European Forest Trees*, trans. F. Andrew Michaux, 3 vols. (Paris: Printed by C. D'Hautel, 1819), 3:119.

Page 26, line 32. the other day} Identified from the source of this passage in Thoreau's journal as 26 November 1860. All references to Thoreau's journal will be to the daily entries; see *The Journal of Henry D. Thoreau*, ed. Bradford Torrey and Francis H. Allen, 14 vols. (Boston: Houghton, Mifflin and Co., 1906). Thoreau wrote most of *The Dispersion of Seeds* from the perspective of 1860, as he did here, but he wrote some passages from the perspective of 1861 and did not live to repair the inconsistency.

Page 27, lines 21–22. one of our ponds} Identified from the journal source of the next paragraph (entry of 20 July 1860) as Walden Pond.

Page 27, line 31. middle of July} Thoreau interlined "(July 20, 1860)" in the MS here.

Page 28, line 5. I noticed lately} Identified as 20 November 1860 from the journal source of that date.

Page 28, lines 27, 29, page 29, line 10. last fall ... one night ... A few days after} Thoreau mentions in the journal source (entry of 20 November 1860) that he had "tried the other night while in bed to account for" the phenomenon to which he refers in these two paragraphs.

Page 29, lines 2–3. I have found ... and fuel} In the "Economy" chapter of *Walden* (published August 1854), Thoreau had written, "The necessaries of life for man in this climate may, accurately enough, be distributed under the several heads of Food, Shelter, Clothing, and Fuel...." (*Walden*, in *The Writings of Henry D. Thoreau*, ed. J. Lyndon Shanley [Princeton: Princeton University Press, 1971], p. 12).

Page 29, line 22. A neighbor} Identified in the journal source (entry of 20 October 1860) as Edmund Hosmer.

Page 30, line 10. last October} Thoreau interlined "1860" in the MS here.

Page 32, lines 7–8. for the same ... its weak side} Thoreau originally wrote "for the stem being removed, this becomes the weak side or point of attack," but he later interlined the clause shown here without deleting the original clause.

Page 32, line 15. April of last year} Thoreau interlined "(1859)" in the MS here.

Page 33, lines 6, 11. some years since.... Eleven years ago} Thoreau interlined "(November 9, 1850)" in the MS and interlined "some years since" over the undeleted original phrase "many years ago."

Page 33, line 15. changed its diet of late} Coal from the anthracite region of Pennsylvania began to be used on a relatively large scale to supply power to locomotives in 1861, primarily as a result of increased use of railroads during the Civil War.

Page 33, line 19. Ten years ago} Thoreau interlined "(July 16, 1851)" in the MS here.

Page 35, line 7. Worcester} The second largest city in Massachusetts, about thirty-five miles southwest of Concord. Thoreau had visited the city on 3–4 November 1859 to deliver his lecture "A Plea for Capt. John Brown."

Page 35, lines 24–25. entrench} MS reads "intrench."

Page 35, line 25. French soldiers in Sevastopol} On 16 September 1854 a large contingent of French soldiers, as well as troops from Britain, Turkey, and Sardinia, landed on the Crimean Peninsula and laid siege to the Russian fortress at Sevastopol. The siege lasted until September 1855 and is regarded by many historians as the first large-scale, prolonged use of trench warfare.

Page 35, line 29. few they may be} Thoreau interlined "other side of wall?" in the MS here.

Page 36, line 31. "little strokes fall great oaks"} John Lyly wrote in *Euphues: The Anatomy of Wit* (1579), "Many strokes overthrow the tallest oaks"; in his *Poor Richard's Almanack* for August 1750, Benjamin Franklin wrote, "Little strokes, / Fell great oaks."

Page 37, lines 18–21. an account of Duxbury ... this growth."} "A Topographical Description of Duxborough, in the County of Plymouth," *Collections of the Massachusetts Historical Society*, 1st ser., vol. 2 (1793): 5.

Page 38, lines 13–15. Loudon . . . several years."} *Arboretum et Fruticetum Britannicum,* 4:2131.

Page 39, line 31. for the squirrels} Thoreau interlined here "Insert Douglas on Lambert getting pine cones," apparently a reference to the botanists David Douglas and Aylmer Bourke Lambert, but the source in Douglas's writings has not been located. Douglas was a collector for the Horticultural Society of London; Lambert was a fellow of the society. These two men were the world's foremost students of conifers during the early nineteenth century.

Page 40, line 17. alive with them.} Thoreau interlined in the MS here "(Perhaps I also saw goldfinches there October 23, November 15, December 31, 1859, and January 7, 1860)."

Page 40, line 26. one day} Thoreau identified the date with the interlineation "(January 20, 1860)" in the preceding paragraph.

Page 41, line 3. One old hunter} Identified in the journal source (entry of 23 January 1860) as George Minott.

Page 41, line 5. The following April} Identified from the journal source (entry of 7 April 1860) as April of 1860.

Page 41, line 7. The same winter} Thoreau interlined "(January 27, 1860)" in the MS here.

Page 41, lines 15–16. the other day . . . the meadow} The day was 28 October 1860, as identified from the journal entry of that date, which also specifies the meadow as being "on the north side the [Cambridge] Turnpike, six to twelve rods from [George] Everett's seed-bearing" larches.

Page 41, line 18. open till spring} Thoreau interlined in the MS here "(Channing brings me some not yet open about March 10, 1861)." The reference is to his friend and most frequent walking companion, William Ellery Channing II (1817–1901).

Page 41, lines 20–23. Wilson . . . pine warbler} Alexander Wilson, *Wilson's American Ornithology, with Notes by Jardine . . . by T. M. Brewer* (Boston: Otis, Broaders and Co., 1840), pp. 291, 28, 79, 82, 91, 180, 207. Thoreau used the 1852 reprint of this edition published in New York by H. S. Samuels. The "two crossbills" are the American and the white-winged. Thoreau's "chickadee" is Wilson's black-capped titmouse. Wilson describes two pine warblers, the pine-creeping and the pine-swamp, but he mentions only the former as feeding on pine seeds.

Page 41, line 22. (Giraud)} Jacob Post Giraud, *The Birds of Long Island* (New-York: Wiley & Putnam, 1844), p. 127.

Page 42, line 21. butterflies.} The drawing here is Thoreau's and has been reproduced from the MS.

Page 43, lines 13–15. Alphonse De Candolle ... among the Alps).} Alphonse Louis Pierre Pyramus De Candolle, *Géographie Botanique Raisonnée; ou, Exposition des Faits Principaux et des Lois Concernant la Distribution Géographique des Plants de L'époque Actuelle ...* 2 vols. (Paris: V. Masson [et al.], 1855), 2:613. Thoreau cited De Candolle's source in the MS as "(*Tabl. de la Nat.*, ed. 1851, volume 2, page 37, [Alexander] Humboldt)."

Page 43, line 30. in Boxborough and in Cambridge} Boxborough is a small town about twelve miles west-northwest of Concord; Cambridge is across the Charles River from Boston, about eighteen miles east-southeast of Concord.

Page 44, line 7. Prichard} The MS was editorially emended from "Pritchard" to reflect the way Moses Prichard spelled his last name.

Page 44, line 31. last summer} Thoreau interlined "1860" in the MS here.

Page 45, line 1. one of our ponds} Thoreau's journal source (entry of 24 August 1860) indicates that he refers here to Walden Pond. The birches were springing up on the shore of Walden's Deep Cove.

Page 45, lines 12–14. Alphonse De Candolle ... in fresh water."} *Géographie Botanique Raisonnée*, 2:985. Thoreau cited De Candolle's source in the MS as "(*Ann. Sc. Nat.*, V[I], page 373)," which appears on page 253 of his Commonplace Book 2 in the Berg Collection at the New York Public Library as "'*Annales des Sciences Naturelles*, 3d series, 1846, VI, page 373[']'" (p. 253).

Page 45, line 26. the other day} No journal source for this passage has been located.

Page 45, line 28. State Street in Boston.} In the mid-nineteenth century, Boston's State Street was considered the center of commerce and finance in New England, much as we regard New York's Wall Street today.

Page 46, lines 1–3. Loudon's *Arboretum* . . . considerable intervals."} *Arboretum et Fruticetum Britannicum*, 3:1691.

Page 46, line 15. as is stated ... before known."} Horace Greeley, in a letter to Thoreau dated 13 December 1860 and printed in the *New-York Weekly Tribune* on 2 February 1861 under the title "Are Plants Ever Spontaneously Generated," pointed out that the season after sweeping fires devastate large pine forests, "up springs a new and thick growth of White Birch—a tree not before known there." He then asked how Thoreau reconciled that phenomenon with his theory "that trees are never generated spontaneously, but always from some nut, or seed, or root, preëxisting in that same locality."

Page 46, lines 18–19. I have had occasion ... wilds of Maine} Thoreau traveled three times to the Maine woods—in September 1846, September 1853, and July–August 1857—spending a total of about thirty-five days there. He wrote an essay for each of his three trips; they are collected in *The Maine Woods*, in *The Writings of Henry D. Thoreau*, ed. Joseph J. Moldenhauer (Princeton: Princeton University Press, 1972).

Page 46, lines 22–25. Blodget ... highest mountains."} Lorin Blodget, *Climatology of the United States, and the Temperate Latitudes of the North American Continent* ... (Philadelphia: J. B. Lippincott, 1857), pp. 78–79. Thoreau added the scrap containing this quotation to the larger *Dispersion of Seeds* MS in April 1861. Since the scrap contains only the quotation and the attribution "Blodget's *Climatology*," the introductory clause ("Blodget, in his *Climatology*, says") is editorially supplied.

Page 46, line 27 to page 47, line 4. Loudon ... blank that occurs."} *Arboretum et Fruticetum Britannicum*, 3:1694, 1696. In the first quotation Loudon refers to Peter Simon Pallas, a Russian botanist; the French author referred to in the second quotation is identified in Loudon as "the author of the article Bouleau, in the *Dictionnaire des Eaux et Forêts*."

Page 47, lines 7, 9, 11. spring of 1859 ... a neighbor ... my neighbor} In the journal source (entry of 30 April 1859), Thoreau mentions collecting one hundred ten birch seedlings, ten of which he planted in his own yard, but he does not identify the neighbor to whom he gave the other hundred seedlings.

Page 47, line 15. In August 1861 I} In the MS this sentence begins "August 1861—found," so "In" and "I" are editorially supplied.

Page 48, line 2. [blank space in manuscript]} Intending, no doubt, to measure the tree later, Thoreau left this space blank and never measured the tree. He did insert a query ("?") in the margin of the MS opposite the blank.

Page 48, line 6. seed is most abundant} Thoreau interlined "(January 20–24, 1860)" in the MS here.

Page 48, line 9. seed in the copses.} Thoreau interlined "(January 8, 1860)" in the MS here.

Page 48, lines 12–17. Mudie . . . losing their perch."} Robert Mudie, *The Feathered Tribes of the British Islands*, 2 vols. (London: Bohn, 1834), 1:148.

Page 48, line 19. in the same manner.} Thoreau interlined "(January 7, 1860)" in the MS here.

Page 49, line 13. on the birch seeds.} Thoreau interlined "(January 29, 1860)" in the MS here.

Page 49, line 19. two parallel lines.} After this sentence in the MS Thoreau wrote "*Vide* sketch," a reference to the drawing following this sentence, the source of which is Thoreau's journal entry of 29 January 1860, which is also the source for the paragraph preceding this drawing.

Page 49, line 20. I even see} Thoreau interlined "(January 24, 1856)" in the MS here.

Page 50, lines 6–7. hold on till winter.} Thoreau interlined in the MS here "(For *dates* of ripening and so on, see *Wild Fruits*)," a reference to the large natural history project he worked on at about the same time he was working on *The Dispersion of Seeds*. A selection from *Wild Fruits* is published in the present volume on pages 177–203; a portion of the project that Thoreau was working into a lecture before he died was published in Leo Stoller, *Huckleberries* (Ames, Iowa: Windhover Press, 1970).

Page 50, lines 8–13. Gerarde's old account ... wings of grasshoppers."} John Gerarde, *The Herball of Generall Historie of Plantes* . . . (London: Adam Islip, Joice Norton and Richard Whitakers, 1633), p. 1485.

Page 50, line 19. to be transported.} The following sentence appears in the MS here: "(One of the two samarae of the sugar maple, as Michaux observed and I have found, is always empty, though as perfectly winged as the other.)" Thoreau placed parentheses around material that he wished to delete, but some parenthetical material he clearly wanted to retain in the text. It is not clear whether he intended to delete or retain this sentence. Michaux's observation is in *North American Sylva*, 1:155.

Page 50, line 24. Patent Office.} During the mid-nineteenth century the U.S. Patent Office, which was operated jointly by the War Department and the Office of the Attorney General, distributed seeds to citizens in small envelopes.

Page 51, line 29. a month later perhaps} Thoreau interlined "(July 9, 1857)" in the MS here.

Page 52, line 11. last September} Thoreau interlined in the MS here the day of the month and the year, "(4th, 1860)."

Page 52, lines 20–21. none of the seed catches} MS reads "none of the seed catch."

Page 52, line 27. its seeds so late} Thoreau interlined "(November 25, 1860)" in the MS here.

Page 52, lines 30–31. Loudon ... devour it.} *Arboretum et Fruticetum Britannicum*, 1:405.

Page 53, line 20. at midsummer} Thoreau interlined "(August 1, 1860)" in the MS here.

Page 54, lines 7–15. Kalm ... seeds ripens for them."} Pehr Kalm, *Travels into North America; Containing Its Natural History, and a Circumstantial Account of Its Plantations and Agriculture in General* ... trans. John Reinhold Forster, 3 vols. (London: The Editor, 1770–71), 2:312.

Page 54, lines 19–20. seeds are said ... often all winter} George B. Emerson wrote of the white ash, "The keys often remain on the tree through the winter" (*A Report on the Trees and Shrubs Growing Naturally in the Forests of Massachusetts* ... [Boston: Dutton and Wentworth, 1846], p. 335).

Page 54, line 27. our river meadows} Thoreau interlined "(June 17, 1852)" in the MS here.

Page 55, line 2. floated in between them.} Thoreau interlined "(February 12, 1850)" in the MS here.

Page 55, line 7. by its beneficiaries.} Thoreau interlined in the MS here "Perhaps speak of the hornbeam and the hop-hornbeam here."

Page 55, lines 13–15. It is said ... are formed here.} Thoreau's source for this reference has not been located.

Page 56, line 26. On June 9th, 1860} MS reads "June 9th, 1860—we had," so the word "On" is editorially supplied.

Page 56, line 28. Mill Dam} The downtown shopping district of Concord.

Page 57, lines 17–18. reminded me of . . . on the seashore} Thoreau refers to his experience at Fire Island, New York, in late July 1850. On 19 July the American bark *Elizabeth*, with Margaret Fuller-Ossoli, her husband, and their son aboard, wrecked on the coast. Thoreau was dispatched to the scene to recover the bodies of the Ossolis and their belongings. He found the beach strewn with the unsalvageable portion of the cargo, which included heaps of white cotton rags that had been destined for American paper mills.

Page 57, line 31. is called *cotton*wood.} Thoreau interlined in the MS here "Down crossing the Mississippi and Minnesota rivers," a reference to the entries for 24 May and 26 June 1861 in his "Notes on the Journey West." These are notes that he took during a two-month trip to Minnesota, where he had gone during his final illness to try to regain his health. In the former entry Thoreau wrote, "Willow down floating horizontally across the [Mississippi] river" between Cassville and Prairie du Chien, Wisconsin; in the latter entry he wrote, "The cotton-wood and black willow shedding down together up the Minnesota [River]" at Red Wing, Minnesota (Walter Harding, *Thoreau's Minnesota Journey* [Geneseo, N.Y.: Thoreau Society, 1962]).

Page 58, lines 1–2. Pliny . . . *araneam abit*."} *Natural History*, bk. 24, ch. 37.

Page 58, lines 2–3. Homer . . . ὠλεσιχάρπου} *Odyssey*, bk. 10, l. 605.

Page 58, lines 3–5. Pliny . . . produces barrenness."} *Natural History*, bk. 16, ch. 46.

Page 58, lines 7–10. Soon shalt . . . o'er the floods.} Homer, *The Odyssey,* trans. Alexander Pope (Georgetown, D.C.: Richards & Mallory & Nicklin, 1813), bk. 10, ll. 602–5.

Page 58, line 11. Styx} The mythical river of Hades (the "Infernal Region").

Page 58, line 12. Saskatchewan and Assineboin} Two rivers of the northern plains of North America, the former flowing east into Lake Winnipeg, the latter (usually spelled "Assiniboine") flowing south and east into the Red River at Winnipeg, Manitoba. The names of both rivers are mentioned in the title of Henry Youle Hind's book (see next note).

Page 58, line 15. Mackenzie to Hind} Mackenzie was among the earliest explorers of inland North America; Hind was, in 1860–61, among the most recent. Thoreau read accounts of their explorations in Sir Alexander Mackenzie, *Voyages from Montreal, on the River St. Lawrence, Through the Continent of North America, to the Frozen and Pacific Oceans; in the Years 1789 and 1793 . . .* 2 vols. (London: Printed for T. Cadell, Jr. [et al.]; Edinburgh: W. Creech, 1802); and Henry Youle Hind, *Northwest Territory. Reports on Progress; Together with a Preliminary and General Report on the Assiniboine and Saskatchewan Exploration Expedition . . .* (Toronto: Printed by J. Lovell, 1859).

Page 58, lines 17–19. some think . . . for nobler forests.} Thoreau's source for this reference has not been located.

Page 58, lines 20–21. I have often noticed . . . on burnt lands.} In *The Maine Woods*, Thoreau mentioned passing over burnt lands that had "occasional strips of timber crossing them, and low poplars springing up" (p. 70).

Page 59, lines 7–8. of all shrubs, is said} Loudon, *Arboretum et Fruticetum Britannicum*, 3:1455. John Lindley said that the *Salix arctica* is the "most northern woody plant that is known" (*A Natural System of Botany; or, A Systematic View of the Organization, Natural Affinities, and Geographical Distribution of the Whole Vegetable Kingdom . . .* [London: Longman, (et al.), 1836], p. 187).

Page 60, line 1. some ten years afterward} Thoreau interlined "(February 14, 1856)" in the MS here.

Page 60, line 6. a natural *Salictum*} Thoreau interlined "(May 14, 1857)" in the MS here.

Page 62, lines 10–11. 7th of June} Thoreau probably meant to write "7th of July," for his journal entry of 9 July 1857 contains this sentence: "I see that the seeds of the *Salix nigra* gathered on the catkin on the 7th, or two days since, put in a tumbler of water in my window, have already germinated! and show those two little roundish green leaves."

Page 63, line 12. One June} Identified from the journal source (entry of 8 June 1856) as June 1856.

Page 64, lines 3–5. they mean who . . . forlorn paramour!"} Edmund Spenser, *Faerie Queene*, bk. 1, canto 1, stanza 9.

Page 64, lines 7, 9–10. willow of Babylon . . . David's tears} "By the rivers of Babylon, there we sat down, yea, we wept, when we remembered Zion. We hanged our harps upon the willows in the midst thereof" (Psalms 137:1–2).

Page 64, lines 10–11. Euphrates ... Alexander's head.} According to Loudon in *Arboretum et Fruticetum Britannicum*, "The branches of one of the weeping willows on the banks of the Euphrates are said to have caught the crown from the head of Alexander the Great, when he passed under the tree in a boat on that river; a circumstance which made the Babylonish diviners predict his early death" (3:1464).

Page 64, lines 18–22. Fuller's *Worthies* ... pay for his saddle."} Thoreau's source, as he notes in the margin of the MS, was John Brand, *Observations on Popular Antiquities of Great Britain: Chiefly Illustrating the Origin of Our Vulgar Customs, Ceremonies, and Superstitions ...* 3 vols. (London: Henry G. Bohn, 1853), 1:122. The quotation can be found in Thomas Fuller, *The Worthies of England*, ed. John Freeman (London: George Allen & Unwin, 1952), p. 47. The Isle of Ely is a district in east England.

Page 64, line 23. Herodotus ... willow rods} *Herodotus, A New and Literal Version, From the Text of Baehr ...* (London: H. G. Bohn, 1854), bk. 4, ch. 67.

Page 65, line 6. weeping sisters of Phaeton, as some pretend} Ovid, *Metamorphoses*, bk. 2, ll. 340–66. Ovid relates the myth that when Phaeton scorched the earth while attempting to drive his father Phoebus' chariot (the sun) across the sky, Zeus killed him with a lightning bolt. As Phaeton's sisters (the Heliades) grieved for him, they slowly turned to trees, presumably weeping willows.

Page 65, lines 12–15. Jardine ... willow catkins."} Wilson, *American Ornithology*, p. 289.

Page 65, lines 16–17. Mudie ... willow down.} *Feathered Tribes*, 1:223.

Page 65, line 17. Wilson ... seeds of the poplar.} *American Ornithology*, p. 79.

Page 65, lines 19–20. Michaux ... in this latitude.} *North American Sylva*, 2:48.

Page 66, lines 4–6. And I read that ... prairie soils."} The first four words of this sentence have been supplied by the editor. Thoreau's source for this quotation has not been located.

Page 66, lines 6–8. Wilson ... seeds in the winter.} *American Ornithology*, pp. 46, 79.

Page 66, lines 8–9. Giraud ... fond of those seeds.} *Birds of Long Island*, p. 127.

Page 66, lines 11–17. Pliny ... gigantic dimensions."} *Natural History*, bk. 17, ch. 14.

Page 66, line 18 to page 67, line 5. Evelyn ... impetuous storms.} John Evelyn, *Sylva, or a Discourse of Forest-Trees* ... 3d ed. (London: Printed for Jo. Martyn and Ja. Allestry, 1679), pp. 273–74.

Page 67, line 7. giant sequoia of California} The General Sherman tree in Sequoia National Park is 272.4 feet high and 36.5 feet in diameter at its base. It takes 48,000 *Sequoia gigantea* seeds to make a pound.

Page 67, line 15. surface of this town} Thoreau interlined in the MS here "Globe containing 263,025,993,120 cubic miles."

Page 69, line 4. nearest cherry tree} Thoreau interlined in the MS here "(as at Assabet Spring, July 14, 1856)."

Page 69, line 20. hilltop in the woods by Walden Pond} The journal source (entry of 25 October 1860) identifies this as Heywood's Peak.

Page 69, line 21. enclosed} MS reads "inclosed."

Page 69, line 22. last fall} The journal source (entry of 25 October 1860) identifies the year as 1860.

Page 70, lines 4–9. Dr. Manasseh Cutler ... cherry trees."} Rev. Mannaseh Cutler, "An Account of the Vegetable Productions, Naturally Growing in This Part of America, Botanically Arranged," *Memoirs of the American Academy of Arts and Sciences*, 1st ser., vol. 1 (1785): 449.

Page 70, lines 10–12. Michaux ... these circumstances.} *North American Sylva*, 2:153.

Page 70, lines 13–15. I have noticed ... camped for a night.} In *Maine Woods*, Thoreau mentions that at the mouth of a small stream where he fished "were the ruins of an old lumbering camp, and a small space, which had formerly been cleared and burned over, was now densely overgrown with the red cherry and raspberries" (p. 106). Under "Small Trees and Shrubs" in the Appendix to *Maine Woods*, he lists "*Prunus pennsylvanica* (wild red cherry), very common at camps, carries, &c., along rivers; fruit ripe August 1, 1857" (p. 306).

Page 70, lines 18–22. Mr. George B. Emerson ... great distance."} *Report on Trees*, p. 452.

Page 70, line 31. ornithologies} As Thoreau's references to them make clear, his principal ornithologies were Giraud's *Birds of Long Island*, John James Audubon's *Ornithological Biography*, and particularly Wilson's *American Ornithology*.

Page 71, lines 6–8. Evelyn ... *suum cacat* ."} *Sylva, or a Discourse of Forest-Trees*, p. 93.

Page 71, lines 9–13. If you would study ... fruits in this town.} See note for page 75, lines 17–23.

Page 71, line 14. this date in 1859} Thoreau's journal source for this passage is his entry of 1 September 1859. He mentions walking that day in the sproutlands behind Britton's Camp.

Page 72, lines 22–25. Wilson ... off the berries"} *American Ornithology*, p. 71. Wilson consistently refers to Thoreau's cherry-bird as the cedar-bird.

Page 72, lines 25–30. Audubon ... taken by the hand."} John James Audubon, *Ornithological Biography, or An Account of the Birds of the United States of America* ... 5 vols. (London: A. Black [et al.], 1831–49), 1:227. Jardine, in his notes to Wilson's *American Ornithology*, p. 71, quotes this passage from Audubon.

Page 73, lines 22–24. it is said ... mockingbird} Thoreau's likely source is Wilson, *American Ornithology*, pp. 184, 21, 391, 108. In the margin of the MS here, Thoreau interlined "(Jenks?)," which is a reference to "The Food of Birds," *New-York Weekly Tribune*, 2 April 1859, wherein it is reported that one Jenks, a professor of zoology, and a committee of the Massachusetts Horticultural Society studied the "habits of the robin" to determine whether "these birds are noxious to farmers." The committee found that "early in November—the robin migrates southward—the few remaining eking out a miserable existence, during the Winter months, on bayberries" and other berries.

Page 73, lines 24–28. Wilson ... extremely fat."} *American Ornithology*, p. 357. Great Egg Harbor is at the mouth of the Great Egg Harbor River in southern New Jersey, near Ocean City.

Page 73, line 30. middle of October} Thoreau interlined "(15, 1859)" here, referring to the journal source (entry of 15 October 1859).

Page 74, lines 2–7. "So fond ... Wilson ... little fatigue."} *American Ornithology*, pp. 21–22.

Page 74, lines 11–13. Loudon ... ripe, as fruit."} *Arboretum et Fruticetum Britannicum*, 2:917.

Page 74, lines 20–22. Evelyn ... sure of their company.} *Sylva, or a Discourse of Forest-Trees*, p. 42.

Page 74, line 29. My neighbor} Not identified in the journal source of portions of this and the preceding paragraph (entry of 22 September 1859).

Page 75, lines 17–23. About the 1st ... bluebirds, and robins.} Thoreau copied all but the last clause of this paragraph and used the material in another location (see page 71, lines 9–13). He then drew lines through the paragraph, which is retained here because the lines appear to have been erased and because he apparently refers to the paragraph when he mentions "the above list" on line 24.

Page 75, line 25. rose-hips} Thoreau interlined "(February 25, 1859)" in the MS here.

Page 75, lines 27–29. Charles Darwin ... seeds of the yew."} *Origin of Species*, p. 184. The *Parus major* is the larger titmouse.

Page 75, line 30 to page 76, line 2. Wilson ... same red color"} *American Ornithology*, p. 22.

Page 76, line 13. I have found} Thoreau interlined "(October 19, 1860)" in the MS here.

Page 76, line 24. kept on horizontally.} The drawing following these words has been reproduced from the MS. An almost identical rendering appears in the journal source for this passage (entry of 19 October 1860).

Page 77, lines 23–26. Wilson ... scarlet tanager.} *American Ornithology*, pp. 71, 65, 126.

Page 77, lines 29–30. George Emerson ... flocks of wild pigeons.} *Report on Trees and Shrubs*, p. 404.

Page 77, line 31. huckleberries extensively} Thoreau interlined in the MS here "Channing says he saw one eating huckleberries this year, 1861."

Page 78, line 2. last September} Thoreau interlined "(1860)" in the MS here; the journal source for the passage is the entry of 23 September 1860.

Page 78, line 14. last October} Thoreau interlined "(25th, 1860)" in the MS here.

Page 78, line 25. the nearest house.} Thoreau interlined "(as in Melvin's Preserve)" in the MS here.

Page 79, lines 5–6, 7. my neighbor ... another ... still another} In the journal source for this passage (entry of 15 November 1859), Thoreau wrote: "William Rice says that [goldfinches] get so much of the lettuce seed that you can hardly save any. They get sunflower seeds also. Are called 'lettuce-birds' in the books." Wilson, in *American Ornithology*, wrote: "During the latter part of the summer [goldfinches] are almost constant visitants in our gardens, in search of seeds.... From these circumstances ... they are very generally known, and pass by various names expressive of their food, color, &c., such as Thistle-Bird, Lettuce-Bird, Salad-Bird, Yellow-Bird, &c" (pp. 8–9). There is no indication in the journal of the identity of the other two neighbors Thoreau mentions.

Page 79, line 15. One winter} Thoreau interlined "(January 4, 1859)" in the MS here.

Page 79, lines 26–28. Wilson ... off to the woods"} *American Ornithology*, p. 97.

Page 79, lines 28–30. Audubon ... deprived them of life."} *Ornithological Biography*, 1:227.

Page 80, line 1. I have elsewhere described} A reference to his lecture-essay "Wild Apples," delivered before the Concord Lyceum on 8 and 14 February 1860, and posthumously published in the *Atlantic Monthly* of November 1862.

Page 80, lines 14–15. In Minnesota} See note for page 57, line 31, above.

Page 80, line 16. One September} Thoreau interlined "(18th, 1859)" in the MS here.

Page 81, lines 6–8. De Candolle ... escaped from gardens.} *Géographie Botanique Raisonnée*, 2:784.

Page 81, lines 16–17. factories above} Teasel was used by factories on streams emptying into the Sudbury and Assabet rivers, primarily to comb manufactured wool.

Page 81, line 23. late in the fall} Thoreau interlined "(November 2 and 8, 1860)" in the MS here.

Page 81, line 25. simpler} "One who collects or gathers simples ['a plant or herb employed for medical purposes']; a herbalist, a simplest" (OED).

Page 82, lines 9–10. in various ways.} Thoreau interlined "(*Vide* if necessary December 1 and 6th, 1856)" in the MS here. In his journal entry for the former date, Thoreau wrote:

Slate-colored snowbirds flit before me in the path ["Abiel Wheeler's wood-path to the railroad"], feeding on the seeds on the snow, the countless little brown seeds that begin to be scattered over the snow, so much the more obvious to bird and beast. A hundred kinds of indigenous grain are harvested now, broadcast upon the surface of the snow. Thus, at a critical season these seeds are shaken down onto a clean white napkin, unmixed with dirt and rubbish, and off this the little pensioners pick them. Their clean table is thus spread a few inches or feet above the ground.

In his journal entry for 6 December 1856, Thoreau wrote:

What variety the pinweeds, clear brown seedy plants, give to the fields, which are yet shallowly covered with snow! You were not aware before how extensive these grain-fields. Not till the snow comes are the beauty and variety and richness of vegetation ever fully revealed. Some plants are now seen more simply and distinctly and to advantage. The pinweeds, etc., have been for the most part confounded with the russet or brown earth beneath them, being seen against a background of the same color, but now, being seen against a pure white background, they are as distinct as if held up to the sky.

Page 82, line 16. readily detect them.} Thoreau interlined here in the MS "*Vide* perhaps Wild Fruits under August 6 (or 16?), how Nature picks her berry seeds," which is a reference to a passage from his *Wild Fruits* MS that has not been located.

Page 82, lines 17–18. Gerarde ... away with the wind"} *Herball of Generall Historie of Plantes*, p. 291.

Page 82, line 19 to page 83, line 3. About the 9th ... their crispy stems.} Thoreau copied this passage from his *Wild Fruits* MS (see page 183, lines 9–25), very likely after he laid that MS aside in the late winter of 1861.

Page 83, lines 1, 3. *generally* gone to seed ... [Half leaf of manuscript missing.] Its highest plot} The MS ending here leaves off with the words "gone to." The five words after "gone to" and the sentence beginning "You see it dotted" are editorially supplied from *Wild Fruits* (see page 183, lines 9–25, as well as the note above). The MS beginning "Its highest plot" is the bottom half of a leaf that was tipped into the flyleaf of volume 1 in set 298 of the Manuscript Edition of *The Writings of Henry D. Thoreau* (Boston: Houghton, Mifflin, 1906). Houghton, Mifflin mounted 520 original Thoreau manuscript leaves (some of which they cut in half) on larger pieces of paper and bound them into 620 sets of the Manuscript Edition and an undisclosed number of specially bound Walden Edition sets. The missing half leaf was also, no doubt, tipped into an as yet unrecovered set of the Manuscript Edition.

Page 83, lines 4–6. Saint Pierre ... of the dandelion."} Jacques Henri Bernardin de Saint Pierre, *Studies of Nature* ... trans. Henry Hunter, 5 vols. (London: Printed for C. Dilly, 1796), 3:xii.

Page 83, lines 7–12. About the 20th ... open to the sun.} Thoreau copied this paragraph from his *Wild Fruits* MS (see page 185, lines 12–17).

Page 83, lines 11–12. Gerarde ... open to the sun."} *Herball of Generall Historie of Plantes*, p. 638.

Page 83, lines 18–21. De Candolle ... become naturalized.} *Géographie Botanique Raisonnée*, 2:619.

Page 83, lines 30–31. De Candolle ... Kasan.} *Géographie Botanique Raisonnée*, 2:831. Kasan is now more widely known as Kazan, a city 450 miles east of Moscow that was made the capital of the Tatar kingdom in the fifteenth century.

Page 83, line 31 to page 84, line 2. Mrs. Lincoln ... the Atlantic Ocean."} Mrs. A. Hart Lincoln Phelps, *Familiar Lectures on Botany, Practical, Elementary, and Physiological* ... 5th ed., rev. and enl. (New York: F. J. Huntington, 1837), p. 100.

Page 84, lines 3–4. Another species ... Gray ... native there.} Asa Gray, *A Manual of Botany of the Northern United States* ... (New York: G. P. Putnam, 1856), p. 481. Thoreau left a blank after "species," apparently intending to insert the Latin name of the species that Gray asserted was native to Europe.

Page 84, lines 5–8. Saint Pierre ... equinoctial winds."} *Studies of Nature*, 3:173.

Page 84, lines 9–10. thenceforward till winter.} Thoreau interlined in the MS here "(as November 20)." In none of his journal entries for 20 November between 1850 and 1860 does Thoreau mention thistledown, but in the entry for 22 November 1860 he wrote, "Every plant's down glitters with a silvery light along the Marlborough Road,—the sweet-fern, the *Lespedeza*, and bare blueberry twigs, to say nothing of the weather-worn tufts of *Andropogon scoparius.*"

Page 84, line 15. pulling them to pieces} Thoreau interlined in his MS here "(as September 4, 1860)."

Page 84, lines 18–21. The Romans . . . Pliny . . . with this genus.} *Natural History,* bk. 10, ch. 57.

Page 84, line 28 to page 85, line 4. Mudie . . . species are soon added."} *Feathered Tribes,* 2:54.

Page 85, line 11. one afternoon last year} Thoreau interlined in the MS here "(1860, also Fair Haven Pond, August 19 another year)." The journal source of passage in the text is the entry of 26 August 1860; he saw thistledown sailing over Fair Haven Pond on 19 August 1858 (see his journal entry of that date).

Page 85, lines 22–25. Theophrastus . . . very high wind"} Theophrastus, *Theophrasti Eresi Quae Supersunt Opera et Excerpta Librorum . . .* 5 vols. (Lipsiae: Sutibus F. C. G. Vogelii, 1818–21), 2:472. Thoreau derived this quotation from a "Fragment" titled *De Signis Pluriarum,* translated from Greek to Latin by Davide Furlano Cretensi. The translation into English is apparently Thoreau's own.

Page 85, lines 25–30. Phillips . . . approaching tempest!"} Henry Phillips, *The History of Cultivated Vegetables . . .* 2 vols. (London: H. Colburn and Co., 1822), 1:103.

Page 85, line 31. Last August . . . Monadnock Mountain} Thoreau and his friend William Ellery Channing left for Mount Monadnock in southwestern New Hampshire on 4 August 1860 and returned on the morning of 9 August. In his journal entry for 9 August 1860 Thoreau reported having seen the thistledown floating over the summit.

Page 86, lines 14–18. Virgil . . . arvis Carduus .} Virgil, *Georgics,* in *Opera . . . ad Usum Serenissimi Delphini . . .* (Philadelphia: M. Carey & Son, 1817), bk. 1, ll. 147–52. The Loeb Classical Library edition of the *Georgics* (*Virgil with an English Translation by H. Rushton Fairclough . . . in Two Volumes,* rev. ed. [Cambridge, Mass.: Harvard University Press, 1978]) translates the lines Thoreau paraphrases: "Ceres was the first to teach men to turn the earth with iron, when the acorns and arbutes of the sacred wood began to fail, and Dodona denied men food. Soon, too, on the corn fell trouble, the baneful mildew feeding on the stems, and the lazy thistle bristling in the fields...." (1:91).

Page 86, lines 23–28. One writer ... each plant."} Thoreau's source for this quotation has not been located, although it was probably also the source for an allusion made by Mrs. Lincoln Phelps in *Familiar Lectures on Botany*: "It has been calculated that a single thistle seed will produce, at the first crop, twenty-four thousand, and at the second crop, at this rate, five hundred and seventy-six millions" (p. 100). Thoreau copied this quotation into his Commonplace Book 1, p. 201. For a facsimile of Commonplace Book 1, see Kenneth Walter Cameron, *Thoreau's Fact Book in the Harry Elkins Widener Collection in the Harvard College Library, Annotated and Indexed* ... 3 vols. (Hartford: Transcendental Books, 1966).

Page 86, line 31. one day} The journal source of this paragraph has not been located.

Page 87, line 8. the comet} A comet whose tail, according to Thoreau, was "at least as long as the whole of the Great Dipper" appeared in the northwestern sky each evening during late September and early October of 1858 (entry of 5 October 1858). Contemporary newspapers indicate that many people were alarmed at what the comet might portend. Thoreau mentions the comet in his journal entries of 23 and 29 September and 1 and 5 October 1858.

Page 87, lines 11–12. out of sight eastward.} Thoreau interlined "(September 29, 1858)" in the MS here.

Page 87, line 17. late in October} Thoreau interlined "(25th, 1860)" in the MS here.

Page 88, line 14. 'change} Clipped form of "exchange," as in "stock exchange."

Page 88, lines 23–24. *hieracifolia ... angustifolium*} Thoreau interlined "(August 13)" over "*hieracifolia*" and "(August 15)" over "*angustifolium*." Strictly speaking, fireweed is *Epilobium angustifolium*; the common name for *Erecthites hieracifolia* is pilewort.

Page 89, lines 17–23. A correspondent ... clean it."} E. G. Waters, "Spontaneous Generation of Plants" [letter to editor dated 7 February 1861], *New-York Weekly Tribune*, 23 March 1861, p. 7, col. 6. Waters wrote to Horace Greeley, the editor of the *Tribune*, apparently to refute a point Thoreau had made earlier in response to a query from Greeley. Both Greeley's query (dated 13 December 1860) and Thoreau's response (dated 30 December 1860) were published under the title "Are Plants Ever Spontaneously Generated?" in the *New-York Weekly Tribune* on 2 February 1861.

Page 90, lines 15–17. Kalm ... instead of feathers."} *Travels into North America*, 3:29.

Page 90, lines 18–19. Alphonse De Candolle ... south of Europe.} *Géographie Botanique Raisonnée*, 2:784.

Page 90, line 22. air in the spring.)} Thoreau interlined in the MS here "? (March 20, 1853)."

Page 90, line 24. stem like a flourish.} Thoreau interlined "(*Vide* Plate)" in the MS here, but the plate to which he refers has not been located.

Page 90, line 26. 4th of October} Thoreau interlined "(1856)" in the MS here.

Page 92, line 3. One of my neighbors} This person has not been identified.

Page 92, line 9. attic window} Thoreau lived in the attic of his parents' house on Main Street in Concord.

Page 92, line 9. end of September} Thoreau interlined "(20th, 1860)" in the MS here.

Page 92, line 13. On August 26th, 1860, I notice} The MS reads "I (August 26, 1860) notice," so the word "On" has been editorially supplied.

Page 92, line 19. one afternoon} Thoreau interlined "(September 24, 1857)" in the MS here.

Page 92, line 21. meadow on Clematis Brook} Thoreau interlined in the MS here "(near the deserted Abel Minott house)."

Page 92, line 22. now point upward} Thoreau interlined in the MS here "(did they before point down?)."

Page 93, line 6. Mr. Lauriat} Obviously an early balloonist, but no biographical information on him has been located.

Page 93, line 23. prophecies of Daniel or of Miller} The apocalyptic visions or prophecies of the prophet Daniel are recorded in the Old Testament, Book of Daniel, ch. 7–12. William Miller (1782–1849), whose followers were known as Millerites, founded the Adventist movement in the United States during the

1840s and predicted that the Second Coming of Christ would take place on 21 March 1844.

Page 93, line 30. end of November} Thoreau interlined "(22d, 1857)" in the MS here.

Page 94, line 6. near the end of April.} Thoreau interlined "(24th, 1856)" in the MS here.

Page 94, line 8. the 18th of September} Thoreau interlined "(1860)" in the MS here.

Page 94, line 12. last of September} Thoreau interlined "(21st, 1860)" in the MS here, but his journal source was actually the entry of 22 September 1860.

Page 94, lines 14–17. It is said of the English ... of their supply."} [John Leonard Knapp], *The Journal of a Naturalist* (Philadelphia: Carey & Lea, 1831), p. 118.

Page 94, line 19. about the same time.} Thoreau interlined "(as October 16, 1859)" in the MS here.

Page 94, lines 20–21. Early in November} Thoreau interlined "(8th, 1859)" in the MS here.

Page 95, line 5. *Adhaerentes* by Linnaeus)} Carl von Linnaeus (Linné), *Amoenitates Academicae; Seu Dissertationes Variae ...* 7 vols. (Holmiae: [n.p.], 1749–69), 2:464.

Page 95, lines 10–11. *Circaea , Galium*} After *Galium* Thoreau interlined what appears to be the word "Spricle."

Page 95, lines 12–17. *Intereunt segetes ...* cultivated fields.} Virgil, *Georgics*, bk. 1, ll. 152–54. In the MS, Thoreau quotes Virgil only to the word "*tribolique,*" but he translates Virgil through the clause ending with the word "*avenae.*" Therefore, the words "*interque nitentia culta / infelix lolium et steriles dominantur avenae*" are editorially supplied. The Loeb Classical Library edition of the *Georgics* translates the passage "The crops die, and instead springs up a prickly growth, burs and clatrops, and amid the smiling corn the luckless darnel and barren oats hold sway" (1:91). The OED notes that "cockle" was often used as a synonym for darnel, or *lolium*.

Page 95, line 21. in October} Thoreau interlined "(20th, 1858)" in the MS here.

Page 95, line 24. Lilliputian army} In Jonathan Swift's *Gulliver's Travels*, Gulliver is shipwrecked on the coast of Lilliput, whose inhabitants are about six inches tall. As he lay on the shore, the Lilliputian army tied Gulliver down before he regained consciousness and shot miniature arrows into him when he attempted to get up. The arrows, he said, "pricked me like so many needles."

Page 96, line 18. in September} Thoreau interlined "(29th, 1856)" in the MS here.

Page 97, line 8. One afternoon ... down the river ... a companion} Thoreau interlined "(September 5, 1860)" in the MS after "One afternoon," and he interlined "(at Ball's Hill)" after "down the river." The companion is identified from Thoreau's journal entry of 5 September 1860 as William Ellery Channing.

Page 97, line 9. walked about through} The MS reads "walked about there through," so "there" has been editorially deleted to avoid redundancy. Thoreau had added the words "by the shore there" later and had neglected to delete the first occurrence of the word "there."

Page 98, line 3. One January} Thoreau interlined "(4th, 1857)" in the MS here.

Page 98, lines 11–16. Wilson ... imbedded with the fleece"} *American Ornithology*, p. 482.

Page 98, lines 16–20. Alphonse De Candolle ... in the country."} *Géographie Botanique Raisonnée*, 2:622. Montpellier is a city in south France west-northwest of Marseilles; Barbary is a region of north Africa on the Barbary Coast extending from the Egyptian border to the Atlantic Ocean and including the former Barbary States (present-day Morocco, Algiers, Tunis, and Tripoli); Syria is a Middle East country south of Turkey; Bessarabia is a region of southeast Europe between the Deinster and Prut rivers, mostly in present-day Moldavia.

Page 98, line 22. was naturalized.} Thoreau interlined in the MS here "(notice about August 1; at height perhaps middle of August)."

Page 98, lines 28, 29 to page 99, line 2. a young lady ... my sister ... young lady's mother} The young lady was Edith Emerson, Thoreau's sister was Sophia Thoreau, and Edith's mother was Lydia Emerson, wife of Ralph Waldo Emerson (journal entry of 6 September 1858).

Page 99, lines 11–14. Pickering ... seeds and plants."} Charles Pickering, *The*

Races of Man; and Their Geographical Distribution (London: H. G. Bohn, 1851), p. 332.

Page 99, line 15. On October 13th, 1860} The word "On" is editorially supplied.

Page 100, lines 2, 3. yellow seeds. . . . vase-like form.} The three drawings here are Thoreau's and have been reproduced from his *Wild Fruits* MS. Thoreau interlined "*vide* sketch—in *Wild Fruits*" in the MS after both "yellow seeds" and "vase-like form."

Page 100, lines 4–5. The seeds are about . . . rather more purplish.} Thoreau interlined this sentence and an alternate sentence in the MS here and deleted neither. The alternate sentence, which has been editorially deleted as redundant, reads "The pods are full of seeds the color of apple seeds but a quarter as big."

Page 100, line 8. plant themselves.} Thoreau interlined in the MS here "*Vide* above still if necessary"; his reference is unclear.

Page 100, lines 9–12. Saint Pierre . . . where they grow."} *Studies of Nature,* 3:192.

Page 100, line 30. this year—1860} Thoreau interlined "(October 10)" in the MS here.

Page 100, lines 5–7. Wilson . . . (*Ardea herodias*).} *American Ornithology,* pp. 528, 536, 556.

Page 101, line 13. On October 18th, 1860} The word "On" is editorially supplied.

Page 102, line 6. development theory} Now better known as the theory of evolution, first comprehensively articulated by Charles Darwin in *Origin of Species.*

Page 102, lines 9–17. Darwin . . . plants to vast distances"} *Origin of Species,* pp. 386–87.

Page 102, line 13. altogether 537} After "537" Thoreau inscribed a caret and interlined "[no *and*]" (his brackets), but his intention is unclear.

Page 102, line 21 to page 103, line 16. Saint Pierre . . . and in reputation.} *Studies of Nature,* 3:192–93. Flora is the Roman goddess of the flowering of plants; Sechelles (usually spelled "Seychelles") is an island group in the west Indian Ocean northeast of Madagascar; Mahé is the largest of the Seychelles Islands; Malabar is a coastal region of southwest India on the Arabian Sea.

Page 103, lines 17–20. Alphonse De Candolle . . . itself in the last.} *Géographie Bo-*

tanique Raisonnée, 2:925. Prâlin and Ronde are islands of the Seychelles; the Maldive Islands are in the Indian Ocean south of the Laccadive Islands and southwest of India's Cape Comorin.

Page 103, line 20 to page 104, line 5. Saint Pierre ... cultivate it.} *Studies of Nature*, 3:194–95, 197, 218. The principal city on the island of Madeira is Funchal, which is located on Funchal Bay. The island of Rodriguez (usually spelled "Rodrigues") was discovered by the Portuguese in 1645 and is 350 miles east of Isle of France (anglicized form of "Ile de France"), which is now the island of Mauritius in the western Indian Ocean. Francis (actually François) Leguat and eight of his companions were abandoned by an unscrupulous sea captain on Rodrigues, not in 1690, but on 1 May 1691. On 29 May 1693, after much hardship and the death of one of their number, they managed to set sail for Ile de France in a barque of their own manufacture (François Leguat, *Voyages et Aventures de François Leguat et de Ses Compagnons en Deuxîles Désertés des Indes Orientales* ... 2 vols. [Amsterdam: (n.p.), 1708]).

Page 104, lines 6–10. One author ... Sloane; and cocoa-nuts."} This passage has been editorially expanded from Thoreau's interlined note in the MS here— "*Vide* American Fruits cast on the shore of Norway, Commonplace Book 1, page 26"—which refers to the following extract: "American fruits cast on the shore of Norway. Some 'so recent as to germinate.'—These fruits are usually the *Cassia Fistula*: *Anacardium*, or Cashew Nuts: *Cucurbitae Lagenariae*, Bottle gourds: Pods of the *Mimosa Scandens*,—called *Cocoons* in the West Indies: Pods of the Piscidia Erythrina, called Dog-wood Tree by Sloane: and Coconuts.' H[enricus] Tonning—[Dissertation 149, "*Rariora Norwegiae*," in William Pulteney, *A General View of the Writings of Linnaeus* ... 2d ed. (London: J. Mawmon, 1805), p. 473.] These from the [chapter] Amoenitates Academicae."

Page 104, line 10. Sloane; and cocoa-nuts."} Thoreau interlined in the MS here "*Vide* Perhaps also Darwin on Plants of Oceanic Islands, Commonplace Book 2, pages 169–171," a reference to the following extracts in his Commonplace Book 2 at the New York Public Library's Berg Collection:

Plants on Oceanic Islands. [Darwin, *Origin of Species*, p.] 339. "The species of all kinds which inhabit oceanic islands are few in number compared with those on equal continental areas: Alph. De Candolle admits this for plants, and Wollaston for insects. If we look to the large size and varied stations of New Zealand, extending over 780 miles of latitude, and compare its flowering plants, only 750 in number, with those on an equal area at the Cape of Good Hope or in Australia, we must, I think, admit that something quite independently of any difference in physical conditions has caused so great a difference in number. Even the uniform county of Cambridge has 847 plants, and the little island of Anglesea 764, but a few ferns and a few introduced plants are included in these numbers, and the comparison in some other respects is not quite fair. . . ."

[P.] 340 "Although in oceanic islands the number of kinds of inhabitants is scanty, the proportion of endemic species (i.e. those found nowhere else in the world) is often extremely large."

Page 104, line 15. One morning some five years ago} Thoreau interlined "(June 3, 1856, and also May 13, 1856)" in the MS here. His journal entries of those dates contain his first explicit and substantive remarks on the topic of the succession of forest trees. The entry for 3 June 1856 is the source of the paragraph beginning here.

Page 104, lines 17–18. a few years before} Thoreau interlined "(1851–52)" in the MS here and queried the interlineation in the margin.

Page 104, lines 18–19. my employer} Identified in the journal source (entry of 3 June 1856) as John Hosmer.

Page 105, line 9. two of my neighbors} In his journal source for the preceding paragraph (entry of 3 June 1856), Thoreau remarks only that he believed Ebenezer Rockwood Hoar had purchased the shrub-oak lot from David Loring.

Page 105, lines 11–12. old farmer with whom I was riding} See note to page 104, lines 18–19, above.

Page 105, line 16. best course, after all.} Thoreau interlined in the MS here "as *vide* 254–5," a reference to five paragraphs in his journal entry of 30 October 1860 explaining the changes that had occurred since June 1856 on the lot he is discussing in the paragraph here, a lot which in the journal entry he calls the "Loring lot" (see note to page 105, line 9, above).

Page 105, line 19. Apparently there were only pines} After these five words in the MS, Thoreau wrote "&c &c as far as two paragraphs on page 15 of printed report." The "printed report" to which he refers is the slightly truncated reprinting of his essay "The Succession of Forest Trees" in *Eighth Annual Report ... of the Massachusetts Board of Agriculture ... for 1860* (Boston: William White, Printer to the State, 1861), pp. 11–23. The sentence here, beginning "Apparently there were only pines," appears on page 13 of that report, and the second paragraph on page 15 of that report ends with the words "which resorted to this wood for shade" (see this volume, page 108, lines 7–8). So Thoreau's note in the MS here is a direction to insert the remainder of this sentence and the thirty-two sentences between this sentence and the third paragraph on page 15 of the "printed report."

Page 108, line 21. Again I examined ... west part of the town} Thoreau interlined "(October 30, 1860)" and "(Tarbell's)" in the MS here.

Page 109, line 12. one afternoon} The afternoon is identified in the journal source for this passage: 27 October 1860.

Page 111, lines 1–5. Nuttall ... New Spain the same number."} Thomas Nuttall, *North American Sylva; or, A Description of the Forest Trees of the United States, Canada, and Nova Scotia ...* 3 vols. (Philadelphia: Robert P. Smith, 1853), 1:17. This sentence has been editorially expanded from Thoreau's interlineation in the MS here—"*Vide* Nuttall on Range of Oaks, Commonplace Book 1, page 190"—which refers to the following extract: " 'Oaks—are confined to the Northern Hemisphere.—the Old World contains sixty-three species, and North America, including New Spain, about seventy-four. Of these the United States possesses about thirty-seven, and New Spain the same number.' Nuttall's North American Sylva. Philadelphia 1853."

Page 111, lines 21–25. Loudon's ... it has ripened."} *Arboretum et Fruticetum Britannicum*, 3:1728, 1718, 1968, 1437. When Loudon uses the phrase "beech mast," he is using "mast" in the sense of "the fruit of the beech ... especially as food for swine" (OED).

Page 111, lines 27–30. Cobbett ... down by the winds."} William Cobbett, *A Year's Residence in the United States of America ... in Three Parts*, (New-York: Clayton & Kingsland, 1819), 2:14.

Page 112, lines 2–3. one botanical writer ... soon vegetated."} Thoreau's source for this quotation has not been located.

Page 112, lines 9–14. Mr. George B. Emerson ... immediately vegetate."} *Report on Trees*, p. 54.

Page 112, lines 16–19. Loudon ... up till the third year.} *Arboretum et Fruticetum Britannicum*, 4:2178, 2224.

Page 112, lines 20–23. The stories . . . hundred years ago} Dr. John Lindley claimed to have raised three raspberry plants "from seeds which were taken from the stomach of a man whose skeleton was found 30 feet below the surface of the earth. He had been buried with some coins of the emperor Hadrian, and it is therefore probable that the seeds were 1600 or 1700 years old" (quoted in Alphonso Wood, *A Class-Book of Botany, Designed for Colleges, Academies, and Other Seminaries*, 23d ed., rev. and enl. [Boston: (n.p.), 1851], p. 61).

Page 112, line 25. Several men of science} In addition to the two botanists Thoreau mentions later in this paragraph, Wood noted the phenomenon in his *Class-Book of Botany*: "Several years ago, in the state of Maine, about 40 miles from the sea, some men, in digging a well, threw up some sand from a remarkable layer, about 20 feet below the surface, and placed it by itself. A year or two afterwards several shrubs sprung up from this sand, grew, produced fruit, and proved to be the beach-plum" (p. 61). Emerson also noted the phenomenon in *Report on Trees and Shrubs*: "Several varieties of [beach] plum are found ... in arid, sandy places, to the distance of twenty miles or more from the sea" (p. 449).

Page 112, lines 29–31. Dr. Carpenter ... upon the seashore."} William Carpenter, *Vegetable Physiology, and Systematic Botany* ... (London: H. G. Bohn, 1858), p. 114.

Page 113, lines 4–5. Dr. Charles T. Jackson ... miles inland in Maine.} "Report of the State Geologist," in *Third Report on the Geology of Maine* (Augusta: Smith & Robinson, 1839), p. 183.

Page 113, line 29. one man} Identified in the journal source of this passage (entry of 22 September 1859) simply as "Temple."

Page 114, lines 8–9. Linnaeus ... he is planting acorns.} *Amoenitates Academicae*, 2:443. Thoreau translates from Linnaeus's Latin.

Page 114, lines 19–20. transported short distances.} Thoreau interlined in the MS here "How River plants are transported—by ice."

Page 115, line 4. This same afternoon} The afternoon is identified in the journal source for this passage: 27 October 1860.

Page 116, lines 5–15. William Bartram . . . all the cleared lands.} Quoted in Wilson, *American Ornithology*, p. 5.

Page 116, line 17. 17th of October last} Identified as 17 October 1860 in the journal source of the same date.

Page 116, line 22. under the acorn, thus:} The drawing here is Thoreau's and has been reproduced from the MS.

Page 116, line 26. On October 16th, 1860} The word "On" is editorially supplied.

Page 118, line 9. bit-stock whose handle} The word "handle" is editorially supplied. A bit-stock is an instrument for turning a bit, composed of a handle and a device for holding the bit.

Page 118, lines 11, 16, 17. side view: . . . down on it: . . . two turns . . . is it rooted.} Each of these four drawings is Thoreau's and has been reproduced from the MS. For nearly identical renderings of three of the drawings, see the journal source for this passage (entry of 17 October 1860).

Page 118, line 19. turn from the manner} MS appears to read "turn for the manner."

Page 118, line 26. October 17th} Identified as 17 October 1860 from the journal source of the same date.

Page 119, line 4. Emerson's lot} Thoreau interlined "(by the Pond)" in the MS here, referring to Walden Pond, on the southwest side of which Ralph Waldo Emerson owned a woodlot.

Page 119, line 4. I examined} Thoreau interlined "(October 24, 1860)" in the MS here.

Page 120, line 30. *old* oak woods} Thoreau interlined "(for instance, Inches)" in the MS here, referring to Inches Wood, sometimes called Stow Woods, which was located between the Harvard turnpike and Stow in Boxborough, about twelve miles west-northwest of Concord.

Page 121, line 2. midst of a dense wood.} Thoreau interlined in the MS here "*Vide* perhaps pages 250 and 280 on bare space under pasture oaks," referring to the following two passages in his journal:

[From entry of 29 October 1860] The site of the last-named pasture oak [one "which Sted Buttrick cut some seven or eight years ago, northeast of" Ebby Hubbard's old black-birch hill] was easily discovered, by a very large open grass-sward where no sweet-fern, lambkill, huckleberry, and brakes grew, as they did almost everywhere else. This may be because of the cattle assembling under the oak, and so killing the bushes and at the same time manuring the ground for grass.

———

[From entry of 5 November 1860] It is evident that the pasture oaks are commonly the survivors or relics of old oak woods—not having been set out of course, nor springing up often in the bare pasture, except sometimes along fences. I see that on the outskirts of Wetherbee's and Blood's lots are some larger, more spreading and straggling trees, which are not to be distinguished from those. Such trees are often found as stragglers beyond a fence in an adjacent lot. Or, as an old oak wood is very gradually thinned out, it becomes open, grassy, and park-like, and very many owners are inclined to respect a few larger trees on account of old associations, until at length they begin to value them for shade for their cattle. These are oftenest white oaks. I think that they grow the largest and are the hardiest. This final arrangement is in obedience to the demand of the cow. She says, looking at the oak woods: "Your tender twigs are good, but grass is better. Give me a few at intervals for shade and shelter in storms, and let the grass grow far and wide between them."

Page 121, lines 6–10. Carpenter ... it is rooted up."} William Carpenter, *Vegetable Physiology, and Systematic Botany* ... (London: H. G. Bohn, 1858), p. 119.

Page 122, line 1. by Thrush Alley} Thoreau interlined "(October 17)" in the MS here, and the journal source identifies the year as 1860 (entry of 17 October 1860).

Page 122, line 4. were becoming trees.} Thoreau interlined "*vide* perhaps page 205" in the MS here, apparently referring to the following sentence from his journal entry of 19 October 1860: "The oldest oak, fairly speaking, in this wood ["the oak lot of Rice's next to the pine strip"] was a black, thirteen years old. Its root, as usual, ran not straight down but with a half-turn or twist (as well as to one side), which would make it harder to pull up at any rate."

Page 122, line 17. October 30th} Identified as 30 October 1860 from the journal source of that date.

Page 123, line 9 to page 125, line 2. Loudon's *Arboretum*. . . . left to unassisted nature."} *Arboretum et Fruticetum Britannicum*, 3:1800–1804.

Page 123, lines 26–27. pines. But, says Mr. Milne: In all cases where} Emended from the MS, which reads "pines, 'but in all cases [says Mr. Milne] where'" (Thoreau's brackets).

Page 125, line 10. If anyone presumes} Thoreau interlined the word "Should" over "If," but the original is retained because he did not alter the verb.

Page 126, line 1. October 17th} Identified as 17 October 1860 from the journal source of that date.

Page 128, line 6. is a seedling} MS reads "a seedling is."

Page 129, lines 9–10. two of a trade never agree.} John Gay, *Fables*, pt. 1, "The Rat-Catcher and Cat" (1727): "In every age and clime we see / Two of a trade can never agree."

Page 129, line 14. A sportsman} Identified as George Melvin in the journal source of this passage, entry of 16 October 1857.

Page 129, lines 20, 23. another . . . his boy. . . . Another} The first two of Thoreau's neighbors have not been identified; the third is identified as George Minott from Thoreau's journal entry of 24 September 1857.

Page 129, line 26. now} Thoreau interlined "(October 31st)" in the MS here. The year is identified as 1860 from the journal source (entry of 31 October 1860).

Page 129, line 28. some weeks of close scrutiny} Thoreau spent almost every day of October 1860 examining woodlots in and around Concord, and he continued his researches almost daily until 3 December 1860, when he was counting tree rings and measuring trees at Fair Haven Hill and caught the cold that led to his death seventeen months later.

Page 130, lines 16–17. dukes of Athol} Thoreau read about the actual James Duke of Athol, and his son and successor, John, whose estates were at Dunkeld and Athol in northern Scotland, in Loudon's *Arboretum et Fruticetum Britannicum*, 4:2358–63, although Emerson's *Report on Trees and Shrubs*, pp. 91–94, contains long extracts derived from Loudon. Duke James planted about two thousand larch trees on the rockiest ground of his estate in Athol, and Duke John dramatically extended his father's larch forests by planting more than fourteen million larch trees on over ten thousand acres. As Loudon's source said, "There is no name that stands so high, and so deservedly high, in the list of successful planters, as that of the late John Duke of Athol" (4:2363).

Page 130, line 29. The noblest trees} At the top of the manuscript page beginning here, Thoreau wrote, "Put this page, perhaps, under Treatment of Forests." The manuscript page ends with the words "and not one kind covering a township" (see page 131, lines 18–19, of the present volume). It is not clear whether Thoreau planned "Treatment of Forests" to be the title of a section, or perhaps a chapter, of *The Dispersion of Seeds*. In any case, he used the phrase in the following sentence from his journal entry of 1 September 1860: "The treatment of forests is a very different question to us and to the English."

Page 131, lines 6–7. of the largest size.} Thoreau interlined in the MS here "*Vide* November 26, 1859," apparently a reference to the following passage in his journal entry of that date:

> In the midst of this wood ["the Colburn Farm woodlot south of the road"] there occur less valuable patches of an eighth of an acre or more, where there is much grass, and cladonia, shrub oaks, and lichen-covered birches, and a few pitch pines only—places of a comparatively sterile character, as if the soil had been run out. The birches will have much of the birch fungus on them, and their fallen dead tops strew the ground.

Page 132, line 2. 3d of December} Thoreau interlined in the MS here "(1860, and they were remarkably abundant that year)."

Page 132, lines 3–4. already been killed.} Thoreau interlined "1860" in the MS here.

Page 133, lines 11–12. still retain their fruit} Thoreau interlined in the MS here "(*Vide* perhaps more December 17, 1859)," apparently a reference to the following passage from his journal entry of that date:

> Under the hill, on the southeast side of R[alph] W[aldo] E[merson]'s lot, where the hemlock stands, I see many tracks of squirrels. The dark, thick green of the hemlock (amid the pines) seems to attract them as a covert. The

snow under the hemlock is strewn with the scales of its cones, which they (and perhaps birds?) have stripped off, and some of its little winged seeds. It is pleasant to see the tracks of these squirrels (I am not sure whether they are red or gray or both, for I see none) leading straight from the base of one tree to that of another, thus leaving untrodden triangles, squares, and polygons of every form, bounded by much-trodden highways. One, two, three, and the track is lost on the upright bole of a pine—as if they had played at base-running from goal to goal, while pine cones were thrown at them on the way. The tracks of two or three suggest a multitude. You come thus on the tracks of these frisky and volatile (semivolitant) creatures in the midst of perfect stillness and solitude, as you might stand in a hall half an hour after the dancers had departed. I see no nests in the trees, but numerous holes through the snow into the earth, whence they have emerged. They have loitered but little on the snow, spending their time chiefly on the trees, their castles, when abroad. The snow is strewn not only with hemlock scales, but, under other trees, with the large white-pine scales for rods together where there is no track, the wind having scattered them as they fell, and also the shells of hickory nuts. It reminds me of the platform before a grocery where nuts are sold. You see many places where they have probed the snow for these white-pine cones, evidently those which they cut off green and which accordingly have not opened so as to drop the seeds. This was perhaps the design in cutting them off so early—thus to preserve them under the snow (not dispersed). Do they find them by the scent? At any rate they will dig down through the snow and come right upon a pine cone or a hickory nut or an acorn, which you and I cannot do.

Page 133, lines 30–31. One winter} Identified as the winter of 1852–53 from the journal sources (entries of 9 December 1852, 10 January 1853).

Page 134, lines 8–12. Loudon . . . course of the winter."} *Arboretum et Fruticetum Britannicum*, 3:1434.

Page 134, line 20. Kane and his companions} Elisha Kent Kane, *Arctic Explorations: The Second Grinnell Expedition in Search of Sir John Franklin, 1853, '54, '55 . . .* 2 vols. (Philadelphia: Childs & Peterson, 1856), 1:128.

Page 134, lines 25–26. dukes of Athol.} See note for page 130, lines 16–17, above.

Page 134, line 28. On March 25th, 1855} The word "On" is editorially supplied.

Page 135, lines 11–12. One who has half-tame red squirrels} Identified in the journal source of this passage (entry of 18 October 1860) as Bronson Alcott.

Page 135, line 15. Another} Identified in the journal source (entry of 20 October 1860) as Edmund Hosmer.

Page 135, line 20. last fall} Thoreau visited "the three principal old oak woods," which he lists in the text on page 160, lines 7–8, as "Wetherbee's, Blood's, and Inches," during the fall of 1860.

Page 135, lines 23–24. several ... one} Of the "several with whom [Thoreau] talked" during the fall of 1860, one was Anthony Wright, who on 23 October 1860 told him about Inches Wood (see journal entry of that date and note for page 120, line 30).

Page 136, line 1. the owner} Identified as D. Wetherbee in the journal source for this passage (entry of 2 November 1860).

Page 136, line 11. this afternoon} Thoreau interlined "(September 24th)" in the MS here, and the journal source of that day in 1860 identifies the year.

Page 137, line 23. Again} Thoreau interlined "(December 2d)" in the MS here, and the journal source of that day in 1860 identifies the year.

Page 138, lines 2–4. I find ... stubs ... surface of the ground.} Thoreau drew a vertical line in the margin beside this sentence in the MS, which indicates that he considered deleting the sentence.

Page 139, line 14. *open* land ... at Walden} During the summer of 1846, his first full summer at Walden Pond, Thoreau cultivated white beans on "two acres and a half of upland" that had been cleared, he said, fifteen years before (*Walden*, p. 156).

Page 139, line 26. walnut} Strictly speaking, a hickory is any of several deciduous trees of the genus *Carya*, and a walnut is any of several deciduous trees of the genus *Juglans*; however, "in the U.S. ['walnut'] often denotes the Hickory ..." (OED). Thoreau uses the two terms interchangeably.

Page 139, line 32. On December 1st} The word "On" is editorially supplied. The year was 1860 (journal source in entry of 1 December 1860).

Page 140, line 23. On December 3d} The word "On" is editorially supplied. The year was 1860 (journal source in entry of 3 December 1860).

Page 142, line 7. they here contend with.} Thoreau interlined in the MS here "More of this on oaks, Journal page 165—[1]89," a reference to the following passages in this journal:

[From entry of 14 October 1860] If you examine a woodlot after numerous fires and cuttings, you will be surprised to find how extremely vivacious are the roots of oaks, chestnuts, hickories, birches, cherries, etc. The little trees which look like seedlings of the year will be found commonly to spring from an older root or horizontal shoot or a stump. Those layers which you may have selected to transplant will be found to have too much of old stump and root underground to be removed. They have commonly met with accidents and seen a good deal of the world already. They have learned to endure and bide their time. When you see an oak fully grown and of fair proportions, you little suspect what difficulties it may have encountered in its early youth, what sores it has overgrown, how for years it was a feeble layer lurking under the leaves and scarcely daring to show its head above them, burned and cut, and browsed by rabbits. Driven back to earth again twenty times—as often as it aspires to the heavens. The soil of the forest is crowded with a mass of these old and tough fibers, annually sending up their shoots here and there. The underground part survives and holds its own, though the top meets with countless accidents; so that, although seeds were not to be supplied for many years, there would still spring up shoots enough to stock it.

———

[From entry of 17 October 1860] It is surprising how many accidents these seedling oaks will survive. We have seen that they commonly survive six to ten years under the thickest pines and acquire stout and succulent roots. Not only [do] they bear the sudden exposure to the light when the pines are cut, but, in case of a more natural succession, when a fire runs over the lot and kills pines and birches and maples, and oaks twenty feet high, these little oaks are scarcely injured at all, and they will still be just as high the next year, if not in the fall of the same year if the fire happens early in the spring. Or if in the natural course of events a fire does not occur, the soil may at last be exhausted for pines, but there are always the oaks ready to take advantage of the least feebleness and yielding of the pines.

Page 142, line 9. hoop-poles} "Smooth straight sapling[s] of green wood for making hoops" (OED).

Page 142, line 17. when I first went to Walden} Thoreau built his house on the shore of Walden Pond during the spring of 1845 and began living there on Independence Day, 4 July 1845.

Page 143, line 3. One squirrel hunter} This person has not been identified.

Page 143, line 24. in midwinter} Thoreau interlined "(as January 7, 1860)" in the MS here.

Page 143, line 29 to page 144, line 27. I am occasionally . . . rocks and stumps.} Thoreau drew a single vertical line through this long passage to indicate that at one time he planned to delete it, but the line appears to have been erased.

Page 145, line 14. found a dozen left.} Thoreau interlined a sentence in the MS here that is difficult to recover; it is written in pencil and appears to read: "They appropriate them all over and completely, as if this property had been conveyed to them—men had signed a grant-claim deed, and after enjoying only a transient vision of their brown shells or husks."

Page 145, line 19. a fortnight past} Thoreau interlined "(August 29, 1858)" in the MS here.

Page 145, line 30. How important the hazelnut} At the top of the leaf that begins here, Thoreau wrote "September 3d, 1858," which is the journal source of this passage.

Page 145, line 5. one November} Identified as November 1857 from the journal source (entry of 14 November 1857). Thoreau mentions in his journal that the limestone quarries in north Concord were on the Old Carlisle Road.

Page 147, line 10. winterberry seeds} Between these two words, Thoreau wrote "(*Prinos?*)."

Page 148, line 4. about a twentieth} MS reads "about the twentieth."

Page 148, lines 24–26. Pennant . . . of the field mouse."} Quoted in Thomas Bell, *A History of British Quadrupeds, including the Cetacea, Illustrated by Nearly 200 Woodcuts* (London: J. Van Voorst, 1837), p. 306.

Page 148, line 27 to page 149, line 10. Bell's *British Quadrupeds* . . . Loudon . . . in these two forests."} Bell reports on these experiments in *History of British Quadrupeds*, pp. 326–28; Loudon's report is in *Arboretum et Fruticetum Bri-*

tannicum, 3:1803–7. Thoreau quotes from Loudon, 3:1806. The Forest of Dean was in Gloucestershire; New Forest was in Hampshire.

Page 149, lines 12–16. Saint Pierre … their own commerce."} *Studies of Nature*, 3:170.

Page 149, lines 19–22. Theophrastus … Latin translator).} *Opera et Excerpta Librorum*, 2:266. The translator, from Greek to Latin, was Theodore of Gaza; the translation of the Latin to English is apparently Thoreau's own.

Page 149, line 20. in the fourth century B.C.} This phrase has been supplied by the editor to fill the blank space Thoreau left after the word "written" in the MS.

Page 149, lines 22–25. Pliny … the art of grafting.} *Natural History*, bk. 17, ch. 22.

Page 149, line 29. *possibly* nuthatches} Thoreau interlined in the MS here "*Vide* if necessary November 26, 1860," a reference to the following passage in his journal entry of that date:

> While I am walking in the oak wood or counting the rings of a stump, I hear the faint note of a nuthatch like the creak of a limb, and detect [it] on the trunk of an oak much nearer than I suspected, and its mate or companion not far off. This is a constant phenomenon of the late fall or early winter; for we do not hear them in summer that I remember. I heard one not long since in the street.

Page 150, line 5. behind a lichen} Thoreau interlined in the MS here "(as number 4, page 144)," a reference to his journal entry of 19 November 1850, in which he wrote: "I once found a kernel of corn in the middle of a deep wood by Walden tucked in behind a lichen on a pine about as high as my head either by a crow or a squirrel. It was a mile at least from any cornfield."

Page 150, line 8. A neighbor} Identified as Reuben Rice in the journal source of this passage (entry of 15 January 1861).

Page 150, lines 25–27. Evelyn … a delicious fare."} *Sylva, or a Discourse of Forest-Trees*, p. 30.

Page 150, line 28. a trapper} Identified in the journal source of this sentence (entry of 16 October 1857) as George Melvin.

Page 151, lines 4–14. Saint Pierre … this kind of food."} *Studies of Nature*, 3:263.

Page 151, line 11. report of a pistol.} Thoreau here wrote "[Father du Tertre's *History of the Antilles*]," which Saint Pierre cited in a footnote.

Page 151, line 14. this kind of food."} Thoreau interlined in the MS here "Perhaps here swine plants acorns?" a reference to the sentence on page 114, lines 8–9, in the present volume.

Page 151, line 27 to page 152, line 5. Herodotus … but perishes entirely."} *New and Literal Version*, bk. 6, ch. 37. Croesus was king of Lydia; Lampsacus was the ancient Greek city of Mysia, Asia Minor, on the Hellespont opposite Gallipoli; Miltiades was a general who commanded the Athenians at Marathon.

Page 152, line 13. stout and spreading.} Thoreau interlined in the MS here "Perhaps describe their thickness and slenderness."

Page 152, line 19. dense pitch-pine wood} Thoreau interlined in the MS here "(Wheeler's blackberry field)."

Page 152, line 27. some thirty years old} Thoreau interlined in the MS here "(H[enry] Shattuck's)."

Page 153, lines 10–11. I have obtained … pitch-pine woods} Thoreau and several assistants planted white pines in Ralph Waldo Emerson's Wyman woodlot during 19–21 April 1859 (see Thoreau's journal entries of those dates).

Page 153, lines 11–12. another} This person has not been identified.

Page 153, line 24. last fall} Identified as the fall of 1860 from the journal source (entry of 30 October 1860).

Page 153, line 26. The proprietor} Identified as J. Hosmer from the journal source of this passage (entry of 30 October 1860).

Page 155, lines 15–16. filling up a pasture} Thoreau interlined in the MS here "(as that near M[artial] Miles's, page 9)," the page number referring to the journal source of this paragraph (entry of 25 November 1860).

Page 155, line 17, enclosing} MS reads "inclosing."

Page 155, line 31. the explorers} Thoreau here refers to those whose job it was to locate stands of white pine for the lumber companies. In *Maine Woods* Thoreau wrote of the white and red pines, and some other trees, "They are of a social habit, growing in 'veins,' 'clumps,' 'groups,' or 'communities,' as the explorers call them, distinguishing them far away, from the top of a hill or a tree, the white pines towering above the surrounding forest. . . ." (p. 210).

Page 156, line 13, enclosed} MS reads "inclosed."

Page 156, lines 29–30. plowed and cultivated.} Thoreau interlined in the MS here "Perhaps here conjectures as to Tarbell hollow one hundred fifty years ago."

Page 157, lines 18–19. Linnaeus's . . . *sterili refertae*"?} Thoreau interlined "(number 9, page 221)" in the MS, referring to the journal source of this passage (entry of 12 March 1852). Linnaeus, *Philosophia Botanica, in Qua Explicantur Fundamenta Botanica ... Editio Altera* (Viennae: Typis J. T. Trottner, 1763), p. 229.

Page 157, line 31 to page 158, line 1. extensively in this town.} Thoreau wrote in the MS here "(as the Great Fields and Rear of Mrs. Dennis['s]—Sandy plains—)."

Page 159, line 7. is very apparent} These three words were recovered from the journal source of this passage (entry of 25 November 1860). Thoreau inadvertently left the words out when transcribing the passage from the journal.

Page 159, line 19. Marlborough road} Thoreau used the clipped form "Marlboro," and interlined "(this side Maynard's)" in the MS here.

Page 159, line 23. white-pine wood} Thoreau interlined "(as the last but one)" in the MS here.

Page 159, line 32. numerously} Thoreau interlined "(north of Cold Pool, page 8)" in the MS here, referring to the journal source of this passage (entry of 25 November 1860).

Page 160, line 7. last fall} Thoreau examined the three old oak woods he mentions here during October–November 1860.

Page 160, line 15. than an oak one.} Thoreau interlined in the MS here "Also at E[bby] Hubbard's, *vide* page 12, number 33," a reference to the following passage from his journal entry of 26 November 1860:

> There are in this wood many little groves of white pines two to four feet high, quite dense and green, but these are in more open spaces and are vigorous just in proportion to the openness. There are also seedling oaks and chestnuts ten to thirty years old, yet not nearly so numerous as the pines. The large wood is mixed oak and pine—more oak at the north and more pine, especially pitch pine, at the south. The prospect is that in course of time the white pines will very greatly prevail over all other trees here.

Page 160, line 30. by oaks but by pines.} Thoreau wrote in the MS here "or elsewhere I *say* (page 13 in E[bby] Hubbard's old wood)," a reference to the following two sentences in his journal entry of 26 November 1860: "Perhaps this is the way that a natural succession takes place. Perhaps oak seedlings do not so readily spring up and thrive within a mixed white-pine and oak wood as pines do—in the more open parts—and thus, as the oaks decay, they are replaced by pines rather than by oaks."

Page 161, line 21. last fall} Thoreau examined the small sproutland he refers to on 16 October 1860 (see journal entry of that date).

Page 162, line 24. open white-pine wood} Thoreau interlined "(as Stow's by Deep Cut)" in the MS here.

Page 163, line 8. mingle with them.} Thoreau interlined "(as beyond Bare Hill)" in the MS here.

Page 163, lines 12–13. oak sprouts may succeed.} Thoreau interlined in the MS here "for instance, R[alph] W[aldo] Emerson's first cutting on hillside."

Page 164, line 3. said by explorers for lumber} See quotation from *Maine Woods*, note to page 155, line 31, above.

Page 164, line 22. I observed today} MS reads "Observed today (October 19, 1851)," so the word "I" is editorially supplied. The parenthetical date in the MS refers to the journal source of this passage.

Page 165, line 4. This afternoon ... October} Identified as 16 October 1860 from the journal source of that date.

Page 165, line 17. I also find} The drawing here is Thoreau's and has been reproduced from the MS.

Page 166, line 15. Given these facts} The drawing here is Thoreau's and has been reproduced from the MS. See the journal source of this passage (entry of 16 October 1860) for a different rendering of this drawing.

Page 167, lines 23–24. entrench} MS reads "intrench."

Page 167, line 26. Zouaves} An elite infantry unit of the French Army recruited from the Kabyte or Zouaova tribe of Algeria in 1831. The Zouaves achieved a reputation during the Crimean War for their hardiness and courage. After the war they were issued colorful uniforms, taught to march in elaborate patterns, and sent on tour. In 1859 they toured the United States and caused a sensation wherever they appeared.

Page 169, lines 13–22. I frequently find ... forest is written.} Thoreau drew a single vertical line through these two paragraphs, which indicates that at one time he planned to delete them, but later he apparently erased the line.

Page 169, line 22. Concord forest is written.} These four words have been recovered from the journal source of this sentence (entry of 19 October 1860). The first thirteen words of this sentence appear at the bottom of a leaf, and Thoreau interlined *"Vide 203"* in the bottom-right margin next to the word "written," referring to the journal page that contains the missing words. At the very bottom of this leaf Thoreau interlined "Insert more here by and by—but first go on with 199—and 200," a clear indication that he intended to add more text after this paragraph in a later draft. His "199—and 200" is a reference to the journal source of the paragraph following the one ending here and beginning "I frequently see an old and tall pine" (entry of 19 October 1860).

Page 171, line 2. A neighbor} This person has not been identified.

Page 171, line 26. axle-tree} "The fixed bar or beam of wood ... on the rounded ends of which the opposite wheels of a carriage revolve" (OED).

Page 172, line 8. does not deserve).} Thoreau wrote in the margin of the MS here, "as at Merriam's field."

Page 172, line 15. with a bushwhack.} Thoreau wrote in the margin of the MS here, "as at Fair Haven Hill."

Page 172, lines 24–25. this October afternoon} Identified as 16 October 1860 from the journal source of that date.

Page 172, lines 29–30. fellow who calls himself its owner} Thoreau mentions in the journal source of this passage (entry of 16 October 1860) that the wood he refers to was "Wheeler's," probably Cyrus Wheeler, although F. A. (Abiel?) Wheeler and William Wheeler also lived near White Pond, which is where Thoreau was walking that afternoon.

Page 173, line 19. "pine-sick."} Richard Peters used this word several times in his article "Departure of the Southern Pine Timber, a Proof of the Tendency in Nature to a Change of Products on the Same Soil," *Memoirs of the Philadelphia Society for Promoting Agriculture*, vol. 1 (1808): 27–40. Thoreau quotes Peters's use of this phrase in the selection on "Forest Trees," page 208, line 21, of the present volume.

Page 173, lines 23–24. by the town—overseers of poor husbandmen.} These seven words were recovered from the journal source of this sentence (entry of 16 October 1860).

Page 177, title. Wild Fruits} This is Thoreau's title, although it does not appear on the title page; instead, Thoreau used the title throughout his late natural history manuscripts when referring to the *Wild Fruits* manuscripts and on a wrapper he used to keep those manuscripts together. That wrapper is now in the Berg Collection at the New York Public Library, at the front of a folder labeled "Notes on Fruits." Thoreau wrote on the wrapper: "Matter to be used in completing Wild Fruits[.] Journal examined as far as Oct[ober] 19 [1860]— only 1st Com[mon] P[lace] book examined." The source for this selection is fifty-five manuscript pages in the Berg Collection. Ten of these pages are in a folder labeled "Portion of Holograph Journal," no accession numbers, and the remaining forty-five are in the folder labeled "Notes on Fruits," paged with accession numbers 399–401, 574–89, [589A], 590, [590A], 591, 599–600.

Page 177, lines 1–4. *Agrestem tenui* ... sing unbidden things.} Virgil, *Eclogues*, 6:8–9.

Page 178, line 8. horse Columbus} Reputed in 1860 to be the fastest horse alive.

Page 178, line 8. Mr. Blank, the Ossian Boy} In his edition of Thoreau's nascent lecture *Huckleberries*, Leo Stoller identifies "Mr. Blank" as "John C. Heenan, the Benecia Boy, who had become notorious in 1860—first by boxing the British champion Tom Sayers to a forty-two round draw, then by marrying the famous actress Adah Menken and afterward charging her with bigamy" (p. 40). Stoller, however, misread "Ossian" as "Oinan," which he took to be a play by Thoreau on *oeno* (sometimes spelled *oino*), the Greek root for "wine."

Page 178, lines 13–14. Pliny ... the least things.} This quotation has not been located in Pliny's works.

Page 178, lines 15–16. Mr. Seward or Caleb Cushing} After Lincoln's election as president of the United States in November 1860, Senators Caleb Cushing (Democrat, Massachusetts) and William Henry Seward (Republican, New York) debated the issue of secession on the floor of the U.S. Senate and at Newburyport, Massachusetts.

Page 180, line 2. Ceram and Amboyna.} Exotic locations mentioned several times in Saint Pierre, *Studies of Nature*. Ceram is an island in the Moluccas, Indonesia, west of New Guinea; Amboyna is the chief city and commercial center of the Moluccas on Amboina Island in the northern Banda Sea.

Page 182, lines 21–24. "several hundred ... of turpentine."} Thoreau's source for this quotation has not been located.

Page 183, lines 5–7. the saying of Cyrus ... valiant in war."} Quoted in Herodotus, *A New and Literal Version,* bk. 9, ch. 122.

Page 183, line 9. 10th of May} Thoreau interlined in the MS here "(from the 7th to the 9th)."

Page 183, lines 14–25. About the same ... their crispy stems.} Thoreau copied this paragraph for use in *The Dispersion of Seeds* (see page 82, line 19 to page 83, line 3), and he then drew a single vertical line through the paragraph, apparently to indicate that he had copied it rather than to indicate that he intended to delete it.

Page 184, line 7. 7th of June.} Thoreau interlined "(and May 30, 1860)" in the MS here.

Page 184, lines 10–14. Gerarde ... silk intermixt."} *Herball of Generall Historie of Plantes,* p. 46.

Page 184, lines 27–29. Gerarde ... this root therein."} *Herball of Generall Historie of Plantes,* p. 47.

Page 184, line 30 to page 185, line 5. Sir John Richardson ... a glass of water."} Sir John Richardson, *Fauna Boreali-Americana; or, The Zoology of the Northern Parts of British America* ... 4 vols. (London: J. Murray, 1829–37), 3:263.

Page 185, lines 12–17. About the 20th ... open to the sun.} Thoreau copied this paragraph for use in *The Dispersion of Seeds* (see page 83, lines 12–17); he then drew a single vertical line through the paragraph, apparently to indicate that he had copied it rather than to indicate that he intended to delete it.

Page 185, lines 16–17. Gerarde ... open to the sun."} *Herball of Generall Historie of Plantes,* p. 638.

Page 185, lines 19–24. Gerarde's account ... grasshoppers."} *Herball of Generall Historie of Plantes,* p. 1485.

Page 186, line 10. now} Identified in the journal source as 16 May 1860 (entry of that date).

Page 186, line 27 to page 187, line 4. Tusser ... prove excellent good.} Thomas Tusser, *Some of the Five Hundred Points of Good Husbandry* ... (Oxford: John Henry Parker, 1848), p. 24. This is stanza 15 in Tusser's poem, "September's

Husbandry"; the first line in most editions reads, "Wife, into thy garden, and set me a plot."

Page 187, lines 5–19. Gerarde ... nourishment is naught."} *Herball of Generall Historie of Plantes*, p. 997, 998.

Page 188, lines 6–7. Virgil ... growing on the ground."} Virgil, *Eclogues*, 3:93.

Page 189, lines 2–3. the ancients speak.} Pliny wrote of the earth exuding a "divine odor" to which "there is no perfume, however sweet, that can possibly be compared" (*Natural History*, bk. 17, ch. 3). Thoreau copied the larger extract from Pliny into his Commonplace Book 2, pp. 133–34, under the heading "Odor of the Earth."

Page 189, line 27. weeded} The MS reads "wed."

Page 191, lines 3–5. "a native ... to the Greeks."} Thoreau's source for this quotation has not been located.

Page 191, lines 19–22. Hearne ... Churchill River"} Samuel Hearne, *A Journey from Prince of Wales Fort in Hudson's Bay to the North Ocean ... in the Years 1769, 1770, 1771, & 1772* (London: A. Strahan and T. Cadell, 1795), p. 452. The clause Thoreau puts in brackets appears in a footnote in Hearne. Churchill River is in Manitoba, its mouth on the west side of Hudson Bay.

Page 191, lines 23–24. Sir John Franklin ... Otei-meena} Sir John Franklin, *Narrative of a Journey to the Shores of the Polar Sea, in the Years 1819, 20, 21, & 22 ...* (Philadelphia: H. C. Carey, [et al.], 1824), p. 78.

Page 191, lines 24–30. Tanner ... Lake Superior.} John Tanner, *A Narrative of the Captivity and Adventures of John Tanner ... During Thirty Years Residence Among the Indians ...* (New York: G. & C. & H. Carvill, 1830), p. 296.

Page 191, lines 30–31. The Dakotahs ... strawberry is red."} Thoreau's source for this quotation has not been located.

Page 192, lines 1–5. William Wood's ... bushel in a forenoon."} William Wood, *New England's Prospect, Being a True, Lively, and Experimental Description of ... New England*, 3d ed. (London: printed 1639; Boston: rpt., Thomas and John Fleet, 1764), p. 16.

Page 192, lines 8–13. Roger Williams ... for many days."} Roger Williams, "A Key into the Language of America ..." *Collections of the Massachusetts Historical Society*, 1st ser., vol. 3 (1794): 221. The "chiefest doctor of England" was

William Butler, called by Fuller in *Worthies of England* "the Aesculapius of our age" (p. 387).

Page 192, lines 14–16. Boucher . . . raspberries and strawberries} Pierre Boucher, *Histoire Véritable et Naturelle des Moeurs et Productions du Pays de la Nouvelle France, Vulgairement Dite la Canada* (Paris: F. Lambert, 1664), p. 64.

Page 192, lines 16–19. Loskiel's . . . fine scarlet cloth."} George Henry Loskiel, *History of the Mission of the United Brethren Among the Indians in North America . . .* trans. Christian Ignatius Latrobe (London: The Brethren's Society for the Furtherance of the Gospel, 1794), p. 79.

Page 192, line 20 to page 193, line 2. Mr. Peters . . . for poetic description."} Richard Peters, "Herbage and Shrubs Spontaneously Produced, after Forest Timber Burnt, by Firing the Woods," *Memoirs of the Philadelphia Society for Promoting Agriculture*, 1 (1808): 238.

Page 193, lines 3–4. historians of New Hampshire . . . first cultivated."} *The History of Dublin, N. H., Containing the Address by Charles Mason, and the Proceedings at the Centennial Celebration, June 17, 1852 . . .* (Boston: J. Wilson, 1855), p. 48.

Page 193, lines 12–18. as one reads . . . *Tsazkoy Chèlè.*"} Thoreau's source for this quotation has not been located. Tsazkoy Chèlè, now more often anglicized to Tsarskoye Selo or simply translated "Czar's Village," is a small town outside St. Petersburg and was the imperial summer residence prior to the Russian Revolution.

Page 194, line 15. pluck this little fruit.} Thoreau interlined a sentence at this point in the MS, but it is very difficult to recover. The sentence appears to read: "Raspberries, as appear from the [recent stories], made part of the food of that unknown primitive people whose [huts] have been [found but in piles at] the bottom of the [major] lakes, probably before the foundation of Rome." The words in brackets are conjectural.

Page 194, lines 15–20. Lindley . . . 1,700 years old."} *Natural System of Botany*, quoted in Alphonso Wood, *A Class-Book of Botany*, p. 61.

Page 194, lines 25–29. Pliny . . . layers and quicksets."} *Natural History*, bk. 17, ch. 21. Multiplying by layers involves bending shoots or twigs to the ground and covering them partly with earth so that they may strike root and propagate; multiplying by quicksets involves setting slips or cuttings of plants in the ground to grow.

Page 195, lines 3–7. Pliny . . . size of the fruit"} *Natural History*, bk. 16, ch. 210.

Page 195, line 25. variant} The MS reads "var."—which is often expanded to "variety."

Page 196, lines 24–25. Pursh . . . black, insipid."} Frederick Pursh, *Flora Americae Septentrionalis; or . . . Description of the Plants of North America . . .* (London: Printed for White, Cochrane, and Co., 1814), p. 429.

Page 196, lines 26–27. it is said . . . of the cranberry."} Thoreau's source was Loudon, *Arboretum et Fruticetum Britannicum*, 2:1161. Enghien is located a few miles southwest of Brussels, Belgium.

Page 198, line 18. *redeemed*} A swamp is said to be "redeemed" after it has been drained and suitably prepared for cultivation.

Page 198, lines 21–22, 23. "touched my trembling ears," "mortal soil"} John Milton, "Lycidas," ll. 77, 78.

Page 199, lines 7–9. Gerarde . . . between the teeth."} *Herball of Generall Historie of Plantes*, p. 1417.

Page 199, line 24. Mithridates} The ancients believed that Mithridates the Great had saturated his body with poisons so that no one could murder him. When the Romans captured him, he tried in vain to poison himself; then he ordered a Gallic mercenary to kill him.

Page 200, line 16. *pennsylvanicum*.} Thoreau interlined "(see July 23, 1854)" in the MS here.

Page 200, line 21. "blueberry hollow"} No mention of this dish has been located, and the word "hollow" is so difficult to recover from the MS that it should be regarded as conjectural.

Page 202, lines 20–21. before the writer was born.} Thoreau interlined in the MS here "*vide* (if necessary) how they bear snow about February 16, 1860."

Page 203, lines 10–16. The earlier low . . . time more earthy.} In the MS Thoreau drew a vertical line in the margin beside these two sentences, which may indicate that he planned to delete them.

Page 203, lines 19–24. By the 1st...still vegetable food.} In the MS Thoreau drew a vertical line in the margin beside this sentence, which may indicate that he planned to delete it.

Page 204, title. Weeds and Grasses} This title is editorially supplied. The source for this brief selection is four manuscript pages in a folder labeled "Dispersion of Seeds" in the Berg Collection at the New York Public Library, paged with accession numbers 233–36.

Page 204, line 1. Pickering, in his work on races, says,} These seven words have been editorially supplied, and the title "Plants of Aboriginal Introduction," which Thoreau copied from Pickering (*Races of Man*, p. 307), has been deleted.

Page 204, line 1 to page 205, line 5. Pickering...*Polygonum persicaria*.} Thoreau quotes from *Races of Man*, p. 307, and selects his remaining facts from pp. 309–12, 332. Gray's Harbor is on the Pacific Coast at the mouth of the Chehalis River in what is now Washington State; Forts Colville and Nisqually were operated by the Hudson's Bay Company, the former in south-central British Columbia and the latter near the mouth of the Nisqually River at the southern end of Puget Sound. Captain James Cook visited New Zealand on four separate occasions, the first time in 1769; his accounts of the visits generated considerable interest in the islands.

Page 204, line 11. gets a foothold)} MS reads "gets foothold)."

Page 205, lines 6–13. Darwin's ... fruits which do not open."} *Origin of Species*, pp. 115, 146.

Page 205, lines 14–21. Darwin ... the aborigines."} Charles Darwin, *Journal of Researches into the Natural History and Geology of the Countries Visited During the Voyage of H.M.S. Beagle Round the World* ... 2 vols. (New York: Harper & Brothers, 1846), 1:125, 123–24 (entry of 19 September 1832). Banda Oriental is the former name of Uruguay, the capital of which is Montevideo, situated on the north shore of the Río de la Plata. In a footnote Darwin identifies his source as "Mr. Atwater's account of the Prairies, in *Silliman's N[orth] A[merican] Journal*, vol. i, p. 177."

Page 205, line 27. Carpenter in his *Vegetable Physiology* says:} The MS reads simply "Carpenter's Physiology—p. 115," so this introductory clause has been editorially supplied.

Page 205, line 26 to page 206, line 7. Carpenter … decay after death.} William Carpenter, *Vegetable Physiology, and Systematic Botany* … (London: H. G. Bohn, 1858), p. 115.

Page 206, line 16. travelling Shaker} Throughout the nineteenth century, members of the Shaker sect traveled around the country selling and giving away small packets of seeds, pots of sprouted plants, and medicinal herbs.

Page 207, title. Forest Trees} This title is editorially supplied. The source for this selection is seven manuscript pages, of which five are in a folder labeled "Dispersion of Seeds" at the Berg Collection, paged with accession numbers 239–43; one is in the George Arents Research Library at the Syracuse University Library, and the other is from an unlocated set of the 1906 Manuscript Edition of *The Writings of Henry D. Thoreau* (Boston: Houghton, Mifflin, 1906). The Thoreau Textual Center at the library of the University of California, Santa Barbara, has a photocopy of the latter manuscript; the copy was acquired when the set was owned by Books with a Past Bookstore in Concord, Massachusetts.

Page 207, line 4. an article by John William Dawson} John William Dawson, "On the Destruction and Partial Reproduction of Forests in British North America," *Edinburgh New Philosophical Journal*, 42.84 (April 1847): 259–71; rpt. *Silliman's Journal* (*American Journal of Science and the Arts*), 2d ser., 4.11 (September 1847): 161–70. The four quotations Thoreau uses were apparently taken from the original printing, pp. 261, 263–64, 267, and 267, respectively.

Page 207, lines 6–8. Mr. Peters … a Mr. Mease, a Mr. Adlum, and a Mr. Caldwell} Thoreau here refers to the following four items in *Memoirs of the Philadelphia Society for Promoting Agriculture*, 1 (1808): Richard Peters, "Departure of the Southern Pine Timber, a Proof of the Tendency in Nature to a Change of Products on the Same Soil," pp. 27–40; J[ames] Mease, "Supplement to the Foregoing," pp. 41–46; Richard Peters, "Herbage and Shrubs Spontaneously Produced, after Forest Timber Burnt, by Firing the Woods," pp. 237–39; and a letter from Charles Caldwell to Richard Peters, 1 April 1808 (pp. 301–7). Mease's article contains a long extract from a letter by John Adlum of Havre de Grace, Maryland.

Page 207, line 8 to page 208, line 3. Hearne's ... could shoot up.} *Journey from Prince of Wales Fort*; pp. 452–53; quoted by Mease, p. 42.

Page 208, lines 4–7. Cartwright's ... after them birch."} George Cartwright, *A Journal of Transactions and Events, During a Residence of Sixteen Years on the Coast of Labrador* ... (Newark, England: Allin and Ridge, 1792), pp. 133–34; quoted by Mease, p. 42.

Page 208, line 14. "a rotation or succession of forest trees."} This phrase appears in John Adlum's letter to Mease (p. 42) and may have provided Thoreau with the title of his essay "The Succession of Forest Trees," first published in the *New-York Weekly Tribune* on 6 October 1860.

Page 208, line 18. Lycoming County} A county in north-central Pennsylvania, the seat of which is Williamsport.

Page 208, line 26. Duxbury} Caldwell spells it "Duxborough" (p. 305).

Page 209, line 31. Miramichi} A river in New Brunswick, Canada.

Acknowledgments

Assembling this book has been a major enterprise that has, for many years, drawn on the time, talents, and goodwill of many individuals and institutions.

For permission and encouragement to publish Thoreau's manuscript, I thank Libby Chenault, Public Services Librarian, Rare Book Collection, University of North Carolina at Chapel Hill; M. N. Brown, Curator of Manuscripts, John Hay Library, Brown University; Mark Weimer, Curator of Rare Books and Manuscripts, George Arents Research Library, Syracuse University; Thomas Whitehead, Head of Special Collections, Samuel Paley Library, Temple University; and Rodney Phillips, Associate Director of Humanities, Social Sciences, and the Special Collections at the New York Public Library, Astor, Lenox, and Tilden Foundations. I am also grateful to Messrs. Brown, Weimer, and Whitehead, Ms. Chenault, and the members of their staff, for assistance during my brief visits to their collections; and I am especially indebted to Stephen Crook and Philip Milito of the Berg Collection for their help and hospitality during the many hours I spent in the Reading Room there.

The late Leo Stoller can almost be said to have discovered Thoreau's late natural history manuscripts when, in the 1960s, he studied those in the Berg Collection well enough to comment knowledgeably about them. His remarks were posthumously published in the introduction to his edition of *Huckleberries* (Ames, Iowa: Windhover Press, 1970). During the mid- to late 1970s Thomas Blanding transcribed almost all *The Dispersion of Seeds* manuscripts in the Berg Collection, and those transcripts, now at the Thoreau Textual Center, were instrumental in heightening interest in Thoreau's late natural history manuscripts. Since 1986 I have benefited from periodic discussions of those manuscripts with Mr. Blanding, Lawrence Buell, Ronald W. Hoag, William Howarth, Joel Myerson, Robert D. Richardson, Jr., Robert Sattelmeyer, Edmund A. Schofield, and Elizabeth Witherell. Dr. Sattelmeyer and Dr. Witherell, and their assistants, Sue Oakes and Louisa Dennis, provided me with much-needed help, often on short notice. Dr. Schofield had Mr. Blanding's transcripts typed onto a computer disk, offered helpful advice on illustrations, and provided early assistance with a few of the annotations and botanical names. Ms. Marcia Moss, Curator of Special Collections at the Concord Free Public Library, was extremely helpful in guiding me through the treasures in that valuable collection.

I owe thanks to David Bullen for his lovely and sensitive design work, to Abigail Rorer for her exquisite drawings, to Vivian Wheeler for expertly editing the manuscript I assembled, and to Beth Beisel, Managing Editor of Island Press, for her patience and support. Howard Boyer, Editorial Director of Shearwater Books, and María Eugenia Quintana very graciously opened their home to me on several occasions so that I could work for extended periods in the Boston area. Their warm hospitality, lively conversation, and rousing good humor made my job far more enjoyable than it would otherwise have been.

For material support that enabled me to carry on my research, I am grateful to Sunstar Inc. of Takatsuki, Osaka, Japan—particularly to Mr. Kunihiro Kaneda and Mr. Toshihiro Funaki.

My greatest debt, certainly, is to my wife, Debra, and our son, David. Without their unstinting patience and support, I simply could not have made much progress on this project, much less brought it to fruition.

B.P.D.

Index

BRADLEY P. DEAN is the editor of the *Thoreau Society Bulletin* and the *Thoreau Research Newsletter* and is the secretary of the Thoreau Society. He has taught English literature at the University of Connecticut, Rhode Island College, and Eastern Washington University. He is currently an adjunct professor of the English Department at East Carolina University. A writer and independent Thoreau scholar, he and his wife, Debra Kang Dean, live with their son, David, in Ayden, North Carolina.

GARY PAUL NABHAN is cofounder and research director of Native/Seeds SEARCH and vice-president of the international Seed Savers Exchange. A MacArthur fellow and noted author, his books include *The Desert Smells Like Rain* and *Gathering the Desert*.

ROBERT D. RICHARDSON, JR., is the author of *Henry Thoreau: A Life of the Mind* and a forthcoming biography of Ralph Waldo Emerson. He lives in Middletown, Connecticut, where he teaches in Wesleyan University's College of Letters.

ABIGAIL RORER resides in Massachusetts and works in various media, including etching, wood engraving, and fine bookmaking. Her illustrations, which are in numerous galleries and collections, have been widely published, including in Vincent Dethier's *Crickets and Katydids, Concerts and Solos* and Roger Swain's *Saving Graces*.